# INVESTING IN RENEWABLE ENERGY

# INVESTING IN RENEWABLE ENERGY

## Making Money on Green Chip Stocks

**JEFF SIEGEL**
WITH
**CHRIS NELDER AND NICK HODGE**

**WILEY**
John Wiley & Sons, Inc.

Published by John Wiley & Sons, Inc., Hoboken, New Jersey.
Published simultaneously in Canada.

For general information on our other products and services or for technical support,
please contact our Customer Care Department within the United States at (800) 762-2974,
outside the United States at (317) 572-3993 or fax (317) 572-4002.

Designations used by companies to distinguish their products are often claimed by
trademarks. In all instances where the author or publisher is aware of a claim, the product
names appear in Initial Capital letters. Readers, however, should contact the appropriate
companies for more complete information regarding trademarks and registration.

Wiley also publishes its books in a variety of electronic formats. Some content that
appears in print may not be available in electronic books. For more information about
Wiley products, visit our web site at www.wiley.com.

***Library of Congress Cataloging-in-Publication Data:***
Siegel, Jeffrey, 1970–
    Investing in renewable energy : making money on green chip stocks/Jeff Siegel;
    with Chris Nelder & Nick Hodge.
        p.   cm.
    Includes bibliographical references and index.
    ISBN 978-0-470-15268-3 (cloth)
    1. Energy industries.   2. Renewable energy sources.   3. Clean energy industries.
    4. Commodity futures.   5. Investments.   I. Hodge, Nick, 1983–   II. Nelder, Chris,
    1964–   III. Title.
    HD9502.A2S486   2008
    333.79'4—dc22
                                                                    2008018566

Printed in the United States of America.

10 9 8 7 6 5 4 3 2 1

# CONTENTS

# PART III: THE SCIENCE AND PROFITABILITY OF CLIMATE CHANGE

# PREFACE

In 2005, I received the following e-mail:

*Dear Jeff,*
*Why the hell would you invest in renewable energy? You have no idea what*
*you're talking about. No one's ever made money from solar and no one*
*ever will!*

Certainly we can look to the solar bull market of 2007 to counter the last sentence of that e-mail. Whether it was the 900 percent gain that First Solar (NASDAQ:FSLR) delivered or the 1,700 percent gain that World Water & Solar Technologies (OTCBB:WWAT) delivered, green chip investors who were properly positioned last year made an absolute fortune.

Still, even with all the money we've made in the past by investing in renewable energy, the question "Why would you invest in renewable energy?" is still quite valid, especially when you consider the fact that there really is a lack of easily accessible and credible information regarding the current state of the overall energy marketplace.

For instance, while the local news has made a habit of reporting on high gas prices every time the summer driving season kicks into high gear, rarely do we hear how these so-called high gas prices are actually quite cheap. The true cost of gasoline is probably closer to about $11.00 a gallon. You may not be paying that price at the pump, but you are paying it. You'll see how in Chapter 1.

We also hear a lot about how the United States is the "Saudi Arabia of coal," boasting a 250-year supply. However, rarely do we hear how these coal-supply numbers are highly inflated, or how the United States most likely passed its peak of coal production nearly 10 years ago. You'll read more about this in Chapter 1, as well.

And what about nuclear energy? President Bush is behind it, and it doesn't have the same $CO_2$ emission issues that are associated with coal. Some have even mistakenly (or intentionally) referred to it as "renewable." But whatever you call it, nuclear capacity is actually set to decrease over the next 25 years. In this book, we'll explain why.

Overall, our once-vast supplies of cheap, conventional, nonrenewable energy resources are shrinking at an alarming rate, while our demand for electricity and transportation fuels is dramatically increasing. As a result, we have created fertile ground for a very real crisis situation, but also a massive opportunity for renewable energy investors.

Just in 2007 alone, venture capital and private equity pumped $8.5 billion into clean energy. Even as the market began to feel the effects of a full-blown mortgage and credit crisis, the clean energy sector totaled more than $117 billion in new investments last year. That's about $20 billion ahead of predictions and 41 percent more than 2006 numbers.[1]

With this kind of big money in play, we have to ask ourselves, "Why are all these people investing in renewable energy?" The answer is quite simple.

The basic fundamentals of supply and demand dictate its profitability!

## ONE CHOICE, ONE OPPORTUNITY

Within the next few decades, our increasingly limited access to cheap, nonrenewable energy resources will present a serious economic crisis. Even today, while the oil is still flowing with few interruptions, gas prices rise with every major or minor refinery disruption, causing the cost of nearly everything else to rise as well. Virtually everything we use and consume today relies on oil. It's the diesel in the trucks that ship our food, clothing, and medicine. It's the gas in our cars that get us to work, school, and the grocery store. It's used in fertilizers, cosmetics, and plastics. It's the stuff that keeps the world's biggest and richest corporations running, providing employment for millions of people around the world. It is the slippery glue that keeps the world moving.

There's also the issue of coal and natural gas. Nearly our entire energy infrastructure, which is aging at an alarming rate, was built around the utilization of these finite resources that are being consumed faster than we can supply them.

Whether we like it or not, the age of conventional fossil fuels is quickly coming to an end. So we have two choices: We can continue to chase an energy economy that's simply unsustainable, and ultimately a long-term failure, or we can use this coming energy crisis as an opportunity to profit from the only other choice we have for power generation: renewable energy.

Renewable energy—which is essentially energy produced from sustainable resources that are naturally replenished—is the only form of energy that will exist beyond oil, coal, natural gas, and nuclear, because the resources used for renewable energy generation are infinite. Moreover, despite the avalanche of misinformation that's constantly spewed from naysayers and mainstream media, we can actually generate enough renewable energy to satisfy *all* of our energy needs. Take a look:

- *Solar:* Enough electric power for the entire country could be generated by covering about 9 percent of Nevada with solar power systems. This is a plot of land roughly 92 miles by 92 miles.

- *Wind:* According to the U.S. Department of Energy (DoE), wind could provide 5,800 quads of energy each year. That's about 15 times the current global energy demand.

- *Geothermal:* According to MIT, there are over 100 million quads of accessible geothermal energy worldwide. The world consumes only 400 quads.

- *Marine energy:* The Electric Power Research Institute has estimated the wave energy along the U.S. coastline at 2,100 TWh per year. That's half the total U.S. consumption of electricity.

- *Biogas:* Your local landfill could be powering your home right now with biogas.

- *Conservation and energy efficiency:* Aggressive energy conservation can save enough electricity every year to avoid building 24 new power plants.

- *Hybrids:* If all cars on the road were hybrids and half were *plug-in hybrids* by 2025, U.S. oil imports could be reduced by about 80 percent.

Of course, most of this information won't be found on any of the dozen or so cable news networks. You'd also be hard-pressed to read about this stuff in most newspapers or magazines. But this is the information that green chip investors (investors who consistently profit from the integration of renewable energy) have been using for years to make smart investment decisions— decisions that have ultimately produced fortunes.

In this book, you, too, will have an opportunity to review the same objective and peer-reviewed data that the most successful green chip investors have been using and still use today. More important, you will also learn about the latest renewable energy projects and technologies that will usher in the next generation of green chip profits, such as:

- Super-efficient, large-scale solar farms that will replace coal-fired power plants. (Chapter 2)

- Offshore wind turbines that could soon power the entire East Coast of the United States, though they're so far removed from shore you'll never even see them. (Chapter 3)

- Geothermal power plants that haven't even been built yet, but already have long-term power-purchase agreements with the utilities. (Chapter 4)

- Dam-less hydropower systems generating electricity in New York City's East River. (Chapter 5)

- Commercial-scale renewable energy systems that produce biogas from agricultural livestock. (Chapter 6)

- Energy management systems that conserve enough energy to close down dozens of coal-fired power plants. (Chapter 7)

- Future biofuel feedstocks that can grow in the desert for years, with little or no water. (Chapter 9)

- Hybrid vehicles that will *never* require a single drop of gasoline or diesel! (Chapter 10)

- A new commodities market that delivers profits by trading CO2. (Chapter 12)

Green chip investors are investing in all of this right now—and making a lot of money in the process. Reading this book will enable you to do the same. But you must read it in its entirety, as this book also clearly outlines the proof any smart investor needs to validate the claim that our fossil-fuel-based energy economy is coming to an end. It may not be the most popular claim to make, but when you're on the receiving end of massive profits from renewable energy stocks, does it matter?

Here's to a new way of life, my friend—and a new generation of wealth!

# INVESTING IN RENEWABLE ENERGY

PART

# TRANSITIONING TO THE NEW ENERGY ECONOMY

*"I'd put my money on the sun and solar energy. What a source of power! I hope we don't have to wait until oil and coal run out before we tackle that."*

—THOMAS EDISON

# CHAPTER

1

# THE GLOBAL ENERGY MELTDOWN

The world is now facing its most serious challenge ever. The name of that challenge is *peak energy*.

If decisive and immediate action is not taken, peak energy could prove to be a crisis more devastating than world wars, more intractable than plagues, and more disruptive than crop failure. We're talking about a crisis of epic proportions that will change *everything*. And rest assured it will not discriminate. Conservative or liberal, black or white, rich or poor, this will be a crisis of equal-opportunity devastation. That may sound hyperbolic to you now, but by the end of this chapter, you will understand why we say it.

Everything we do depends on some form of energy. Our entire way of life, and all of our economic projections, are built on the assumption that there will always be more energy when we want it. But global energy depletion has already begun, although few have realized it.

You're one of the lucky ones, because after reading this book, you will understand both the challenge of peak energy and some of the solutions early in the game—allowing you the opportunity to be well-positioned to not only profit from the renewable energy revolution that is already under way, but to thrive.

By the time you've completed this chapter, you will have a full understanding of what peak energy is, how it affects the future of the entire global economy, and why it is imperative that this challenge of peak energy is met head-on with renewable energy solutions. This will ultimately lead you to profits via the companies that are providing the solutions both in the near-term and well into the future.

## PEAK ENERGY

Before we begin discussing the particulars of peak oil, gas, coal, and uranium, we must first discuss what we mean when we use the term *peak energy*.

The production of any finite resource generally follows a bell curve shape. You start by producing a little, and then increase it over time; then you reach a peak production rate, after which it declines to make the back side of the curve. Between now and 2025, we could see the peak of *every single one* of our finite fuel resources. But why is the peak important? Because after the peak, we witness the rapid decline of these fuels, leaving us vulnerable to what could amount to the biggest disruption the global economy has ever witnessed. This would be a disruption that could spark an international crisis of epic proportions.

### Peak Oil

The first resource that will peak is oil, which is also our most important and valuable fuel resource. We have an entire chapter devoted to oil—Chapter 8—so we will merely summarize here. Here are some simple facts about peak oil:

- The world's largest oil reservoirs are mature.

- Approximately three-quarters of the world's current oil production is from fields that were discovered prior to 1970, which are past their peaks and beginning their declines.[1]

- Much of the remaining quarter comes from fields that are 10 to 15 years old.

- New fields are diminishing in number and size every year, and this trend has held for over a decade.[2]

Overall, the oil fields we rely on to meet demand are old, and their production is shrinking, thereby bringing the oil industry closer to the peak and our entire global economy closer to the brink of catastrophe. Because when these fields dry up, so does everything else. And unfortunately, while today's oil fields are struggling at this very moment to keep pace with demand, new field discoveries are diminishing.

Before you can tap a reservoir, you must discover it. Here, too, the picture is clear: The world passed the peak of oil discovery in the early 1960s, and we now find only about one barrel of oil for every three we produce.[3] The fields we're discovering now are smaller, and in more remote and geographically challenging locations, making them far more expensive to produce. And the new oil is of lesser quality: less light sweet crude, and more heavy sour grades. These trends have held firmly for about four decades, despite the latest and greatest technology, and despite increasingly intensive drilling and exploration efforts.

This should be no surprise to anyone. It's the nature of resource exploitation that we use the best, most abundant and lowest-cost resources first, then move on to smaller resources of lower quality, which are harder to produce.

Global conventional oil production peaked in 2005. For "all liquids," including unconventional oil, the peak of global production will likely be around 2010.

With a little less than half the world's total yet to produce, which will increasingly come from ever-smaller reservoirs with less desirable characteristics, peak oil is not about "running out of oil," but rather running out of *cheap* oil.

The outlook for oil exports, on which the United States is dependent for over two-thirds of its petroleum usage, is even worse. Global exports have been on a plateau since 2004. This poses a firm limit to economic growth.

In sum, demand for oil is still increasing, while supply is decreasing; the absolute peak of oil production is probably within the next two years; and net importers like the United States are not going to be able to maintain current levels of imports, let alone increase them. This is a very serious situation, because without enough imports to meet demand, we simply cannot function. We will find it increasingly difficult to transport food, medicine, and clothing; to fuel our planes, trains, automobiles, and cargo ships; to provide heat in the winter and cooling in the summer; and to manufacture plastics and other goods that rely on petroleum as a key ingredient.

While the world's top energy data agencies have all commented on the threat of peak oil, along with many of the leaders of the world's top energy producers, the U.S. Government Accountability Office (GAO) may have said it best:

> [T]he consequences of a peak and permanent decline in oil production could be even more prolonged and severe than those of past oil supply shocks. Because the decline would be neither temporary nor reversible, the effects would continue until alternative transportation technologies to displace oil became available in sufficient quantities at comparable costs.[4]

Even so, peak oil is just the first hard shock of the energy crisis that will soon be unfolding. Right after peak oil, we will have peak gas.

## Peak Gas

In many ways, the story of natural gas is similar to that of oil. It has a bell-shaped production curve (although compared to oil, it hits a longer production plateau, and drops off much faster on the back side), and the peak occurs at about the halfway point.

Like oil, new gas wells are tapping smaller and less productive resources every year, indicating that the best prospects have already been exploited and that we're now relying on "infill drilling" and unconventional sources, such as tight sands gas, coalbed methane, and resources that are deeper and more remote.

Like oil, the largest deposits of gas are few in number and highly concentrated. Just three countries hold 58 percent of global gas reserves: Russia, Iran, and Qatar. All other gas provinces have 4 percent or less.[5]

And like oil, there is the quality issue. It appears that we have already burned through the best and cheapest natural gas—the high-energy-content methane that comes out of the ground easily at a high flow rate. We're now getting down to smaller deposits of "stranded gas" and the last dregs of mature gas fields, and producing gas that has a lower energy content.

Assuming that world economic growth continues, that estimates of conventional reserves are more or less correct, and that there will not be an unexpected spike in unconventional gas, the world will hit a short gas plateau by 2020, and by around 2025 will go into decline.[6]

To illustrate our argument, consider the forecast for natural gas and oil combined, from Dr. Colin Campbell of the Association for the Study of Peak Oil (ASPO), which is shown in Figure 1.1.

However, the local outlook for natural gas is far more important than the global outlook. Natural gas production is mostly a landlocked business, because it's difficult to store and expensive to liquefy for transport. In the United States, we import only 19 percent of the natural gas we use, of which 86 percent is transported by pipeline from Canada and Mexico, both of which are past their peaks. Imports from Canada account for about 17 percent of our total gas consumption,[7] but Canada may have as little as seven years' worth of natural gas reserves left.[8]

Because it's difficult to store, there is little storage or reserve capacity in our nation's web of gas pipelines and storage facilities. In the United States, we have only about a 50-day supply of working storage of natural gas.[9] There isn't much cushion in the system; everything operates on a just-in-time inventory basis, including market pricing.

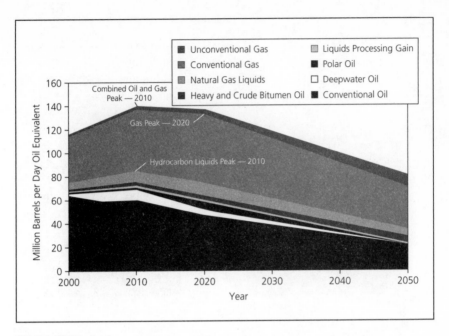

**FIGURE 1.1** *Campbell's (2003) Forecast of World Oil and Gas Production*
*Sources:* Data: C.J. Campbell and Anders Sivertsson, 2003; chart: David J. Hughes slide deck, "Can Energy Supply Meet Forecast World Demand?," November 3, 2004.

Therefore, our main concern with gas is the domestic production peak. North America reached its peak of gas production in 2002, and has been declining ever since—the inevitable result of mature gas basins reaching the end of their productive lives.[10] (See Figure 1.2.)

The onset of the U.S. production peak was in 2001, and production is now declining at the rate of about 1.7 percent per year—far below the projection of the Energy Information Administration, as shown in Figure 1.3.

The declining plateau of production has held despite the application of the world's most advanced technology, and a tripling of producing gas wells since 1971, from approximately 100,000 to more than 300,000. (See Figure 1.4.)

The same is true for Canada, where they've been drilling more than ever, but production is still declining. Consequently, in recent years, gas rigs have been leaving Canada, and going to locations elsewhere in the world where rental fees are higher.

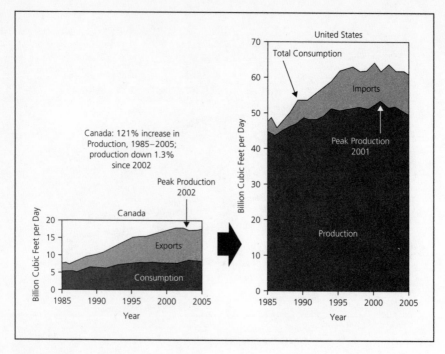

FIGURE 1.2 *North American Gas Production, 1985–2005*
*Source:* J. David Hughes, "Natural Gas in North America: Should We Be Worried?,"
October 26, 2006, http://www.aspo-usa.com/fall2006/presentations/pdf/Hughes_D_
NatGas_Boston_2006.pdf.

In North America, the best and cheapest natural gas at high flow rates is gone. For the United States, this is again a very serious situation. Current supply-and-demand forecasts indicate that a shortfall in natural gas supply is looming, possibly by as much as 11 trillion cubic feet (tcf) per year by 2025, or *about half of U.S. current usage* of 22 tcf/year.

When we passed the North American gas peak, as seen in Figure 1.5, the price of gas imports skyrocketed. Yet demand has continued to increase, in part due to increased demand for grid power, but also in part due to switching over to gas from petroleum, which has increased in price even more rapidly than gas. Now we're needing more imports every year, but getting about the same amounts, and paying more for them. This trend shows no signs of abating.

Therefore, North America will increasingly have to rely on *liquefied natural gas* (LNG) imported by sea.

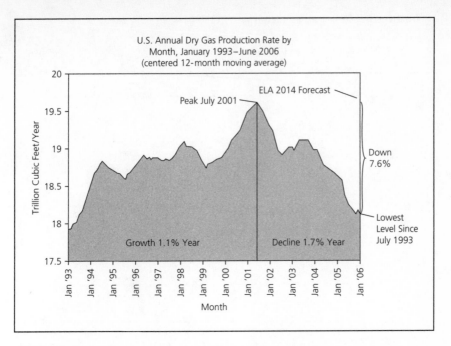

**FIGURE 1.3** *U.S. Gas Production Rate, 1993–2006*
*Source:* J. David Hughes, "Natural Gas in North America: Should We Be Worried?,"
October 26, 2006, http://www.aspo-usa.com/fall2006/presentations/pdf/Hughes_D_
NatGas_Boston_2006.pdf.

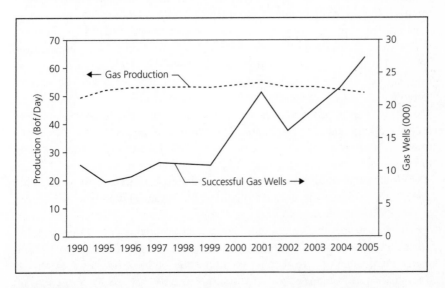

**FIGURE 1.4** *U.S. L48 Gas Production versus Successful Drilling*
*Source:* "Balancing Natural Gas Supply and Demand," notes from Department of
Energy Meeting, December 2005, http://www.fossil.energy.gov/programs/oilgas/
publications/naturalgas_general/ng_supply_overview.pdf.

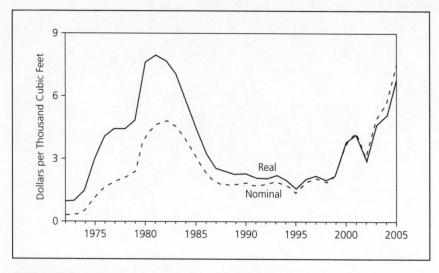

**FIGURE 1.5** *Cost of Gas Imports, 1970–2005*
Source: EIA *Annual Energy Review,* 2005.

**Liquefied Natural Gas** LNG is made by carefully cooling natural gas to minus 260 degrees Fahrenheit, at which point it condenses into a liquid. It then must be kept under controlled temperature and pressure to stay liquefied, with some of it "boiling off" along the way, and transported in superinsulated, very expensive, pressurized tanker vessels. Then when it reaches its destination, it must be slowly *regasified*—warmed back up—before it can be sent through a pipeline to the end-user.

All of this requires significant inputs of energy and large facilities for both liquefaction and regasification. The whole LNG process, from cooling to transporting to regasification, entails a 15 to 30 percent loss of the energy in the gas. It also makes the gas more expensive than domestic gas.

What is the potential LNG supply for the United States? At present, it's uncertain. Consider the outlook for the three countries with the largest gas reserves: Russia, Iran, and Qatar.

In Russia, the investment climate for international energy companies has turned less than hospitable after a vicious round of resource renationalization under President Putin in recent years, and the outlook for LNG exports is dubious. Russia's planned gas exportation capacity appears to be focused on pipeline transport, and a dispute with Royal Dutch Shell over the rising costs of Russia's very first LNG plant at the Sakhalin II field has delayed progress on the project.

As for Iran, it seems unlikely that the geopolitical standoff over its nuclear development program will be resolved any time soon, such that it might become a hospitable investment climate for gas exportation projects. So we can probably rule out Iran as a major source of LNG for North America, at least for now.

That leaves Qatar, which is friendly to the United States and making significant investments in its LNG export capacity. Unfortunately—again due to rising costs—plans to build several much-anticipated LNG export facilities in Qatar were canceled in February 2007, such as a proposed $15 billion LNG facility in partnership with ExxonMobil. "Right now, everyone around us is postponing and delaying projects," Qatari Oil Minister al-Attiyah commented.[11]

At the same time, a rising sentiment of NIMBYism (Not In My Backyard) has nixed planned LNG import facilities in the United States, from Louisiana to Long Beach.

This is not a scenario to inspire hope for a dramatic increase in LNG imports. But according to respected Canadian geologist J. David Hughes, who provided the figures referenced earlier on gas, to cover the projected 2025 gas shortfall of 10 to 11 tcf/year in the United States alone, we would need to *double* (or, after competition sets in, *triple*) the *world's* current LNG capacity. Hughes estimates that this would require:

- Two hundred new LNG tankers, each with capacity of three billion cubic feet (bcf).
- Thirty new North America–based receiving terminals, each with capacity of one bcf per day.
- Some 56 new foreign-based 200 bcf/year liquefaction trains.
- Capital investment on the order of $US100–200 billion.
- Time to build total capacity = 10 to 20+ years.[12]

Even if we had no difficulty at all in building new gas liquefaction and receiving plants, this stretches the imagination and is virtually impossible.

**The End of the Line**  Where does this leave us? In short, when it comes to natural gas, we're on our own in the United States. Although new drilling in the Lower 48, the Gulf, and, eventually, in Alaska will produce some additional gas, it won't be nearly enough to change the basic peak production profile. At best, it will thicken and extend the tail. That leaves one remaining option: switching fuels.

Natural gas is commonly used for heating and cooking, because it is safe, clean burning, efficient, and easy to control. Switching those uses to something else, like coal, wood, or fuel oil, means really stepping backward in time and technology, and comes with high carbon emissions.

But 29 percent of the natural gas used in the United States is for generating grid power, and accounts for 20 percent of the grid power produced.[13] That portion we can shift: to renewables!

Recognizing the serious threat that the natural gas supply poses to grid power generation, and the importance of renewables to fill the gap, former IEA chief Claude Mandil remarked in May 2007:

> A heavy investment cycle in power generation is looming in most IEA countries and governments need to play an assertive role in reducing uncertainty and making sure appropriate investment takes place. . . . A window of opportunity now exists to push for a cleaner and more efficient generation portfolio that will have significant impact on the energy sector and the environment for the next 40–50 years.[14]

This window is yawning wider every year, as we approach the end of the line for natural gas–fired power plants.

The next obvious choice would be to increase our reliance on coal, the dominant fuel used for grid power. However, there may be a slight problem with that.

## Peak Coal

Coal is by far the dirtiest form of fossil fuel we use, but it's also the most readily usable fuel that we still have in relative abundance. Coal provides about one-quarter of the total energy the world uses. Worldwide electricity production is 40 percent powered by coal. Two-thirds of the steel industry relies on it for fuel, and that coal must be high-energy "black coal."

Like oil and gas, the best deposits of coal are highly concentrated. The major deposits of coal—about 90 percent—are located in just six countries: the United States, which has the most, plus Russia, India, China, Australia, and South Africa.

The United States has 496.1 billion tons of demonstrated coal reserves, 27 percent of the world total,[15] and thus is often called "the Saudi Arabia of coal." Our coal endowment has been widely estimated to be a 250-year supply. But that estimate was based on a USGS study from the 1970s, which assumed that 25 percent of the known coal could be recovered with current technology and at current prices. Now the USGS believes that only 5 percent is recoverable with today's technology and at current prices.[16]

This startling conclusion came from a 2007 study by the National Academy of Sciences. The researchers looked at recent updated surveys from the

United States Geological Survey (USGS) and determined that some of the old assumptions were wrong. "There is probably sufficient coal to meet the nation's needs for more than 100 years at current rates of consumption," the study says. "However, it is not possible to confirm the often-quoted assertion that there is a sufficient supply of coal for the next 250 years."[17]

Note that the 100-year estimate is based on our *current* consumption rate: about 1.1 billion tons a year. By 2030, due to users switching over to coal from other rapidly depleting fuels, the rate of coal consumption could be as much as 70 percent higher than it is today, in which case that "100-year" supply could be depleted much more quickly.[18]

Similarly, a separate study of world coal reserves in March 2007, which was conducted by a German consultancy called the Energy Watch Group (EWG), found that the United States does not have anywhere near its claimed 250-year supply of coal.[19] Indeed, EWG claims that in terms of energy content, the United States passed its peak of coal production in 1998!

The distinction is based on the fact that various types of coal contain different amounts of energy. Anthracite (also known as black coal) from Appalachia and Illinois has 30 megajoules of energy per kilogram (30 Mj/kg), but it has long been a tiny fraction of our overall coal production, and has been in decline for over half a century.

Our supposedly vast reserves are mainly of lower-quality bituminous coal, delivering 18 to 29 Mj/kg, and subbituminous coal and lignite ("brown coal"), delivering a mere 5 to 25 Mj/kg. (See Figure 1.6.)

For comparison purposes, EWG translated the energy content of the coal produced into *tons of oil equivalent*. In terms of *volumes of stuff mined*, they found that U.S. coal production can continue to grow for about another 10 to 15 years. But in terms of *energy*, which is the only metric that really matters, U.S. coal production peaked in 1998 at 598 million tons of oil equivalent, and had fallen to 576 million by 2005.

Just as we have burned through the world's best sources of oil and natural gas, we have burned the best sources of coal. The remaining coal we produce will be of progressively lower quality, and will be progressively more expensive to transport due to the escalating cost of diesel.

In a replay of the well-worn debate about oil reserves, it appears that the global reserve numbers for coal have been vastly overstated. The information we've had for the world, like the U.S. data, is decades old and unreliable, and modern reassessments by nice, transparent countries like Germany and the United Kingdom have resulted in 90 percent reductions!

The reserve numbers from Asia are particularly suspect, some dating back to the 1960s. China hasn't reduced its reported reserve numbers in

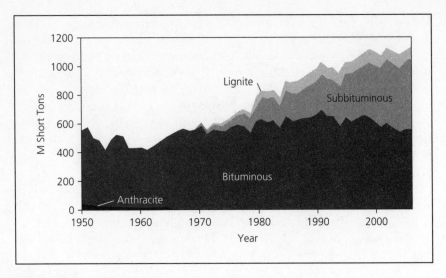

**FIGURE 1.6** *Coal Production in the United States*
*Source:* Energy Watch Group.

15 years, even though we know it has produced some 20 percent of its reserves since then.

In fact, for the past 20 years, *all* major coal-producing nations that have updated their reserve numbers have adjusted them downward. And in the past 25 years, the global total reserve estimate has been cut by 60 percent.

The EWG report concludes, "The present and past experience does not support the common argument that reserves are increasing over time as new areas are explored and prices rise."

Let's look at the data.

■ Total global reserves stand at about 909 billion tons.

■ The world's largest producer of coal is China, which will likely peak between 2012 and 2022, followed by a steep decline.

■ The next-largest producer is the United States, which will likely peak between 2020 and 2030.

Figure 1.7 is EWG's chart of possible worldwide coal production. Based on this scenario, the EWG estimates that the absolute peak of global coal production will occur around 2020, about 10 years after peak oil, and at about the same time as peak gas!

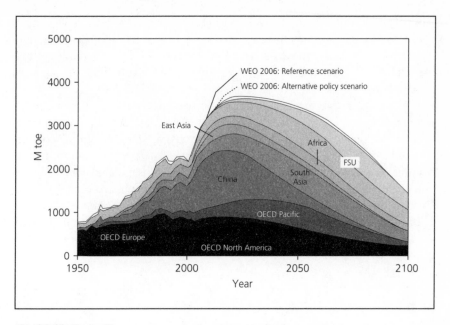

**FIGURE 1.7**  *Worldwide Possible Coal Production*
*Source:* Energy Watch Group.

Although coal depletion is another prong of the threat of global energy depletion, in terms of the long-term survival of life on Earth, it's a good thing. Coal is a greenhouse gas nightmare, and is the second-dirtiest form of hydrocarbons (after oil sands and shales). As we will see in Chapter 11, the problem of global warming demands that we reduce our consumption of coal. Even scaling up coal-to-liquids (CTL) production would require a large increase in emissions.

Many governmental and business leaders have expressed hope for dramatically expanding coal usage while avoiding an explosion of greenhouse gas emissions through the use of carbon capture and sequestration (CCS). CCS technology has been available for years, but it has failed to really catch on because it has always been considered to be too expensive. Before we assume that it will become a common feature of coal-burning plants in the future, we must ask ourselves what will be different in the future such that the cost of CCS will be deemed acceptable. At this point, we must view "clean coal" strictly as a sound bite. In real-life, commercial power doesn't yet exist.

There is also a cost attached to CCS that is almost never mentioned: that of energy. An interesting and detailed study by oil industry analyst Rembrandt

Koppelaar of ASPO-Netherlands looked at the energy cost of CCS, and compared that to the aforementioned EWG study, which had projected a gentle slope past the peak. Koppelaar determined that adding CCS technology shifted the peak of coal forward five years, to between 2015 and 2025, and significantly sharpened the slope of the decline. (See Figure 1.8.)

We can therefore imagine a scenario in which we push for increased coal usage due to peak oil and peak natural gas, but we do it responsibly by requiring CCS technology on every coal plant—only to advance the date of peak coal.

With or without CCS, peak coal suggests that powering the grid may become a challenge within a decade, leaving many observers to conclude that a nuclear energy renaissance may be the next best solution. According to the Energy Information Administration (EIA)'s *International Energy Outlook 2007*, world electricity generation will need to nearly double from 2004 to 2030.[20] Can nuclear energy meet that massively surging demand?

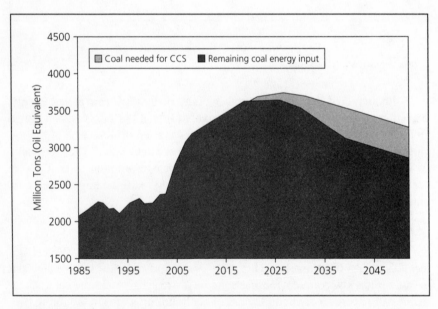

FIGURE 1.8 *Coal Production Scenario with Energy Input Costs for Carbon Dioxide Capture and Storage (CCS)*
*Sources:* Chart: Rembrandt Koppelaar, http://europe.theoildrum.com/node/2733; production scenario: Energy Watch Group, www.energywatchgroup.org/files/Coalreport.pdf.

## Peak Nuclear

By now, you can probably guess what the story is with nuclear power: The best ores of uranium have been mined, leaving mainly low-quality ores left to exploit.

To the casual observer, this might seem at first like a ridiculous statement. Uranium is a very common element, found in about the same abundance as tin worldwide, in everything from granite to seawater. Almost all—99.3 percent—of the uranium found on Earth is uranium-238, an isotope of uranium containing 238 protons per atom. The remaining uranium—0.7 percent—is uranium-235, and that's what is used as fuel for our "light water" nuclear reactors.[21]

In a light water reactor, a chain reaction causes the fission (breaking apart) of the nuclei of the uranium-235 atoms, which generates an enormous amount of heat. (Some of the uranium-238 atoms also contribute, by converting to plutonium-239, of which about half is consumed in the process.) The heat is used to turn water into steam, which is then used to turn a turbine and generate electricity. Water is used as a moderator, to slow down the neutrons in the nucleus sufficiently to support the chain reaction.

The most common type of nuclear plant today, and the ones currently being planned, are pressurized water reactors, which use pressurized water as a coolant and neutron moderator. This type of reactor is generally considered to be the safest and most reliable.

In the early days of nuclear energy, it was assumed that the industry would quickly move beyond simple water reactors and develop *breeder* reactors, which can use the far more abundant uranium-238. Breeder reactors are so called because they generate more fuel than they consume, by neutron irradiation of uranium-238 and thorium-232 or plutonium. With breeder reactors, the initial fuel charge is gradually consumed and then the reactor runs on the fuel it has generated itself. Breeder reactors are cooled by liquid metal (such as sodium or lead) and have the advantage of being able to use depleted uranium-238 and uranium formerly used in weapons as fuel.[22]

After it is used, the fuel must be taken out of a breeder reactor and reprocessed in order to be reused. In this step, it is conceivable that some plutonium could be diverted from the reprocessing and fall into the hands of illicit weapons builders, which is why breeder reactors have aroused fresh fears of terrorists armed with nukes. Although reprocessing spent fuel is the foundation of France's robust nuclear energy program, concerns about safety, nuclear weapons proliferation, and economics have halted nuclear fuel reprocessing in the United States for over 30 years.[23]

There are actually dozens of different types of nuclear reactors, each with its own fuel needs and pros and cons. But all commercial nuclear reactors in use today are either water reactors or some type of fast breeder reactor.[24]

**Limits to Nuclear Power** As of 2007, there were 435 commercial nuclear reactors operating in 30 countries, providing 370,000 MW of capacity—that's 6.2 percent of the total energy produced worldwide, or about 16 percent of the world's base-load electricity.[25]

The United States supplies more commercial nuclear power than any other nation in the world, and currently has 104 commercial nuclear-generating units licensed to operate,[26] which constitute a mere 11.5 percent of the nation's energy needs.

Can nuclear energy be substantially scaled up? According to the EIA's *International Energy Outlook, 2007*, nuclear power will remain a bit player. Figure 1.9 illustrates the EIA's projection.

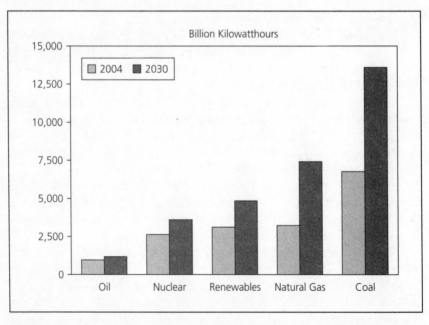

FIGURE 1.9 *World Electricity Generation by Fuel, 2004 and 2030*
*Sources:* www.eia.doe.gov/oiaf/ieo/pdf/electricity.pdf; 2004: derived from Energy Information Administration (EIA), *International Energy Annual, 2004* (May–July 2006), www.eia.doe.gov/iea; 2030: EIA, *System for the Analysis of Global Energy Markets* (2007).

The long lead times for nuclear plants, plus their high cost of construction and fuel production, necessarily limit their future. Part of the problem is shortages in building materials and skilled labor—the same limits that face the oil and gas industries. Coal and natural gas power plants, despite their environmental consequences, are far easier, faster, and cheaper to build, so the EIA is probably correct in this forecast.

But perhaps the most effective limit on the nuclear power industry is NIMBYism—that is, "Not in my backyard." It's nearly impossible, at least in the United States, to find any community willing to host a new nuclear plant or a nuclear waste storage site.

The last reactor built in the United States was ordered nearly four decades ago, took three decades to approve and build, and became operational in 1996. That's a very long lead time. Even if the political will can be mustered to grease the skids for new plants, it's hard to imagine that lead time being shortened by much, if at all, as environmental review requirements and community resistance are greater now than they were then.

Then there is the problem of just maintaining our current nuclear capacity. Of the 103 reactors currently operating in the United States, many are approaching the end of their intended life spans. Even with 20-year extensions of their planned life spans, all existing reactors will be decommissioned by the middle of this century. Just replacing them will require building two reactors a year for the next 50 years—in itself a dubious prospect.[27]

The aging of nuclear plants is a major factor worldwide. A 2007 paper by leading researchers at the Oxford Research Group suggests that over the next 25 years, nuclear power capacity is actually set to decrease, as many of the world's operational reactors are nearing the end of their lives. However, replacement reactors aren't forthcoming: There are only 25 new nuclear reactors currently being built, with 76 more planned and another 162 proposed but hardly certain. Even if all of them materialized in the next 25 years, we'd still be nearly 40 percent shy of replacing all of today's reactors.[28]

## Peak Uranium

Life span and NIMBYism aside, however, the most unyielding limit to nuclear power is the prospect of peak uranium production. As new sources become harder and harder to find, the prospect of future nuclear growth becomes dimmer.

Gerald Grandey, the president and CEO of Cameco Corporation, the largest uranium producer in the United States, believes that demand for uranium will exceed supply for the next eight or nine years, forcing utilities to depend on inventories for fissionable fuel rather than new production. In a June 2007 press conference, he indicated that he expects demand to grow at 3 percent annually for the next decade, but doesn't see uranium mining being able to keep pace with demand. Nor does he see much in the way of opportunity to acquire smaller producers in order to increase his company's output: "There isn't a whole lot out there to acquire that's meaningful," he said.[29]

This is a complex topic, but essentially, like coal, uranium comes down to a question of *energetics*. Only the highest-quality ores are net energy positive when used in a typical fission reactor. And like coal, we may be past peak uranium in terms of energy content.

According to independent nuclear analyst Jan Willem Storm van Leeuwen, when the uranium-235 content of the ore is under 0.02 percent, more energy is required to mine and refine the uranium than can be captured from it in a nuclear reactor, so it's not worth doing.

In a 2002 paper by van Leeuwen and Philip Smith, "Can Nuclear Power Provide Energy for the Future; Would It Solve the CO2-Emission Problem?," the authors predict that the diminishing availability of high-grade uranium ores will pose a hard limit to the future growth of nuclear energy: "Another way of putting it is to say that if all of the electrical energy used today were to be obtained from nuclear power, all known useful reserves of uranium would be exhausted in less than three years."[30]

Naturally, as they are consumed, the world's reserves of high-grade ore are dropping. The vast majority of the remaining uranium, and the largest deposits of it, have ore grades lower than 0.1 percent. That is 100 to 1,000 times poorer a fuel than the ore used today, making it uneconomical to mine.[31] (See Figure 1.10.)

As Figure 1.10 shows, van Leeuwen estimates that at current rates of consumption—again, not anticipating any massive upscaling of nuclear energy usage—high-grade uranium ore will last only to about 2034, and nuclear energy will become a net energy loser by 2070.[32]

The remaining sources of uranium, from lower-quality ores to seawater, are ultimately net energy losers because it takes so much energy taken from fossil fuels to mine and produce the fissionable material that it would be pointless to use those fuels for mining and processing uranium to drive a reactor. It would be far better just to burn them.

The Oxford Research Group paper supports the conclusion that there are adequate reserves of high-grade uranium ores for only about another 25 years of operation, and that any increases beyond that point will have to come from breeder reactors, which primarily use the much-more-abundant plutonium for fuel.[33]

A 2006 study by the Energy Watch Group (the same group that did the coal report), "Uranium Resources and Nuclear Energy," indicates that even

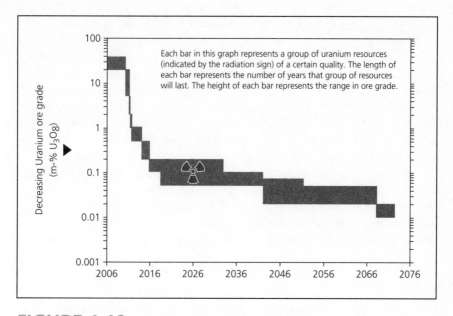

Each bar in this graph represents a group of uranium resources (indicated by the radiation sign) of a certain quality. The length of each bar represents the number of years that group of resources will last. The height of each bar represents the range in ore grade.

**FIGURE 1.10**  *Uranium Ore Grade, 2006–2076*
*Source:* Jan Willem Storm van Leeuwen, Oxford Research Group.

under the best-case estimates of uranium resources, production will peak before 2050, assuming today's relatively minuscule rate of use.[34] Increase the rate of use, or use a less optimistic reserve number, and that date moves forward quickly.

The EWG study's conclusion was sobering:

*The analysis of data on uranium resources leads to the assessment that discovered reserves are not sufficient to guarantee the uranium supply for more than thirty years.*

*Eleven countries have already exhausted their uranium reserves. In total, about 2.3 Mt of uranium have already been produced. At present only one country (Canada) is left having uranium deposits containing uranium with an ore grade of more than 1%, most of the remaining reserves in other countries have ore grades below 0.1%, and two-thirds of reserves have ore grades below 0.06%.[35]*

The Energy Watch Group estimates that the uranium peak would be around 2025 for "probable reserves" and 2030 for "possible reserves,"[36] the latter being more or less in line with van Leeuwen's estimate.

Figure 1.11 is their chart of *possible reserves*—in other words, their best-case scenario.

As shocking as this projection is, if the world significantly expands its use of nuclear power, the reality could be worse. EWG's assumptions about the rate of use were based on the nuclear plants and uranium mining operations currently in existence, plus those that were planned or under construction at the end of 2006. If the ambitions of government leaders to radically increase nuclear-generating capacity are realized, then the rate of use will be higher, and the peak sooner.

To put a final nail in the nuclear coffin, the authors of the EWG report note that alternative reactor designs won't substantively affect their calculation, saying, "At least within this time horizon, neither nuclear breeding reactors nor thorium reactors will play a significant role because of the long lead times for their development and market penetration."[37]

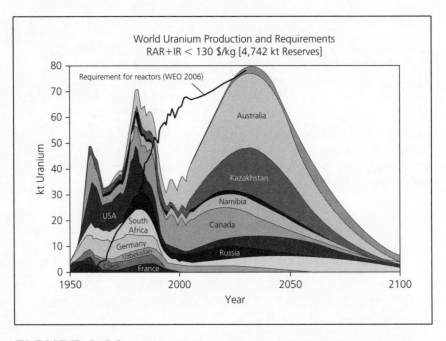

FIGURE 1.11 *Future Production Profile of Uranium—All Possible Reserves*

*Source:* Energy Watch Group, "Uranium Resources and Nuclear Energy," December 2006, EWG Series No. 1/2006, www.lbst.de/publications/studies__e/2006/EWG-paper_1-06_Uranium-Resources-Nuclear-Energy_03DEC2006.pdf.

Nuclear energy has other challenges, too, apart from the availability of fuel. The true cost of building nuke plants, from planning all the way through decommissioning, are never accounted for, nor paid, by the operators of the plants. The decommissioning costs are invariably externalized, or foisted onto the public, while we have yet to deal with the past 60 years' worth of toxic spent fuel, some quarter of a million tons of it, now scattered around the globe. Once all costs are taken into account, nuclear energy may in fact be a net energy loser.

To conclude, alternative reactor designs are not ready for prime time, and for traditional reactors, the world has 30 years or less of uranium reserves left, at current rates of usage. The global peak of uranium production will likely be around 2025 to 2030, perhaps 5 or 10 years after peak coal.

## CRISIS OR OPPORTUNITY?

We have now seen a few scenarios for peak oil, peak gas, peak coal, and peak uranium, which together account for 98 percent of today's energy usage. These scenarios, built on objective and peer-reviewed data and research, illustrate the urgency of a complete overhaul of our energy economy. Within the next century, most of our conventional power-generating resources will fade or simply become too expensive to find, extract, produce, and consume. This leaves the entire global community with a significant challenge to rapidly develop new energy technologies and a new energy infrastructure. Because, as you can see below, the global fossil fuel production and forecast does not look good.

Putting them all together (with slightly different forecasts), it might look something like the image depicted in Figure 1.12. That's why we call peak energy a crisis. Given that the bell curves of production for all of today's dominant fuels tail off to perhaps one-quarter of the peak supply by the end of the century, we presume that we'll have to accomplish the renewable-energy revolution in perhaps 75 years' time—a breathtaking challenge.[38]

With peak energy occurring by 2025, where does that leave us? It leaves us with an incredibly huge gap to fill with renewables. Consider today's overall energy mix by referring to Figure 1.13.

The largest renewable energy source in the world is hydropower, but there is very little hydroelectric power left to exploit worldwide, and many of the existing plants have struggled to continue operating in the last few years due to reduced rainfall—a phenomenon that has been tied to global warming.

Therefore, with 98 percent of today's fuels in irreversible depletion by 2025, we're going to have to start growing that 1.4 percent wedge of "Geothermal and Other" as fast as we possibly can, starting yesterday, until it takes over

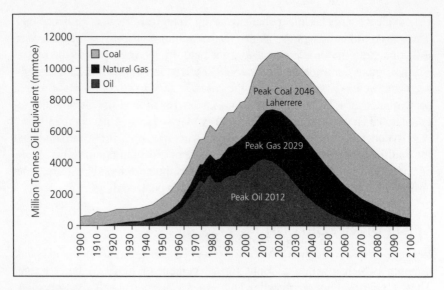

**FIGURE 1.12** *Global Fossil Fuel Production and Forecast*
*Source:* Euan Mearns and Luís de Sousa.

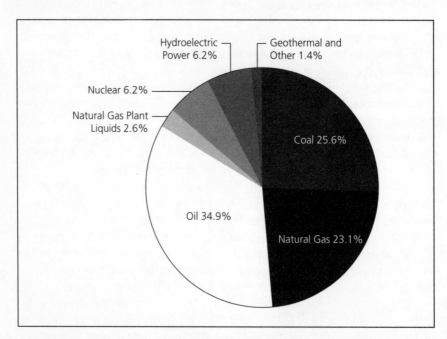

**FIGURE 1.13** *World Energy Production by Source, 2004*
*Source:* EIA, "World Primary Energy Production by Source, 1970–2004," www.eia.doe.gov/emeu/aer/txt/stb1101.xls.

nearly the whole pie. Unless some amazing, unexpected, paradigm-changing breakthrough happens in the meantime, it is literally our only choice (after reducing consumption).

This raises an important question: Since the foregoing analysis suggests that peak oil will occur in the next two years (if it hasn't already) and that the peak of all energy production is a scant 17 years off, do we have enough time to pull it off?

One of the most well-respected studies on how long it will take to prepare for peak oil was published in February 2005 by veteran energy analysts Robert L. Hirsch, Roger Bezdek, and Robert Wendling, in a report titled "Peaking of World Oil Production: Impacts, Mitigation, and Risk Management,"[39] which they did for the U.S. Department of Energy.

Their approach was elegantly simple: First, they determined how much oil could be offset by various mitigation strategies. They made some reasonable assumptions about the future potential of all exploitable sources of energy, and about the amount of savings that might be achieved through conservation and higher efficiency, and charted each as a wedge on an aggregate chart. Then they charted that against what they considered to be a reasonable forecast of world oil production under three different scenarios, in which intensive mitigation begins at the peak, 10 years before the peak, and 20 years before the peak.

Their conclusion was blunt: Only if we commence our efforts a full 20 years before the peak can we manage a smooth transition. If peak oil is truly only two years off, then we are already facing an inevitable, roughly 20-year shortfall in supply, simply because it takes that long to replace infrastructure and make other necessary adjustments to live within a reducing, rather than expanding, energy budget.

In their words:

*If mitigation were to be too little, too late, world supply/demand balance will be achieved through massive demand destruction (shortages), which would translate to significant economic hardship. . . . The world has never faced a problem like this. Without massive mitigation more than a decade before the fact, the problem will be pervasive and will not be temporary. Previous energy transitions (wood to coal and coal to oil) were gradual and evolutionary; oil peaking will be abrupt and revolutionary.[40]*

The lead author of the report, Robert Hirsch, a longtime energy consultant for Science Applications International Corporation (SAIC), sums up the situation simply: "Peak oil: the more you think about it, the uglier it gets."[41]

The paucity of alternative fuels, and the relative immaturity of renewable energy and of strategies for reducing energy consumption, prompted noted peak oil analyst and oil investment banker Matthew Simmons to remark, "There are no magic bullets, only magic BBs." Rather than pursuing some single new source of energy, like the ever-elusive cold fusion, we need to be thinking about a thousand small solutions that together can solve the energy-depletion dilemma.

## THE SOLUTIONS

In the next 11 chapters, we will discuss many of these "small solutions." We will review the various renewable energy technologies that are at the forefront of transitioning our energy economy, we will show you the companies that got an early lead in the renewable energy sector, and explain why they delivered for investors and why they're now some of the most important energy companies operating today. But most importantly, we will show you how you can profit from the next generation of renewable energy companies that are poised to take over where fossil fuels leave off.

# CHAPTER

## 2

# THE SOLAR SOLUTION

Of all the energy sources available to us, the Sun is our largest source by far, dropping 970 trillion kWh worth of free energy on us every day. Enough solar energy strikes the United States each day to supply its needs for one and a half years. Put another way, the amount of solar energy the Earth receives every minute is greater than the amount of energy from fossil fuels the world uses in a year![1] Nearly all energy forms on Earth come from the Sun, either directly or indirectly.

To begin with, all fossil fuels are the product of organic life-forms on Earth that drew their energy from the sun. Algae and plants harvested solar energy via photosynthesis, and after accumulating and being cooked for millennia, became the substances that we know today as oil, coal, gas, shales, tar sands, and so forth—what author Thom Hartmann has called the "last hours of ancient sunlight."

Likewise, modern solar energy technologies harvest the sun's energy waves. Photovoltaic (PV) cells make electricity from photosensitive materials that respond to the visible light spectra of sunlight. Solar thermal technologies, such as solar hot-water systems and concentrating solar power (CSP) systems, directly capture heat from infrared light spectra.

Wind energy comes from the uneven heating of the planet as it spins through the day and night, being warmed and cooled by the sun. Hydropower depends on rain, which is the result of the sun warming the surface of the planet and causing evaporation. Even nuclear energy owes its origin to a long-dead sun somewhere. About 6.6 billion years ago, our uranium was formed in a supernova explosion—the colossal collapse of a star. Even the heat at the core of our planet is the result of uranium, thorium, and potassium decaying, causing convection and continental drift. Therefore, even geothermal energy ultimately comes from a sun. In fact, just about the only kind of energy we use that doesn't derive from the Sun is tidal energy, which is primarily generated by the gravitational pull of the Moon.

We'll get to tidal energy later in this book. For now, let's focus our attention on solar, as this is probably the most popular and well-covered sector of the renewable energy market.

In this chapter, we will discuss a number of key points to demonstrate that solar will be a significant source of power generation in the future. We will also focus on the next round of opportunities solar will present to investors like you. First, let's quickly review some background information on solar so you'll have the necessary tools to invest in this sector wisely.

## A SHORT HISTORY OF SOLAR TECHNOLOGIES

Modern attempts to harvest the sun's energy directly date back to the 1870s, and the first solar motor company was founded in 1900. The first documented design was a concentrating solar power (CSP) device, which focuses the heat of the sun using lenses or mirrors to drive thermal engines or generators. In the 1870s, CSP systems were used to drive steam engines, which in turn were used to do something else, usually to pump water (although they were also used to make ice, in order to impress investors and astonish the public).

Today, CSP plants have been radically improved. Modern plants usually use huge arrays of parabolic trough mirrors to superheat oil or molten salts to around 750 degrees Fahrenheit, which is then used to drive a turbine. Such designs have two key advantages: They can provide their own power storage and continue operating when the sun goes down; or when the sun isn't shining, they can be switched over to run on natural gas.[2] This is one reason why CSP plants have become the technology of choice for utility-scale projects.

Probably the most familiar kind of solar equipment to most people is solar hot water systems, which provide domestic hot water, pool heating, and space heating. Solar hot water experienced an explosion of popularity in the 1970s, thanks to generous federal and state incentives made available under the Carter administration. Unfortunately, the flood of money, directed at a less-than-fully-developed technology and market, led to a Wild West atmosphere in much of the industry. A goodly number of badly made systems were installed, which functioned for a while and then quit, usually sitting ugly and useless on the roof for many years longer than they worked (if at all). The experience gave the solar industry a black eye, from which it has only recently begun to recover.

But recover it has, and how! Today's solar hot water equipment is dramatically improved, of much higher efficiency, and well tested after three decades of experience in the field. With the return of rebates, tax credits, and other incentives, the solar hot water industry is experiencing a rebirth. Increasingly, green building standards are making it a required part of residential and commercial construction as well.

A new generation of direct solar thermal devices is aimed at space heating and process heat. Such large-scale solar thermal systems are most often used for large commercial buildings, such as hotels or breweries. One of the largest such systems heats the million-gallon swimming pool built for the 1996 Atlanta Olympics, saving an estimated $12,000 per year.[3] However, innovative, small rooftop designs are also gaining popularity, helping to heat homes and businesses without greenhouse gas emissions.

The next most common application of solar energy is photovoltaics (PV), in which photons of light are converted into electricity in a semiconductor similar to a computer chip. The first PV chip was made in 1883, using a semiconductor made of selenium and gold. In 1954, the modern age of PV arrived, when Bell Labs engineers discovered—quite accidentally—that silicon doped with certain impurities was very sensitive to light. Since then, the technology has steadily improved. Today's everyday silicon cells boast efficiencies as high as 24 percent, and the race is on for higher efficiency, lower cost, and greater durability.

Of the three major types of solar-energy systems, PV is by far the largest and most rapidly growing market. Let's take a closer look at it.

### Silicon Solar

Traditional solar modules are made with photovoltaic cells made from silicon. The silicon is "grown" in ingots and either sliced into thin wafers to make monosilicon cells or sliced into thin chips that are then assembled into polysilicon cells.

Making solar cells is a very high-tech process, the first stages of which are essentially the same as for making computer chips. In furnaces, silicon is melted down and refined to 99.9999 percent purity so that it will make a good conductor. Then the silicon is applied to a substrate to make a wafer. Traditional silicon solar cells are built up from layers of silicon wafers that have been doped with other substances, which is what causes them to produce electricity that can be harvested by a wire running through the cells.

Next, the wafers must be baked in furnaces as hot as 1,350 degrees centigrade. While they're baking, and while they're being unloaded from the furnace, many factors must be carefully controlled: oxygen, moisture, and airborne particles.

The materials involved are delicate and must be handled carefully, the temperatures are dangerously high, and the whole process must be done in a "clean room" environment so the product will be free of any contaminants. Consequently, making silicon solar cells is an expensive process, and one that can produce only relatively small batches of finished product for a relatively great expenditure of effort.

The PV industry used to rely on the scraps from the semiconductor (computer chip) industry for its feedstock, as it started to take off during a slump in the computer industry. However, the latter's recovery led to a chronic shortage of refined silicon for PV beginning in 2005, which in turn led to a shortage of solar modules in some parts of the world, particularly the United States.

This led to two things, both good for the business: First, the silicon refining and chip manufacturing segments received a big influx of investment to address the supply crisis. The global production of solar cells increased in 2006 by 33 percent over 2005, for a total of 2,204 megawatts, and the production of polysilicon increased by 16 percent.[4]

The second effect was to spur the development of thin-film PV.

## Thin Film

So-called *thin-film* PV devices are usually based on mixtures of elements other than silicon—most notably copper indium gallium selenide (CIGS)—applied in a thin layer to plastic, even organic, components. Using nanotechnology and advanced materials science, thin film is able to produce power with a fraction of the materials. Similar techniques are being tried using ultrathin layers of silicon on a glass substrate, reducing what is now a 250-micrometer ($\mu$m)-thick wafer to less than 20 $\mu$m.

Thin film also has the potential to be mass-produced for a fraction of the cost of mono- or polycrystalline silicon, because the film can be applied to long rolls of substrate and manufactured in continuous processes, unlike the laborious process of making wafers. And because highly refined silicon is so expensive to make—about 45 percent of the cost of a solar cell—thin film also represents the greatest potential for cutting the cost of PV.[5]

Such innovations have the potential to make solar so cheap and cost effective that it can be deployed anywhere, from the first world to the developing world. Already, Kenya buys more than 30,000 small panels each year for as little as $100 each.[6]

While thin-film solar is considerably cheaper than traditional polysilicon solar, it has also suffered from low efficiency. Most of the thin-film products brought to market in the past 10 years had only 4 to 5 percent efficiency—less than half that of their traditional counterparts—so they took up twice as much space or more to achieve the same output. If you wanted to use thin-film solar, you needed the same amount of money but twice the surface area—not a recipe for huge success.

However, intensive research over the past two years or so is changing all that. Exciting innovations in PV are cropping up everywhere. Researchers in the Materials Sciences Division of Lawrence Berkeley National Laboratory recently made an unexpected discovery that could enable solar cells to convert the full spectrum of sunlight—from the near infrared to the far ultraviolet— into electricity.[7]

Some commercially available thin-film solar cells have achieved efficiency levels as high as 9 percent, putting them within competitive reach of traditional silicon modules, but at a lower cost. And in the lab, we're seeing efficiencies as high as 19.5 percent. That particular efficiency was achieved by Ascent Solar (NASDAQ:ASTI).

Other solar cell manufacturers such as Arise Technologies (TSX:APV) and SunPower (NASDAQ:SPWR) are taking a different approach, combining both traditional polysilicon and thin-film PV wafers in a hybrid cell with 18 percent efficiency—right at the top end for commercially available traditional solar cells.

Another player in the thin-film space is Nanosolar, a privately held Silicon Valley company that is building its first manufacturing plant, which will churn out a kind of solar foil in long rolls using a modified printing press. If successful at commercial scale, the process could slash PV production cost to one-tenth of what it is today, on a rapid production line, and build fabrication plants for one-tenth the capital outlay.[8]

The ultimate goal of this PV, however, is what is known as *building integrated photovoltaics* (BIPV), which incorporates PV directly into roofing and other materials, eliminating solar panels entirely. BIPV modules not only produce power, but also function as a roofing membrane, just like composite asphalt shingles. Some models integrate very well aesthetically with composite shingles, making the solar portion hardly noticeable.

Solar roofing tiles are already being installed on some new homes, and their popularity far exceeds their availability. Initiatives like California's SB 1, part of Governor Schwarzenegger's Million Solar Roof campaign, requires solar to be offered as an option for single-family home developments of more than 50 units as of 2011, and other incentives in the state are already leading developers to offer solar as a standard option.[9] With such mandates in place, BIPV has a guaranteed market. Thanks to the steady demand outlook, manufacturers now have the green light and the confidence to invest the hundreds of millions of dollars it will take to scale up the production of BIPV modules to commercial levels.

Beyond standard BIPV, a new generation of solar called *hybrid photovoltaic/thermal* (PV/T or PVT) is also emerging, which uses a layer of PV material over a thermal collector to heat air or hot water. Not only does this capture more solar energy overall, but it actually increases the efficiency of the PV layer by keeping it cool. This is because photovoltaics lose efficiency, or *derate,* as they heat up. Research into PVT has been going on intensively for the last several years, and now a few manufacturers are starting to bring it to market, usually as BIPV equipment, where the house can be designed around it from the beginning.

## THE SKY'S THE LIMIT

With the advent of higher oil and gas prices beginning around 2000, more consumers and businesses began looking for clean, green, domestic alternatives, causing a boom in the solar industry. Annual growth rates of 35 percent or more drove the global market to $11 billion and climbing.

Demand for solar power has been on a steady climb, growing about 25 percent every year for the past 15 years, and about 48 percent per year on average since 2002. That's exponential growth, effectively doubling global production every two years!

Worldwide, PV production increased by 3,800 MW in 2007, an estimated 50 percent jump over 2006. At year end, the global solar PV capacity had reached 12,400 MW.[10] (See Figure 2.1.)

The growth of PV cell production worldwide has been equally outstanding: a sixfold rise since 2000, and 41 percent growth in 2006 alone.[11] In the United States, the growth rate of installed PV has been similar, with a 33 percent gain in 2006 over 2005[12] and a whopping 83 percent gain in 2007.[13]

Of course, all of this growth requires money—and lots of it. According to Nth Power LLC, a cleantech venture capital group, and Clean Edge, Inc., a leading research and publishing firm on clean and green technologies, venture capital going into the U.S. solar business has soared from $68 million in 2004, to $156 million in 2005, to $264 million in 2006. Globally, they estimate that solar PV will grow more than fourfold in 10 years, from a $15.6 billion industry in 2006 to $69.3 billion by 2016.[14]

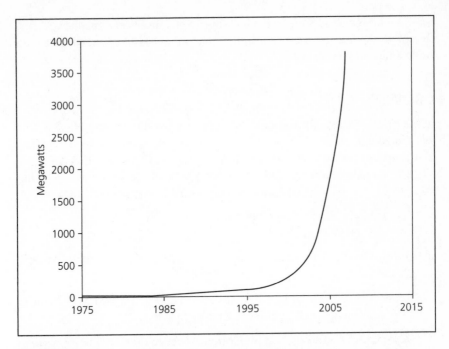

**FIGURE 2.1** *World Annual Photovoltaic Production, 1975–2007*
*Source:* "Solar Cell Production Jumps 50 Percent in 2007," December 27, 2007, Earth Policy Institute, http://www.earthpolicy.org/Indicators/Solar/2007.htm.

China in particular is poised to become a dominant player in the solar arena. With its immense capacity to manufacture silicon-based electronics quickly and cheaply, making solar products is an easy reach for China. In 2006, China passed the United States to become the world's third largest producer of the cells, after Germany and Japan—the latter two being the two most solarized nations in the world.

And they're not done yet: "To say that Chinese PV producers plan to expand production rapidly in the year ahead would be an understatement," said Travis Bradford, president of the Prometheus Institute, in May 2007. "They have raised billions from international IPOs to build capacity and increase scale with the goal of driving down costs. Four Chinese IPOs are expected to come to market this month alone."[15]

While the growth of the industry is impressive, solar power still accounts for less than 1 percent of worldwide electricity consumption. Given the impending realities of declining energy from fossil fuels, the sky is the limit for the solar industry. Some estimates say it could produce as much as 20 percent of worldwide electricity consumption in as few as 35 years, which would be an amazing growth story.

## GROWING CAPACITY

In the United States, utility station PV capacity as of 2005 was 11,000 kW, and distributed (i.e., nonutility capacity) was 485,000 kW. Solar thermoelectric (i.e., CSP) capacity was 400 MW, of which 354 MW is in California (EIA data).[16]

The Golden State is already the largest solar producer in the world, but more large CSP projects will soon be under way, including:

- A 400 MW plant by BrightSource Energy in a dry lakebed just over the border from Primm, Nevada.

- A 553 MW plant by Israeli company Solel Solar Systems in the Mojave Desert.

- An 850 MW plant in San Bernardino County and a 900 MW plant in Imperial County built by Stirling Energy Systems.

- A combined 660 MW plant by Florida Power & Light in San Bernardino County.

- A 175 MW plant by Ausra, a California-based solar thermal company, in a location to be determined.[17]

In total statewide, six new large projects totaling 2,400 MW of power have been proposed, and another 1,770 MW are under discussion. And right-of-way requests have been filed for federal land for 34 potential projects that could produce 24,000 MW of new solar power, enough to power 18 to 24 million homes![18]

Ausra has even grander ambitions. In their plants, hot water is used as a working fluid instead of molten salt or other more expensive media, which opens the possibility of having enough steam storage to run the plant for 16 hours. Should the design become a commercial success, Ausra expects to deliver grid power at the competitive rate of 8 cents per kWh. According to the company's founder and chief scientist, physicist David Mills, the plants could supply 96 percent of the national electricity demand. "The entire energy use of 2006, the current technology including storage would use a patch of land 92 miles by 92 miles," Mills says. "Ten percent of the [Bureau of Land Management] land in Nevada is enough."[19] The main limitation on this scenario is having sufficient grid capacity to transmit the power from the Southwest to the rest of the country.

As for worldwide CSP plants that are either under construction or in planning, the World Energy Council expects capacity to grow to 3,000 MW, of which 2,000 MW will be in Spain, thanks to abundant sunshine and government support.[20]

Corporate America has jumped on board in the last few years as well, recognizing that solar power now makes good economic sense, in addition to the benefits of green cachet. Rolling blackouts in 2001 quickly led Google, Microsoft, and Yahoo! to pursue solar energy as an option for powering large server installations.[21]

Large investments in corporate campuses are also starting to be made, such as Google's recent announcement that it will build a 1.6 megawatt solar installation on its corporate campus—the largest on any corporate campus in the United States, and one of the largest on any corporate site in the world.

Three major factors are fueling the new solar energy boom: lower costs, improved performance, and incentives.

### Cost Reductions

As with any new technology, as the industry grows, costs are coming down.

When solar PV first started taking off in the 1970s, the price of a watt of capacity was around $20; in 2004 that had dropped to $2.70. (Likewise, wind power has dropped from $2 per kWh to 5 to 8 cents now.) With coal-fired power currently running about 2 to 4 cents per kWh, clean energy is rapidly closing the gap on dirty energy.[22]

According to a recent study by the Worldwatch Institute in Washington, D.C., and the Prometheus Institute in Cambridge, Massachusetts, the cost of PV will decrease another 40 percent by 2010, just two years from now![23] Part of the cost reduction owes to simple economies of scale: The more output a plant has, the lower the cost per unit. The production costs of PV solar cells are dropping 8 percent per year in Japan, and 5 percent per year in California.[24]

However, much of the cost reduction in recent years has come from incremental improvements in the manufacturing process. Manufacturers have found savings by reclaiming the residues from sawing expensive silicon ingots into wafers; "debottlenecking" their plants to improve the efficiency of their production processes; and reducing losses from breakage by moving toward more automated handling of materials, and continuous *belt-to-belt* (or in the case of thin film, *roll-to-roll*) fabrication processes.

While such efforts are continuing to squeeze a few percent more productivity out of the fabrication plants every year, a new thrust of cost reduction is focusing on labor costs in the field. Typically, 15 percent or more of the total cost of a solar PV system is installation labor, which can be fairly easily reduced by simply reducing the number of parts that a contractor needs to install.

In a traditional roof-rack mounting system, for example, a mounting foot is bolted to the roof every 48 to 72 inches. Then the mounting rails must be cut to length and installed on the feet using nuts and bolts. Then as many as four clips or clamps are attached to each module with nuts and bolts to mount the module on the rack. Still more labor is needed to run the conductor and ground wiring, plus a grounding lug, which must be carefully screwed into the frame. Many of the clips, screws, nuts, and bolts are very small and easily fumbled or dropped, costing valuable time.

One prominent installer, Akeena Solar (NASDAQ:AKNS), is tackling these issues by integrating the conductor wiring, grounding wire, and racking components directly into the modules, in what they are calling the Andalay system. "The result is a rooftop solar power system with superior built-in reliability with outstanding aesthetics in an all-black, streamlined appearance," says Barry Cinnamon, the CEO of Akeena. "Moreover, an installed Andalay system uses 70 percent fewer parts and requires 25 percent fewer attachment points than traditional solar systems, meaning better long-term performance."

The Andalay system has been licensed by Suntech Power Holdings Co., Ltd. (NYSE: STP), one of the world's leading manufacturers of photovoltaic (PV) cells and modules, for distribution in Europe, Japan, and Australia. Suntech's Managing Director of BIPV Products, Len May, described the benefit: "Andalay is a significant innovation that directly addresses the need to reduce the cost of solar systems, and we are confident that there will be significant demand for this attractive and high performance solar solution in markets outside of the U.S."[25]

**Cost Parity: The Holy Grail** As costs continue to drop for PV, it is rapidly closing in on cost parity in all markets. In fact, solar PV is already economically competitive in states where electricity is expensive, including Hawaii, Massachusetts, and New York, and states with good solar exposure and lots of land, like California, Nevada, and Arizona.[26]

*Cost parity* and *economically competitive* are loaded terms, and few appreciate the subtleties they encompass. It's generally understood that we're comparing solar and other renewable technologies to grid power pricing, but what powers the grid? It is primarily coal! Consider the current and projected breakdown of energy sources used for electricity generation given in the EIA's *International Energy Outlook 2007*, shown in Figure 2.2.

Not only is coal the predominant source of grid power today—about 40 percent of the total—it is expected to be even more so in the coming years. In fact, the graph in Figure 2.2 is likely optimistic about the future role of oil and natural gas, as the EIA has still not admitted to peak oil and gas in its projections. Which leads us to wonder: If oil and gas fall short of the EIA's expectations, will coal or renewables fill the gap? (Like the EIA, we do not believe that nuclear power will be able to scale up significantly from current levels, due to many factors, including peak uranium.)

This means that most analyses of the cost effectiveness of solar PV are comparing it against coal. However, there are a number of problems with that approach.

First, we believe that the cost of coal will rise substantially over the coming years. How fast, we don't know; but it appears that past estimates about the abundance and quality of coal reserves worldwide have been vastly overstated. As mentioned earlier, this startling announcement was made in

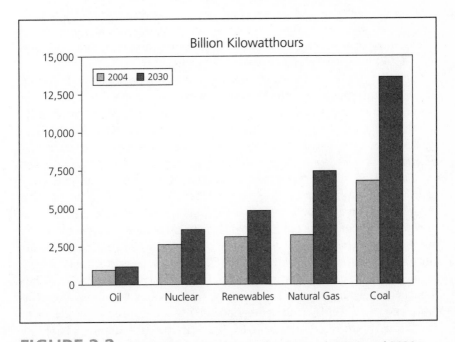

FIGURE 2.2   *World Electricity Generation by Fuel, 2004 and 2030*
*Source:* "International Energy Outlook 2007," Energy Information Administration, http://www.eia.doe.gov/oiaf/ieo/pdf/electricity.pdf.

March 2007 by a German consultancy called the Energy Watch Group.[27] They scrutinized the world's coal resources and concluded that the United States did not have anywhere near its claimed "250-year supply" of coal.

Indeed, they claimed that, in terms of energy content, the United States passed its peak of coal production in 1998. This is due to the varying energy content of different types of coal. Like oil, natural gas, and uranium, we have (naturally) used the best and cheapest resources (anthracite, or "black coal") first. Now we're getting down to lower grades of coal (bituminous, subbituminous, and lignite), which have lower energy content. So even though the actual volumes of coal mined are still increasing in the United States, the energy content is falling, from 598 million tons of oil equivalent in 1998, to 576 million in 2005.

On a global scale, the study estimates that the absolute peak of global coal production will likely be around 2020, approximately 10 years, maybe less, after the global peaks of oil and gas. If you installed a solar-energy system right now, 2020 would be about halfway through its typical 25-year warranty period.

And yet nobody—and we mean *nobody*—factors this into their solar purchasing decisions, even though peak coal would likely radically increase its price, which would increase the price of grid power, and hence the comparative ROI of the solar-energy system.

Instead, not recognizing the radical changes we are about to face, solar buyers assume that the cost of grid power will increase in the future at about the same rate as it has in the past. So we know straight off that the economics of solar are nearly always miscalculated. We expect that as the post-peak reality dawns on everyone, they will quickly recognize the economic superiority of solar power.

Second, as we have seen, the cost of solar will continue to decline, especially in the thin-film arena. For example, Nanosolar hopes to deliver a solar product to the market at $0.99 per watt, which is less than half the current price of traditional solar modules. While their predictions of time to market and manufacturing capacity have proved to be overstated in the few years since they started up, they also raised $150 million in private capital right out of the gate, have no intentions of going public, and have some very big names in technology and investing behind them. Within a few years, their expectations may very well be fulfilled—a potentially paradigm-shifting development. Yet, future solar purchasing expectations are almost always based on today's prices for traditional solar equipment.

Third, the hidden subsidy of not assigning any cost to emissions from fossil fuel–burning power plants is going away. How fast, and by what mechanism, remains to be seen. But we have little doubt that its days are numbered, given that some of the country's largest manufacturers and utilities are now backing everything from carbon cap-and-trade schemes to carbon taxes. Why? Because as the chief of Duke Energy, James Rogers, put it, "If you're not at the table when these negotiations are going on, you're going to be on the menu."[28]

Over the next several decades—again, within the life of a solar PV system—costs will be assigned to carbon emissions. Eventually, those costs will be passed through to grid power pricing. If the knock-on effects of emissions, such as the loss of healthy ecosystems, the loss of natural resource–dependent industries like forestry, health costs, and so on are somehow taken into account, grid power costs could increase further.

Fourth, we are still in the earliest days of incentive programs for renewables, which are changed, added, or removed at both the state and federal level almost annually. As voters become more literate about the politics of energy, we expect the available incentives to become more favorable to solar, especially as we reach the point where it becomes clear that today's largely coal-fired grid is untenable in the long term, and that renewables are the obvious next choice.

Fifth, solar buying decisions for homeowners are very different from what they are for utilities. A homeowner can simply compare his or her historical utility bills to the anticipated cost of the solar system. But for utilities, the decision is much more complex. Utilities must buy a certain amount of baseload generation—that is, power generation that's on all the time, typically from coal and nuclear plants—as well as bursts of generation that will be used only at times of peak demand, which is usually satisfied by natural gas–fired plants. Solar power is usually generated in excess in precisely the same time and place that peak demand occurs: in sunny areas on hot summer days.

So PV really should be compared to natural gas–fired grid pricing, which is going to increase much sooner and faster than coal, and coal-fired baseload capacity really should be compared to suitable renewable baseload generation such as geothermal energy, which can have 98 percent uptime, or CSP plants with storage capability. Such important distinctions, however, are lost when considering only *average* grid prices.

Sixth, the structure of the grid itself is changing. In the coming years, we believe that many innovations will change the way the grid works, including islanding for microgrids, smart metering, automated demand-response management, time-of-use pricing, more deregulation of utilities, and so on. Most of these changes will ultimately benefit any sort of distributed power generation, and in particular solar.

Finally, consider a best-case scenario for solar, where individual communities can function using their own distributed generation and storage within self-islanding microgrids—a very possible scenario. Compare that to the reality we face today, where a single falling tree branch in Ohio took down much of the Northeastern and Midwestern United States, and Ontario, Canada, within two hours on Thursday, August 14, 2003. This was the largest blackout in North American history, affecting about one-third of the population of Canada and one-seventh of the population of the United States.

Such vulnerability can be extremely costly. The cost of the 2003 blackout has been estimated between $4 billion and $10 billion dollars.[29] But opportunity costs of this sort are rarely considered in utility-scale purchases of solar generation. Of course, policymakers are now beginning to take them into account as they lay down the rules for future development and utility procurement. We believe that eventually this will lead to increased support for distributed generation and storage across the grid, particularly for solar energy.

### Better Performance

At the same time that costs of PV are coming down, the technology itself is being improved. Much of the energy absorbed by solar cells is wasted as heat, but recent research is dramatically improving PV efficiency. Ten years ago, the best solar cells available had efficiency levels of only 12 to 15 percent (14 percent is generally considered the minimum profitable performance for standard silicon solar cells).[30] Today's commercially available solar cells are 15 to 22 percent efficient. And new, experimental multijunction solar cells, which combine different types of photosensitive materials that respond to different wavelengths of light, have achieved efficiencies of up to 40 percent.[31,32]

That number is likely to climb even higher as large semiconductor and solar companies pour billions of dollars into solar research and development (R&D).

Applied Materials (NASDAQ:AMAT), the world's largest producer of chip-making equipment, is one such company that is making serious investment in its solar business. CEO Mike Splinter estimates that the PV manufacturing equipment sector will triple from about $1 billion today to more than $3 billion by 2010. "I don't see any reason that Applied Materials can't capture between 15 percent and 20 percent of this total capex over that period, and grow a business that is profitable at $500 million," he says.[33] And the company's vice president, Dr. Charles Gay, wrote in a January 22 editorial, "In some regards the industry has reached a 'tipping point' where the demand, infrastructure, and number of manufacturers have reached a high enough level that makes large-scale production viable, and in fact facilitates still more growth."[34]

The U.S. Department of Energy (DoE) has also funded a slate of research on solar cells, as well as other energy and efficiency research projects.

In November 2007, the DoE announced that it would invest $21.7 million into R&D for advanced PV technology, for 25 projects in partnership with 15 universities and 6 companies; including cost sharing, the total investment will be up to $30.3 million.[35] The projects are expected to produce commercial results by 2015, reducing costs and increasing performance.

## Incentives

As with any new energy source, incentives are crucial to getting the industry off the ground, to round up the necessary capital for basic R&D and to establish enough capacity that it can approach economic viability.

Solar is no exception to this. The U.S. government has been inconstant in its support of solar energy, which in some cases has caused more harm than good. However, with escalating energy costs, increasing environmental concerns, and a need to secure more energy options, many states aren't waiting any longer for the federal government to kick-start solar energy programs, opting to establish their own incentive programs instead.

It's win-win-win: The states win because it means increasing their clean, green, local production, often a requirement of their renewable portfolio standards (RPS), which we will discuss in a moment; consumers win, because they get tax breaks and the power cost insurance of solar; and solar manufacturers win because the incentives provide the security of demand that is crucial to motivating a large electronics company to pony up a cool couple-hundred-mil for a new manufacturing plant.

California currently has some of the strongest incentive programs in the country. The Golden State has passed legislation making solar panels a standard option for new-home buyers by 2012, and has set a goal to install 400 MW of solar electric capacity on new homes, with solar electric systems on 50 percent of all new homes built in California by the end of 2016, and one million homes with solar panels by 2018.[36] California has also joined Germany and Japan in the hope of adding 3,000 megawatts of residential rooftop capacity by 2018.[37]

The enthusiasm for state RPS has actually created an overhang of demand, leaving utilities to scramble to find enough renewable energy capacity to satisfy the requirements.

As of August 2007, 29 states had established RPS requiring that some portion of the overall energy mix must be supplied from renewable sources by a future date.[38] But the available supply of renewable energy is far less than mandated. According to an October 2007 study by the National Renewable Energy Laboratory (NREL), the renewable energy capacity will fall 28 million megawatt-hours (MWh) short of the total RPS requirements by 2010 in the base case, and 8 million MWh short in the high case.[39]

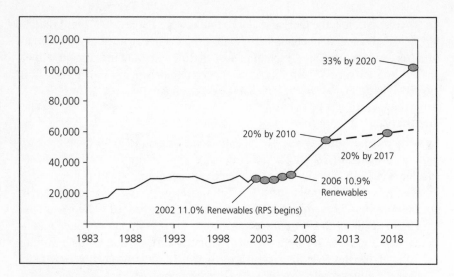

**FIGURE 2.3** *Progress Toward California's Renewable Energy Goals*
*Source:* "2007 Integrated Energy Policy Report," Executive Summary, December 5, 2007,
California Energy Commission, http://www.energy.ca.gov/2007_energypolicy/index.html.

California, the national leader in renewable energy development, exemplifies the problem. With an RPS that calls for 20 percent of its power to be produced from renewables by 2010, and 33 percent by 2020, but only about 11 percent currently produced from renewables, there is an enormous demand to be satisfied, as shown in Figure 2.3.[40]

Meeting the 2020 target will require 17,000 MW of renewable generation, at a cost of around $50 billion.[41] Since nearly half of the state's current generation from renewables comes from the massive Geysers geothermal plant, which can't be significantly enlarged, a great deal of that new generation will have to come from utility solar plants, which currently contribute only 0.2 percent of the total.[42]

The California Energy Commission admits that the RPS goals really cannot be met without further changes:

> So far, however, the RPS results have not kept pace with its mandate due principally to insufficient transmission infrastructure and complex administration. . . . The utilities are not expected to be able to serve 20 percent of their retail load with renewables by 2010 although they may have contracted for the necessary amount by that date. The 33 percent goal by 2020 is feasible but only if the state commits to significant investments in transmission infrastructure and makes some key changes in policy.[43]

In order to satisfy the RPS, the commission recommends substantially upgrading the grid, better planning, and most importantly, the establishment of a *feed-in tariff* (FiT).

**Feed-in Tariff** A FiT legislates that utilities must buy green power at a substantially higher price than standard market rates. For example, if the normal price of grid power is 10 cents per kWh, then the rate for green power might be 40 cents per kWh. Such incentives avoid the pitfalls of other incentive programs, which tend to create limited markets that fail when the incentives are withdrawn. Therefore, FiTs have proven to be the most effective type of incentive for renewable energy.

Germany, Spain, and Denmark have all used FiTs to great effect, quickly ramping up their shares of energy produced from renewables, particularly wind.

The greatest success story for FiTs has been Germany, where the program made it possible for anybody with a decent site to install PV. The guaranteed price paid to a solar generator by a utility is 54 to 57 cents per kWh, but the price of buying grid power is only 20 cents per kWh, so customers are effectively getting paid to install solar!

Consequently, their solar industry has been red-hot in recent years, and consumed over half of the world's entire output of solar modules. This leaves the United States literally unable to get solar modules from time to time. Germany accounted for 960 MW of new installations in 2006, or 55 percent of the world total, while the United States installed only 140 MW, or 8 percent.[44]

Japan is another example of extremely successful solar incentives. The initial 70,000 Roofs Program begun in 1994 paid for half the installation costs of PV. The Japanese have also shelled out hundreds of millions of dollars to boost the rest of the value chain, from R&D to net metering to other market incentives. All of these incentives contributed to making Japan the world leader in PV manufacturing and installation—accounting for nearly half the world market—in about a decade.[45]

The cost of PV is now so low, and the equipment so ubiquitous, that the Japanese are phasing out their incentive program altogether—even as the number of installations has continued to rise. (See Figure 2.4.)

We may expect other markets with aggressive incentive programs, like Germany and Spain, to phase out their incentives as well when their markets become saturated. Meanwhile, if California, which has been cited as anywhere from the tenth to the fifth largest economy in the world,[46] were to establish a feed-in tariff, it could easily pick up the slack from these mature markets and guarantee a robust demand for solar.

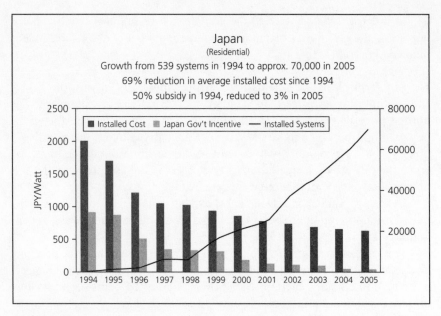

**FIGURE 2.4** *Japan's PV Growth versus Incentives*
*Source:* Sharp solar slide deck, "Creating a Stable Investment Climate for Solar," 2005,
http://eesi.org/briefings/2005/Climate%20&%20Energy/10.6.05Solar/OBrien10.4.05.pdf.

At some point in the relatively near future, we expect the solar industry to be able to support itself, providing clean green and worry-free power at a price that is competitive with grid power generated from other sources.

## INVESTING IN SOLAR

Over the past decade, we've seen a direct correlation between technological innovation and solid, sustainable growth in the solar market. With every new breakthrough has come another opportunity for investors.

This is a trend that's not expected to slow down for at least the next 10 to 15 years, because when it comes to efficiency and cost reduction, there's still so much room for this sector to grow.

Certainly the cost-reduction angle allowed green chip investors to profit handsomely back in 2005 after picking up shares of a small solar company called Evergreen Solar (NASDAQ:ESLR).

In 2003, the industry's growth projections were staggering. Solar manufacturers were gearing up for large-scale expansions to keep up with what would prove to be unprecedented demand. The only problem was that because the market was about to grow so much, and so fast, it would be faced with a very serious shortage of a key ingredient in PV production—highly refined silicon. This stuff was going to be consumed faster than it could be supplied.

The silicon shortage was going to push production costs for PV way up, and solar manufacturers that relied on silicon would soon be scrambling to find supplies cheap and abundant enough to keep them in business.

Obviously, this was critical information for potential solar investors, because any company that could hedge against the coming shortage would certainly have the upper hand. At the time, Evergreen Solar was that company.

Evergreen had developed a "String Ribbon" technology that made it a solar darling for investors. With this technology, silicon was processed as a high-temperature liquid. Then, between two strings, the liquid silicon formed a film, similar to a bubble, which gradually crystallized and "grew" a wafer (ribbon) out of the silicon melt. In contrast, conventional production processes cut wafers from large silicon blocks, which result in a substantial waste of valuable silicon.

Evergreen's String Ribbon technology produced a solar wafer with much less silicon, cutting waste. As a result, the company was able to manufacture high-quality cells with just two-thirds of the silicon of conventional methods. That alone made Evergreen a major force. From 2003 to 2006, the stock delivered gains in excess of 960 percent for green chip investors, as shown in Figure 2.5.

Of course, Evergreen Solar wasn't the only company to use the coming silicon shortage to attract investors. In fact, the most obvious way to take advantage of the silicon shortage was to go straight to the source—the silicon manufacturers.

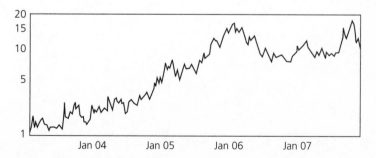

**FIGURE 2.5**  *Evergreen Solar, Inc.*

MEMC (NYSE:WFR), Hoku Scientific (NASDAQ:HOKU), and Renewable Energy Corporation (which trades on the Oslo Stock Exchange) are three leading silicon suppliers that have cleaned up over the past few years. As you can see from the charts in Figures 2.6, 2.7, and 2.8, investors who got in early on these made a fortune.

As seen in Figure 2.6, a $10,000 investment in MEMC in August 2004 was worth about $110,100 by the end of 2007.

As seen in Figure 2.7, a $10,000 investment in Hoku Scientific in August 2006 was worth about $50,700 by the end of 2007.

As seen in Figure 2.8, a $10,000 investment in Renewable Energy Corporation in May 2006 was worth about $23,800 by the end of 2007.

Overall, with just these three plays, Green Chip investors had the opportunity to turn $30,000 into $184,600. Double up, and you're looking at $369,200. That's more than a quarter of a million dollars on just three solar stocks in less than four years.

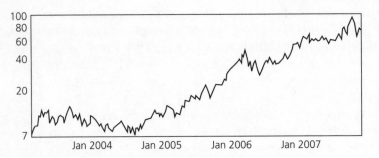

**FIGURE 2.6** *MEMC Electronic Materials*

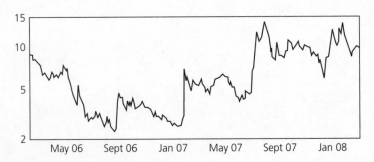

**FIGURE 2.7** *Hoku Scientific*

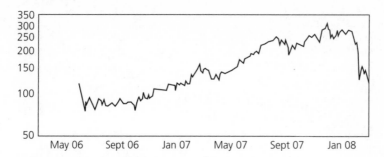

**FIGURE 2.8**  *Renewable Energy Corporation*

Companies that can provide solar-grade silicon for PV manufacturers will continue to do well. However, this is a fast-growing industry, and the technology slows for no one. That's why, while conventional PV will still provide opportunities for investors well beyond the next decade, we also continue to focus on the next generation of solar technology, which we believe will offer even more opportunities over the long term.

In early 2007, investors got a glimpse of just how well a publicly traded solar company can perform when it boasts new, disruptive technology. The company was First Solar (NASDAQ:FSLR), and before it went public, analysts were predicting the stock would open somewhere between $16 and $18 a share. But on the morning of November 17, 2006, shares of First Solar opened at $24.50 a share and never looked back. By December 2007, the stock hit a high of $256.45, as shown in Figure 2.9.

Because the company's technology represented the next generation of solar manufacturing, insiders knew that its perceived value would be much higher than that of a conventional solar manufacturer. While conventional solar manufacturing relied heavily on large quantities of silicon, First Solar's edge was its thin-film solar technology, which required no silicon at all.

In an instant, investors had a solar play that was immune to the silicon shortage. Even better, the efficiency of First Solar's modules was nearly double that of the competing thin-film technology of the time.

While there were still a couple of smaller, publicly traded, thin-film companies out there, First Solar was boasting contracts that none of the others could touch. These included a bundle of five agreements the company landed in early July that were expected to bring sales of approximately $1.28 billion.

FSLR Daily

M A M J J A S O N D 07 F M A M J J A S O N D 08

FIGURE 2.9 *First Solar*

For almost any kind of manufacturing company, $1.28 billion worth of contracts is huge. For a relatively new, publicly traded solar company, this was absolutely massive. Investors who jumped in early made a fortune.

Today, we continue to monitor the progress of new thin-film developers that will offer increased efficiency, disruptive pricing, and increased aesthetic value. While First Solar was really one of the first thin-film developers to deliver such significant gains for investors, they won't be the last. There are now dozens of companies developing their own thin-film solutions that could soon mirror the kind of success First Solar had in 2007. From publicly traded companies like Daystar Technologies (NASDAQ:DSTI), Ascent Solar Technologies (NASDAQ:ASTI), and Powerfilm, Inc. (which trades under the symbol PFLM on the London Stock Exchange), to private companies, like HelioVolt and Konarka, this is an area of solar development that's just now starting to heat up. Incidentally, Konarka works in the field of *organic photovoltaics* (OPV), too—a technology that offers the promise of significant disruption in pricing and aesthetics, as well as impressive efficiencies in low light conditions. OPV materials are also flexible and form-fitting, and can be wrapped around or even painted onto various materials.

Historically, OPV never has been taken too seriously, and is often criticized as having limited potential. But in 2000, OPV researcher Alan Heeger, along with two other scientists, Alan MacDiarmid and Hideki Shirakawa, was awarded the Nobel Prize in Chemistry for the discovery and development of conductive polymers. This is the work that provides the foundation for OPV. Certainly we've seen a lot of advancement since then.

Still, in order for OPV companies to even consider competing, they have to measure up to the efficiency of today's thin film, which runs from 9 percent in the field to 19.5 percent in the lab. In 2007, the DoE's Office of Energy Efficiency and Renewable Energy released a report that identified a demonstrated OPV efficiency of 5 percent. At an OPV conference that same year, researchers at Northwestern University claimed as much as 6.25 percent. It is estimated that 10 percent would make OPV commercially viable.

Organic photovoltaics also have issues with degradation due to prolonged exposure to sunlight. With OPV, the degradation occurs much faster than with conventional solar cells.

The technological advancements that address these challenges will lead us to our future solar investments. Back in 2004, we read a number of reports that disregarded advancements in thin film due to lower efficiencies. But Green Chip investors who focused on the future, instead of muddling around in the present, jumped on First Solar when it first went public—and made a fortune. So it should be no surprise that today we watch any company working to advance OPV technology. It could be these companies that will deliver significant solar profits tomorrow.

As mentioned earlier, Konarka is a private company currently doing quite a bit of research in OPV. In 2007, Konarka was one of two recipients of a $4.7 million investment from the National Institute of Standards and Technology to develop technology that would allow windows and other building applications to be converted into solar panels. The company is using these funds to develop its module architecture, while the second recipient, Air Products (NYSE:APD), will develop high-conductivity polymers with more efficient charge injection capability in OPV cells.[47]

In January 2008, Konarka announced a development agreement with SKYShades, a supplier of shade and tension membrane structures, to integrate OPV material into tension fabric material. And in March 2008, Konarka conducted the first-ever demonstration of manufacturing organic bulk heterojunction solar cells via inkjet printing. This demonstration confirmed that organic solar cells can be processed with printing technologies, and with little or no loss compared with certain semiconductor technologies, like spin coating.

It will be interesting to see how OPV plays out, since the companies that nail the required efficiency and costs, as well as overcome degradation obstacles associated with OPV, will reward early investors handsomely. One promising consortium announced in June 2007, including the German government and companies such as Bosch, BASF, Merck, and SCHOTT will invest a total of 360 million euros in OPV.[48]

One angle that could really help propel OPV forward initially will be applications that don't require significant efficiencies. For example, imagine OPV applied to your cell phone. Under low light conditions, like those in your office, home, or conference room setting, OPV could continuously trickle-charge your phone, which conventional solar can't do. With such an application, you'd never have to worry about your phone completely losing power. Or imagine OPV applied to the roof of a hybrid or plug-in hybrid electric vehicle, charging its battery while it's sitting out in a parking lot all day.

Over the next three to five years, we expect to see more peer-reviewed data and more development agreements that will provide us with the information we need to make the right investment decisions. When this stuff finally hits, and it will, Green Chip investors will already be positioned to profit.

## Concentrating on Solar

Another solar sector that will gain continued momentum is concentrating solar power (CSP).

CSP plants are typically extremely large, able to produce massive amounts of solar energy cheaper than PV. One of the most recent CSP plants built in the United States, Nevada Solar One, cost roughly $220 to $250 million, making its price per kWh between $0.09 and $0.13. As more of these plants are built and scaled up, researchers and analysts expect that cost to come down to about $0.07 per kWh,[49] which puts them within reach of cost parity with coal- and nuclear-fired power.

The Nevada Solar One project was the first CSP project to be installed in the United States in more than 15 years. One reason it took a decade and a half is simply that it took that long to see the increase in demand for clean, efficient, and renewable energy. The other reason is—you guessed it—better technology.

Before Nevada Solar One, there were nine similar projects in the Mojave Desert. All of these plants still operate above and beyond original expectations, but the latest technology has drastically improved overall efficiency and cost. While the older plants required a 25 percent natural gas–fired backup to keep the heat transfer fluid temperature from fluctuating, Nevada Solar One is more efficient in holding its temperature and requires only a 2 percent natural gas backup.[50]

As we start to see more CSP development in the future, we'll also see a wealth of opportunities stemming from the companies providing the most advanced components for these projects. That's why we monitor the progress of new CSP projects, and keep an eye on the money trail and power purchase agreements (PPAs). Once these projects get the necessary funding and PPAs, a little digging uncovers the companies that will provide the heat exchangers, the turbine generators, the receivers, and so on.

Nevada Solar One is a perfect example of this. On September 21, 2005, the new Solargenix CSP plant (aka Nevada Solar One) got its PPA amendments approved. This approval allowed Solargenix to complete the project.

A few weeks later, SCHOTT announced that it had received its first large volume order for its solar receiver tubes. By January, Solel Solar Systems announced it had signed a $10 million contract with Solargenix to supply Solargenix with its solar receivers and thermal conduction units. On February 2, Spanish renewable energy and construction company Acciona (which trades on the Madrid Stock Exchange), announced it was buying a 55 percent stake in Solargenix. On February 11, 2006, Acciona and Solargenix broke ground.

As you can see, a lot of money was made almost instantly once the PPA was approved. In July 2007, we informed our readers that the Electric Power Research Institute (EPRI) had announced a new project to study the feasibility of CSP in New Mexico. This was initiated by the New Mexico utility, PNM, which is now interested in building a CSP plant in New Mexico by 2010.[51]

We'll be following three phases: The first includes the formation of a group of experts from engineering firms, national laboratories, and electric utilities. The second includes a comprehensive feasibility assessment to examine the site and regulatory issues surrounding the development of the plant. The third is plant construction.

In between the second and third phases is when savvy solar investors will be honing in on the companies that will profit from this project. Certainly we'll be reporting on it to all our readers so they can get in early on these, too; this will give them an opportunity to take an early position, then cash out once the rest of Wall Street catches up and pushes the stock north.

## COMBINING FORCES, ADDING PROFITS

We advise that investors pay close attention to any new agreements between solar companies. Sometimes, just combining forces in this market can send a stock soaring.

For instance, consider WorldWater & Solar Technologies Corporation (OTCBB:WWAT). In May 2007, WorldWater and Solargenix signed a strategic memorandum of understanding that was expected to lead to the expansion

FIGURE 2.10 *WorldWater & Solar Technologies Corporation*

and increased efficiency of marketing and sales forces. Green Chip investors sitting on shares of WorldWater at the time watched the stock pick up gains in excess of 65 percent within a month following the announcement. (See Figure 2.10.)

We're quite confident that we'll see more agreements like this one as CSP continues to heat up. We're equally confident that solar investors smart enough to tap these stocks early will enjoy similar gains.

# CHAPTER

**3**

# GLOBAL WINDS

Wind energy comes from the uneven heating of the planet as it spins through the day and night, being warmed and cooled by the Sun. Temperature gradients between land and sea, and physical obstacles like mountains, also play a role in the complex dance of wind.

Wind power dates back to at least 5000 B.C.E., when it was used to propel boats along the Nile River. By 200 B.C.E., simple windmills were pumping water in China and grinding grain in the Middle East.

Windmills designed to generate electricity, known as *turbines*, first appeared in Denmark around 1890. They operate on a simple principle: Two or three propeller-like blades are attached to a rotor, which is in turn connected to an electrical generator. When the wind blows, the propeller turns the rotor, spinning the generator and creating electrical current. Utility-sized wind turbines are familiar horizontal-axis units, typically mounted on a tower 75 feet or more off the ground, to take advantage of faster, less turbulent winds. Smaller vertical axis turbines without towers are also used, particularly for low-speed winds.

## BENEFITS OF WIND POWER

Wind power is primarily a utility-scale technology, with hundreds of turbines arrayed in large "wind farms." Wind offers a number of advantages over fossil fuel in powering the grid:

- Wind is a vast, free, and inexhaustible resource.

- Wind helps reduce our use of the primary fuels for grid power: natural gas, coal, and to a lesser extent, petroleum. Recognizing that all fossil fuels will peak within the next 20 years, and skyrocket in cost, it is important that we reduce their consumption as much as possible.

- Electric power from wind in most cases is already cheaper than power from natural gas, coal, and nuclear plants. Even locations that do not have adequate wind resources can benefit from wind generation elsewhere, which helps to hold down grid power costs overall.

- Once a turbine is erected, wind requires no fuel.

- Like solar and geothermal power, most of the costs are up front to build a wind system. After that, the maintenance and operation costs are minimal and predictable. So financing wind-power projects can be low-risk compared to fossil-fueled plants, where the cost of the fuel is volatile and unpredictable, and thus an investment risk.

- Deploying more wind reduces climate change. Once in place, a wind farm creates no greenhouse gas emissions.

- Wind power needs no water. Traditional power plants of all kinds require significant amounts of water, as much as several billion gallons per day each, which is used in the condenser cycle to turn steam back into water. During hot summers, such as the 2006 heat wave in Europe, and periods of drought like the American Southeast experienced in 2007, power plants have been shut down due to a lack of water.[1]

- Wind power can be a large part of a diversified energy mix. The more diversified the supply, the better for energy security, by reducing conflict over energy resources and adding resiliency to the grid.

- Wind production is fairly predictable, so its costs are fairly steady. This helps to buffer the impact of volatile fossil fuel costs.

- The wind industry is a major economic boost and a source of well-paying new jobs.

## VAST RESOURCES

Like solar and geothermal resources, the available global wind resource is positively vast. According to the U.S. Department of Energy, wind could provide 5,800 quadrillion BTUs (quads) of energy each year—about 15 times the current global energy demand of roughly 400 quads.[2]

The World Energy Council calculated in 2007 that using just 1 percent of the million gigawatts or so available "for total land coverage"[3] with wind farms running at 15 to 40 percent of the time,[4] wind power could supply all of the world's current electrical needs. Offshore capacity is also enormous, enough for Europe to supply all of its electrical needs within 30 km off shore.[5]

As with most renewable energy technologies, the site is everything. Winds are particularly variable, thanks to topography. The important characteristics for a good wind site are having strong enough winds to start up the generator, and winds that are relatively steady. A site with moderate, steady winds is far preferable to one with low overall wind and powerful gusts.

Modern turbines are designed to start up with winds of around 3 to 5 meters per second (m/s),[6] and reach a maximum operating limit at around 20 to 25 m/s.[7] This makes an average wind speed of about 5 m/s desirable for a wind farm site, which can be found offshore of all five continents. In coastal regions, 7 m/s is available, and in mountain passes, some coastal waters, and islands, 8 m/s is typical.[8]

## FORECAST: WINDY AND PROFITABLE

In 2006, total world wind generating capacity was around 72,000 MW, producing some 160 terawatt-hours (TWh) per year of electricity.[9] As of the end of 2006, the top wind producers were Germany, with 20,622 MW; Spain, with 11,615 MW; and the United States, with 11,575 MW.[10]

Even so, wind accounts for only about 1 percent of the world's total energy use.[11] So the sky is the limit, given the enormous need to replace depleting traditional fuels.

Wind is the fastest growing of all renewable power sources, increasing at a rate of about 25 percent per year worldwide in recent years. Since 1990, wind generating capacity has doubled roughly every three and a half years;[12] that's about a 20 percent per year growth rate.

Worldwide wind energy capacity grew 27 percent in 2007, a record pace, to a total of 94 GW, according to a new report from the Global Wind Energy Council. New installations were up 30 percent over 2006, and the global wind market is now estimated to be worth about $36 billion per year in new generating equipment.[13]

In economic terms, that's double the size of the wind industry in 2006, which stood at $17.9 billion according to a 2007 report by Clean Edge. They anticipated that the business would grow to $60.8 billion by 2016,[14] which would represent a 13 percent annual growth rate over 10 years, but now that looks like an underestimate.

One important factor to bear in mind about the prospects for the wind industry is that, as we've already mentioned in Chapters 1 and 2, as far as we have seen, *nobody takes into account fossil fuel depletion* in their projections. Studies do place certain constraints on fossil fuels in their models, based on assumptions about the future of emissions controls, geopolitical factors, climate change, historical production rates, industry investment, and so on, but it appears that most analysts have yet to fully grasp the coming energy crisis—or if they do, they aren't saying so.

Consequently, we believe that for the next two decades or more, the growth of the industry will be strong and sustained, surpassing previous estimates. We estimate that, conservatively, we'll continue to see 25 percent annual growth rates for the foreseeable future, creating more than $4 billion in new wind projects annually, until the resource is more fully exploited. At that point, the growth rate could slow down, but wind will still have to grow to compensate for the loss of other fuels.

A 2005 study from the Global Wind Energy Council is even more optimistic, showing that by the year 2020, when world electricity demand will have increased by two-thirds, wind could realistically meet 12 percent of world electricity demand—equivalent to powering 600 million average European households. By then, they believe the wind industry will be an €80 billion (about $118 billion) annual business![15]

Several projections of wind power capacity are shown in Figure 3.1.

### Wind in the United States

Europe has built a flourishing wind industry over the last decade, but the same explosive growth curve is just getting started here in the United States. If the grid were able to support it, the state of North Dakota alone could generate more wind power than all of Germany,[16] but Germany has more installed wind capacity than the entire United States. Wind power currently supplies less than 1 percent of all electrical power in the United States, but our potential resources are much greater, especially in the Great Plains states.[17]

According to Xavier Viteri, the head of Spanish utility Iberdrola's renewable energy business, wind energy in the United States resembles the early days of the European wind industry. "There's a lot of room for development there, and there is a lot of expertise here."[18]

Not surprisingly, the U.S. wind market has been the fastest-growing wind power market in the world since 2005,[19] accounting for 16 percent of new worldwide wind generating capacity in 2006—more than the power equivalent of two nuclear reactors. In 2005, total generating capacity surged 27 percent to 9,100 MW. In 2006, wind grew by another 26 percent, adding 2,454 MW

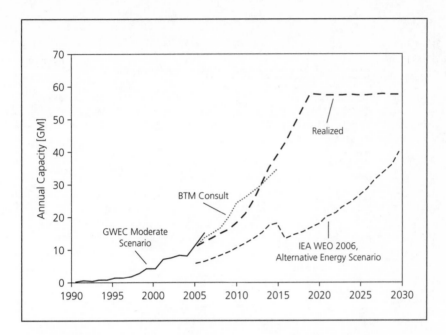

**FIGURE 3.1**  *Different Estimates for Annual Wind Power Capacity*
*Source:* Slide deck, "Continental Wind Resource and Variation," Juha Kiviluoma, Energy
Technology Innovation Policy (ETIP) research fellow. ETIP seminar series November 6, 2007.

(surpassed only by new natural gas plants!), representing $4 billion in investment.[20] And in 2007, wind installations shattered expectations, adding an estimated 5,244 MW of new capacity, a 45 percent increase over 2006, representing $9 billion in investment.[21] Growth in 2008 isn't slowing down either, and is expected to match that of 2007. Sixty-one percent of the U.S. capacity in 2006—over 7,300 MW—has been installed since 2001.[22]

By the end of 2007, the installed wind capacity in the United States stood at over 16,800 MW.[23] Another 3,506 MW are already under construction as of January 2008.[24] Wind farms are expected to generate an estimated 48 billion kilowatt-hours (kWh) of wind energy in 2008, enough to power over 4.5 million homes.[25]

Texas, Washington, and California are leading the nation in new wind capacity growth. Somewhat ironically, given its long history of fossil fuel production, Texas is the largest and fastest-growing wind market in the country, boosting its wind capacity by 59 percent in 2007, to 4,356 MW, as evidenced in Figure 3.2.[26]

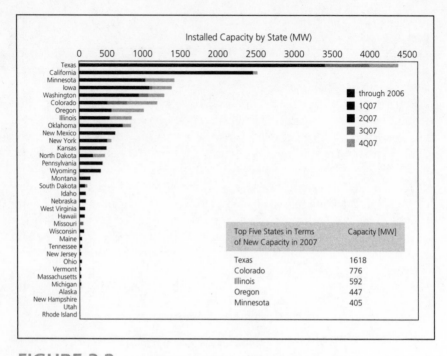

**FIGURE 3.2** *U.S. Wind Installed Capacity by State*
*Source:* American Wind Energy Association, *4th Quarter Market Report,* January 2008.

The recent surge in Texas wind power has nothing to do with environmental issues or a sudden outbreak of "green" feeling. It's simply a profitable business, especially in the coast and panhandle regions, where the wind blows reliably year-round. Russel E. Smith, executive director of the trade group Texas Renewable Industries Association, is bullish: "At this point, we think 10,000-plus megawatts in the next five to eight years is doable," he said.[27]

The Horse Hollow Wind Energy Center is the latest in a series of mega-wind projects in Texas. At 47,000 acres and 735 MW, it's the largest of its kind in the world. The operator, FPL Energy, is the largest owner and operator of wind turbines in the world, and generates more than 1,600 megawatts of wind power in Texas alone. Their total U.S. wind portfolio has 4,100 megawatts of capacity, enough to power more than a million homes. FPL Energy dropped $1 billion on wind power in Texas in 2006 alone, and they have grand plans for expansion.[28]

In addition to such large, utility-scale wind projects, the residential wind market is gaining ground. Residents of windy states with at least half an acre (and friendly neighbors) spent more than $17 million on small wind-power systems in 2005, up 62 percent from 2004. Some reported a savings of 35 percent or more.

As impressive as American wind energy production is, it's really just getting started. According to a joint report issued in May 2007 by 18 organizations including trade associations, universities, research groups, and the U.S. government energy agencies, and coordinated by the American Council on Renewable Energy (ACORE), wind energy could supply the majority—248 GW, or nearly 40 percent—of renewable energy produced in America by 2025.[29] The authors took pains to point out that long-term policy support from the government is key to the successful expansion of wind capacity.

The American Wind Energy Association (AWEA) made a similar forecast in 2007, asserting that it's both possible and affordable to supply 20 percent of the nation's electricity with wind power by 2030. This would mean over a 20-fold expansion, from 16.8 GW today to 350 GW. The grid would also need to be beefed up substantially to support the additional power transmission, generating new demand in everything from cables to transformers. This would be good for America, AWEA contends, by not only making a substantial reduction in emissions, but creating some three million jobs.[30]

Combining the ACORE forecast and AWEA historical data, we see the amazing exponential growth picture for wind in the United States in Figure 3.3.

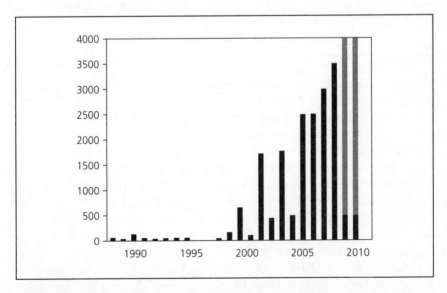

**FIGURE 3.3**  *U.S. Wind Power Installations (MW/Year), 1989–2010*
*Source:* "The Outlook on Renewable Energy in America," ACORE, January 2007, http://www.acore.org/pdfs/Outlook_Preview.pdf.

### Wind in the EU

In Europe, where member countries have been far more aggressive about setting binding goals to decrease greenhouse gas emissions and increase renewable energy production, the wind industry is already huge, and poised for further growth.

Between 1994 and 2005, wind power in the European Union skyrocketed from 1,700 to 40,000 MW. Germany has been particularly aggressive, and now boasts more than 18,000 MW of capacity.

In January 2008, as part of a larger proposal to battle climate change, the European Commission presented draft laws setting a new, ambitious target calling for 20 percent of the overall energy mix to be provided by renewable energy by 2020, plus a 20 percent reduction in carbon emissions, with specific targets set for each of the EU's 27 countries. Considering that only 8.5 percent of the EU's energy consumption came from renewables in 2005, this means the sector will need to more than double within 12 years.[31]

Most of that growth will come from wind. Europe has relatively abundant wind, compared to its solar, geothermal, and biomass resources. The British Wind Energy Association (BWEA) estimates that Britain could generate 25 percent of the country's electricity from wind alone by 2020, increasing its number of onshore turbines from around 1,800 today to 5,000, and its offshore turbines from around 150 today to 7,000.[32,33] This would increase Britain's wind capacity 13-fold, from 2.5 GW to 33 GW.[34]

## FALLING COSTS

The driving force behind the wind industry's massive growth is simple: It makes good economic sense. Although renewable energy continues to be labeled by opponents as too expensive, wind energy has already reached parity with grid power from traditional fuels.

"We still have elected officials who believe renewable energy cannot power this country, and I think that is incorrect," said ACORE president Michael Eckhart upon the release of the council's 2007 report. "We can deliver huge amounts of energy in an environmentally sustainable way."[35]

Even without federal tax credits, wind power is now the cheapest form of electricity generation. This is due in part to the rapidly increasing prices of coal and natural gas in recent years.

A 2007 report by the U.S. Department of Energy on the U.S. wind power market supports this assertion. Entitled "Annual Report on U.S. Wind Power Installation, Cost, and Performance Trends: 2006," it analyzed project costs, turbine sizes, and developer consolidation, and concluded that "Wind power is competitive and has provided good value in wholesale power markets. Wind power has consistently been priced at, or below, the average price of conventional electricity (coal, nuclear, natural gas, etc.)."[36]

Figure 3.4 from the National Energy Renewable Laboratory (NREL) shows the relative costs of grid fuels.

In Europe as well, wind has already achieved cost parity with nuclear power, at 6.6 euro-cents per kilowatt hour. According to a 2007 report from the Energy Research Centre in Netherlands, achieving grid parity means that wind will soon overtake nuclear power worldwide as the cheapest alternative to fossil fuels. The group claims that technological advances in the coming years will further improve the economics of wind even as security costs make nuclear energy less financially attractive.[37]

Wind energy is superior to nuclear energy in every way except one: the need for storage. Wind is intermittent, and nuclear energy is extremely steady, which is what makes it desirable for "baseload" supply. But we believe this disadvantage will be alleviated thanks to intensive research now under way into storage systems both large and small. As grid operators begin to reform their networks, beefing them up while making them more distributed and smarter, these new storage solutions will help wind energy to leap over the final hurdle and become a vital and significant part of the future's baseload energy capacity.

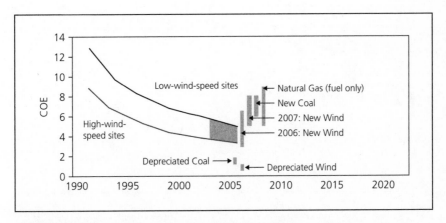

**FIGURE 3.4**  *Grid Power Costs for Wind, Coal, and Natural Gas*
*Source:* "Wind Energy Update," NREL, January 23, 2008, http://www.eere.energy.gov/windandhydro/windpoweringamerica/pdfs/wpa/wpa_update.pdf.

## Innovation

Several factors are contributing to a steady reduction in the cost of wind power. The first is size: The newest wind turbines are far larger and more efficient than earlier designs, capable of producing electricity for as little as four to six cents per kilowatt-hour—about the same as burning coal.

Generally speaking, the bigger the turbine, the cheaper and more efficient it is, because taller towers can reach much faster, much stronger winds. This owes to the fact that power increases as the cube (power of three) of the wind speed. (Consequently, all turbines are designed to reduce their speed when they reach a maximum design rating, in order to prevent damage.) This has led to a steady increase in the size of turbines, from small 100 kW machines 25 years ago to 2.5 MW offshore monsters today.[38] (See Figure 3.5.)

Accordingly, the 2007 report from the DoE found that the performance of wind projects has been increasing due to improved placement and technological advances in the turbines.[39]

The cost of wind power is also declining due to increased research and development and advances in materials science. In addition, the life span of turbines is improving, thanks to materials innovations, improved technology for avoiding damage in high winds, and going to frictionless maglev bearings. These improvements have helped to lower the costs of operations and maintenance dramatically, from $30/MWh in the 1980s to around $8/MWh today.[40]

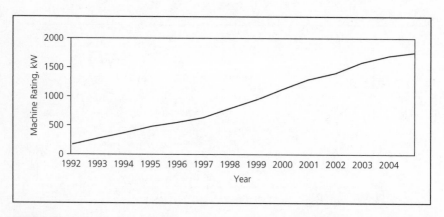

FIGURE 3.5   *Average Size of Wind Turbines Installed in Germany, 1992–2005*

Source: German Wind Energy Institute, via the *2007 Survey of Energy Resources,* World Energy Council 2007.

Together, these efforts are progressively producing wind machines that are lighter, stronger, more durable, and more efficient, which all contribute to reducing costs and increasing deployment, as shown in Figure 3.6.

Interestingly, although the overall cost of wind power has declined, and is expected to continue to do so with further technological improvements and better siting, the cost of the turbines themselves has been rising slightly since 2002, due to the rising costs of materials and energy from fossil fuels.[41] Developers report that they're already sold out for 2008, signaling a seller's market. But supply is soon expected to increase to meet the growing demand. The AWEA claims that at least 14 new manufacturing facilities were opened or announced in the United States in 2007, and existing plants are being expanded, even in states with low wind resources.[42] So we expect costs to resume their decline in short order.

While we're on the subject of innovations in wind, we must mention one of the more curious recent innovations—or rather a revival of the oldest wind technology: using it to power boats. From worldwide merchant fleets to the U.S. Navy, intensive efforts to reduce the use of petroleum fuels have spawned a resurgence of interest in wind power. Only instead of using tall masts and sails, they're using giant kites to assist a ship's engines and save a little fuel.

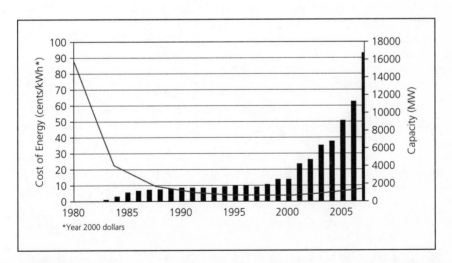

**FIGURE 3.6**  *Cost of Energy and Cumulative U.S. Domestic Capacity*
Source: "Wind Energy Update," NREL, January 23, 2008, http://www.eere.energy.gov/windandhydro/windpoweringamerica/pdfs/wpa/wpa_update.pdf.

In January 2008, the world's first commercial ship to use kite-assisted power was launched in Venezuela. A champion of the technology, inventor Stephen Wrage believes he can displace 20 percent of the ship's daily fuel bill.[43]

## Wind and Climate Change

Of course, a truly fair accounting of the cost of wind power would include greenhouse gases. The emissions of wind power are minimal, deriving only from the manufacturing and installation of the turbines. After that, they just produce clean power. In Europe, where $CO_2$ emissions can run $30/ton, wind offers a financial benefit for avoided emissions, but in the United States, where emissions have no cost assigned, fossil fuels essentially have a big thumb on the scale when compared to wind costs.

According to UCS/Black & Veatch, when the cost of emissions is included at $30/ton, wind costs about the same as nuclear power, and far less than gas or coal, even with carbon sequestration. When the price of $CO_2$ is $50/ton, which we wouldn't rule out for the next decade, only the most extreme off-shore wind production will be more expensive than nuclear, gas, and coal.[44]

A European Commission project called ExternE studied externalized costs, and estimated that if externalized costs such as environmental damage and health costs were included, the cost of producing electricity from coal or oil would double, and the cost of power from gas would increase by 30 percent. Adding in externalized costs such as the impacts of climate change would instantly make wind and most other renewable energy cost-competitive without any incentives whatsoever. The project estimates that wind power in the EU avoided approximately €5 billion in external costs in 2005 alone.[45]

Even without the participation of the United States, the international Kyoto Protocol agreement to control carbon emissions has given birth to an exploding worldwide market in greenhouse gas credits. The carbon market nearly doubled in 2007 to $60 billion, and the volume of carbon traded grew 64 percent.[46]

Since the indirect (and mostly unacknowledged) subsidy of free emissions in the United States has such a large potential future cost attached, we must ask ourselves where we think the trends are headed when evaluating the cost-effectiveness of wind power. Will the United States finally step up and commit to binding targets on emissions, in cooperation with the international community?

It seems all but inevitable at this point. As the 800-pound gorilla on the world stage, consuming one-quarter of the world's energy and creating one-quarter of the world's $CO_2$ emissions but having only 5 percent of the global population, America is in an indefensible position. The United States now stands completely alone among developed countries (and indeed, most of the world) in refusing to commit to a binding international effort to reduce CO2 emissions.

Meanwhile, a growing urgency among the general population to do something about climate change seems likely to make it politically and economically correct at last. Large manufacturers, financial and insurance companies, automakers, regional and state governments, international alliances, even power plant operators are not waiting for the feds to come around, preferring instead to get ahead of the issues by tackling the climate challenge head-on.

The ongoing fight over emissions controls between California and 15 other states and the EPA is a politically charged microcosm of the larger trend. Even after the Supreme Court ruled against the EPA's refusal to regulate CO2 in 2007, the EPA continues to defy the will of the states to permit tighter controls. As of this writing, a lawsuit, a petition, several legal challenges, and Congressional inquiries have been launched against the agency over its stance on CO2, which by all accounts is not based on science, but politics. Jeffrey Holmstead, a 20-year veteran of the EPA who at one time was responsible for overseeing clean air issues, said the Supreme Court ruling is a signal that the fight will continue. "That really dominates everything that goes on now," Holmstead said. "And it's certainly going to affect everything EPA does . . . as far forward as you can imagine . . . probably for the next 20 years."[47]

It doesn't take a genius to see which way the wind is blowing on climate change. In the balance between protecting the environment and the public health on the one hand, and protecting narrow business interests on the other, the weight of public opinion is shifting toward the former by all indications. Our bet is that the United States will soon have the leadership and the public support to finally play ball with the rest of the world. Numerous proposals and pieces of draft legislation have been circulating in the halls of Congress in support of carbon taxes, carbon cap-and-trade schemes, fuel economy standards, and many other emissions-reducing strategies. We are absolutely confident that carbon emissions will soon come with a cost, which will radically reshape the economics of energy in favor of wind and other emissions-free renewables, and we'll be covering those opportunities in *Green Chip Stocks*.

## THE COMPETITIVE ADVANTAGE

Like any emerging energy technology, the evolution of wind power has depended heavily on incentives to level the playing field and encourage its growth, in order to reduce costs and improve performance.

Essential wind power incentives are not just monetary. Policy support is crucial, such as setting binding targets for renewable energy generation and carbon emissions; removing barriers to deployment and reducing investor risk; reforming markets to remove discriminatory access and transmission tariffs and to encourage, rather than discourage, distributed generation technologies like wind; and ending direct and external subsidies to fossil fuel power. With a truly level playing field, the data suggests that no monetary incentives would be needed for renewable energy to compete with fossil fuels.

In the United States, state incentives have played an important role, particularly in encouraging small (residential and commercial-sized) wind systems. Incentives to install small wind systems are available in California, Massachusetts, New Jersey, New York, Pennsylvania, Ohio, and Wisconsin, and the list is growing rapidly.

Utility-scale wind farms are now receiving a big boost from the huge overhang of demand owing to state *renewable portfolio standards* (RPS). As we discussed in Chapter 2, the nation's renewable energy capacity will fall 28 million megawatt-hours (MWh) short of the total RPS requirements by 2010 in the base case, and 8 million MWh short in the high case. California needs to nearly double its production of renewably generated electricity in the next two years to satisfy its RPS. Europe has its own overhang of demand for renewables, in order to meet carbon emissions targets.

The most important incentive for domestic wind power, however, is the federal *production tax credit* (PTC), a 1.9-cent-per-kilowatt-hour deduction that investors can claim for a period of 10 years. The PTC has been a key driver in the growth of the U.S. wind industry. As part of the Energy Policy Act of 2005, the PTC was extended through December 2008, which had much to do with the amazing growth of wind production over the last two years.

As incentives go, the PTC has not only been effective, it's also been very low-cost. Compared to Europe's CO2 costs—a different sort of incentive for renewable energy—NREL comments, "The PTCs are a bargain."[48]

But the PTC is scheduled to lapse at the end of 2008, plunging the U.S. wind industry back into another low point in the incentive-driven boom-and-bust cycle that has plagued the renewable energy industry for decades. This cycle is dramatically demonstrated by Figure 3.7, which shows the devastating effect that expiring PTCs have.

As of this writing, it is too early to guess what the future of the PTC will be. It is our ardent hope that Congress will recognize that continuing the PTC for wind is essential to letting the industry grow enough to help fill the coming gap in energy production.

As a final point, we cannot overlook the enormous economic stimulus that the wind industry provides. It comes at a critical time for the U.S. economy, creating jobs and economic growth while also helping to reduce the

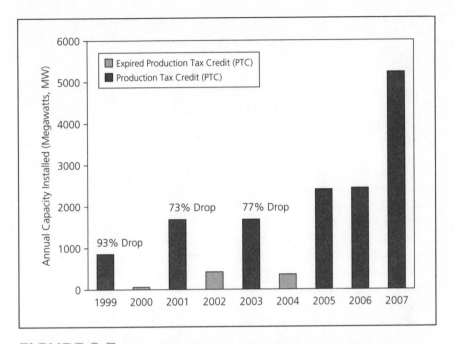

**FIGURE 3.7**  *Annual Installation of Wind Capacity, 1999–2007*
*Source:* AWEA press release, "Installed U.S. Wind Power Capacity Surged 45% in 2007," January 17, 2008, http://www.awea.org/newsroom/releases/AWEA_Market_Release_Q4_011708.html.

country's greenhouse gas emissions. According to the NREL, wind farms provide 100 to 200 new jobs during construction, and 6 to 10 permanent jobs for operations and maintenance, for each 100 MW deployed. By their calculation, the cost and benefits of achieving 20 percent electrical generation from wind by 2030 would add up as follows:[49]

| | |
|---|---|
| Incremental direct cost to society | $43 billion |
| Reductions in emissions of greenhouse gases and other atmospheric pollutants | 825 million tons (2030), $98 billion |
| Reductions in water consumption | 8% total electric, 17% in 2030 |

*(Continued)*

| Jobs created and other economic benefits | 140,000 direct, $450 billion total |
| Reductions in natural gas use and price pressure | 11% ($150 billion) |
| *Net Benefits* | $205 billion + water savings |

Call us crazy, but a nearly five-times return on the investment, reduced water consumption in a drought-stricken country, a more stable and distributed grid power mix, *and* reduced reliance on foreign energy suppliers sounds like a pretty good deal!

Indeed, it appears that for those who are already years ahead in deploying wind power, it is a good deal. Consider Denmark, which generates the largest proportion of its energy from wind of any country in the world, and which is on the absolute cutting edge of offshore wind development. Researchers with the Danish Wind Energy Association estimated that in 2007, wind power actually saved consumers money, after paying the subsidy. The economics are clear: According to the Dutch utility Nuon, in 2005 the average spot market price for electricity was €45/MWh with no wind, but under €30/MWh when the winds were good (over 13 m/s!).[50]

## A Long-Term Outlook

However we design the incentives, we should look to the long-term picture, because power plants are long-term investments, and the dependencies we develop around them last even longer. Instead of just looking at the comparative costs of power today, we should try to imagine what it will be in 20 or 50 or 100 years if we don't replace fossil fuels with renewable power as quickly as possible.

The trends are clear: As we saw in Chapter 1, all fossil fuels and nuclear power will go into terminal decline at various points over the next 20 years, some quite rapidly, and we have only just begun the task of substituting renewable energy.

As the price of generating grid power from fossil fuels and coal rises, the cost of that power must also rise. Whereas the cost of producing power from wind is already cheaper than traditional power, and will remain constant, so the cost advantage should increasingly favor wind.

Meanwhile, the world is moving toward reducing carbon emissions one way or another, and incentives are growing. Even against a headwind of intense lobbying by the coal industry, we expect that public support for wind, and public concern about air quality and global warming, will only grow.

Finally, renewable energies such as wind are truly sustainable for the long term. If we manage our remaining fossil fuels wisely, we could conceivably produce wind turbines and grid parts for centuries into the future, and that's not something you can say about any of the traditional fuels.

In time, we think even the Kennedys will welcome the sight of offshore turbines in the distance from their estate on Cape Cod.

So hold onto your hat; the wind's picking up!

## INVESTING IN WIND

Investing in wind energy can seem a bit frustrating if you focus only on wind turbine manufacturers. After all, two of the biggest players in this sector are GE (NYSE:GE) and Siemens (NYSE:SI). GE actually supplied 45 percent of all the new U.S. installed capacity in 2007.[51] But neither can be considered early investment opportunities.

And as far as pure-plays go, the biggest players here don't trade domestically. This has been especially frustrating for U.S. investors, who typically don't have the ability or know-how to trade in foreign markets, especially when they get a glimpse of the performance of some of these stocks.

Take Vestas Wind Systems (which trades on the Nordic Stock Exchange), for instance. This is a Danish company that has watched its stock gain in excess of 1,400 percent in just under five years. (See Figure 3.8.)

Vestas has been manufacturing wind turbines since 1979, and has installed more than 33,000 wind turbines in more than 60 countries. It has about a 25 percent market share of the industry.[52]

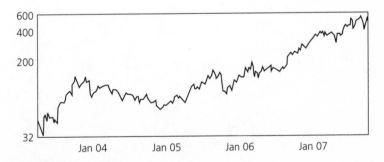

**FIGURE 3.8** *Vestas Wind Systems*

Gamesa Corporation is another foreign wind-investment opportunity. This Spanish company (which trades on the Madrid Stock Exchange) has watched its stock pick up 285 percent over the past three years, as shown in Figure 3.9.

Because renewable energy momentum transcends borders, and really represents a wealth of opportunities on a global scale, Green Chip investors don't have to limit themselves only to U.S. and Canadian markets. But because a detailed review of the international market for renewable energy would really require a separate book altogether, we will focus only on domestic opportunities here. That being said, you can learn more about international renewable energy opportunities through our sister publication, *Green Chip International*, a service that not only provides research and data on international renewable energy markets, but also makes recommendations and instructs readers on how to invest in these international renewable energy stocks.

In the meantime, let's look at a few different ways you can play the wind energy sector here in the United States.

### Thinking Outside the Turbine

Back in December 2004, one of the biggest wind turbine manufacturers in the market announced that it put in an order for a new, low-cost carbon fiber manufactured by a company called Zoltek (NASDAQ:ZOLT).

The company announced that it had concluded a long-term supply agreement whereby Zoltek would provide Vestas Wind Systems with $80 to $100 million worth of carbon fiber and carbon fiber materials for the manufacture of rotor blades and turbine generators. Within six weeks of that announcement, Zoltek's stock shot up more than 90 percent.

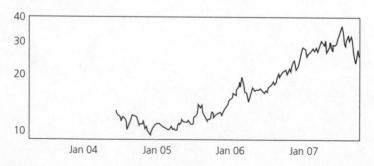

**FIGURE 3.9** *Gamesa Corporation*

Following that deal, Zoltek landed another deal with Fiberblade S.A. (a business unit of Gamesa Eolica) to provide Fiberblade with $65 to $75 million worth of carbon fiber and carbon fiber materials to be used in the manufacturing of large-scale rotor blades.

By mid-2007, the stock had risen from about $10 per share in December 2004 to as high as $51.77 a share. That's a gain of 417 percent in only two and a half years.

Of course, like most of the renewable energy industry, increased demands in efficiency and cost reduction continue to dictate the evolution of the marketplace. And this certainly affects the materials angle for wind as well, because as the industry progresses, blade sizes continue to increase in an effort to provide more power. However, with larger blades comes additional weight. And this has made weight reduction extremely important. If you're able to reduce weight, you can reduce stress on the turbine and the blade during operation. A lighter, more efficient blade also decreases the demands on the hub components and tower structure, thereby allowing for a decrease in capital and operating expenses for the turbine.

So now blade manufacturers are looking for new materials and designs that provide a reduction in blade weight while providing the necessary stiffness and compression strengths required. And that's where we see the next opportunity for materials in the wind sector.

In February 2006, at the European Wind Energy Conference in Athens, a new product called WindStrand™ was announced by Owens Corning. WindStrand would potentially allow turbine manufacturers to increase blade lengths by as much as 6 percent and deliver up to 12 percent more power by using a hybrid of carbon and glass fibers. This carbon–glass hybrid solution would allow for the increase in blade lengths and necessary stiffness while controlling weight. As well, it's estimated that the cost would be about 20 percent less than any competing carbon–glass hybrid solution on the market.[53] It's this kind of innovation that'll lead investors to the next wave of materials profits in the wind sector. We also suspect that we'll see improvements in strength-to-weight ratio of composite materials used in blades from the tech sector.

## Storing Wind

Another way to play the wind sector is via storage solutions. While the production cost for wind may be competitive with conventional sources, its usage cost can still be quite high because of the intermittent nature of wind. But one way to counter this—and make the wind energy sector even more lucrative—is through storage technologies.

A storage system connected to a wind turbine could effectively store energy whenever the wind blows during low-demand, non-peak hours, and then send it during the higher-priced peak hours, which are typically during the middle of the day. Essentially, this turns wind energy (which uses an *unscheduled resource*) into a higher-value generating system that *can* provide consistent power.

At this point, there are a number of storage systems being developed for this purpose. And although high cost and reliability issues are still present, there's a race to perfect these various storage technologies, some of which include:

- Compressed air energy storage (CAES)

- Flywheels

- Ultracapacitors

For investors, it can be confusing as to which holds the most potential. Certainly each company operating in its respective segment will tout its solution as the best. But the proof will be in the press release, because the minute any one of these companies has proved its technology as the clear leader, it's going to saturate the media with press releases.

Of course, as investors, we want to be on top of it before the rest of the crowd, and before those press releases start flying. That's why we spend so much time talking with company representatives and R&D folks. Granted, they always try to sell their technology. But you'd better believe that when these guys have proof—and I'm talking real numbers—they'll tell you all about it. As well, it's important to see how system operators and state regulators react to these systems. Sometimes, this information can be exactly what you need to make a smart investment decision.

For instance, look at Beacon Power Corporation (NASDAQ:BCON). This is a company that develops an energy storage technology that provides frequency regulation. In January 2007, the California Independent System Operator (an organization that manages the flow of electricity along California's open-market wholesale power grid) announced it had certified Beacon's flywheel technology for use as a frequency-regulation resource in the state. The stock gained 44 percent in about four weeks.

We also took a close look at the California Energy Commission's report, "In the Public Interest: Developing Affordable Clean and Smart Energy for 21st Century California," which was released in May 2007. Here's what appeared in the report:

*A new flywheel energy storage system, developed by Beacon Power of Wilmington, Massachusetts, with funding from the Energy Commission, can provide the same service more efficiently without burning fossil fuel. Beacon's system works by spinning a carbon-fiber composite flywheel at a very high speed to store electricity in the form of kinetic energy.*

*The beauty of this technology is that it can respond almost instantaneously to frequency excursions. Whereas it takes conventional power plants up to five minutes to respond to California ISO signals, the flywheel storage energy system takes only four seconds to respond, greatly improving the frequency regulation of the transmission network.*[54]

At the time this report came out, shares of Beacon were falling. In fact, by May 24, 2007, the stock got as low as $0.77. With the stock down nearly 70 percent from its high in February, the low level below $0.80 provided an excellent entry point. Less than four months later, the stock hit $2.49 a share, as shown in Figure 3.10.

Considering the stock was so speculative, most investors were more interested in trading this stock at the time, rather than adopting a longer-term strategy for buying and holding it. But this little piece of information gave investors a signal that the company was at least being identified by the California Energy Commission. Given such a young and volatile market, but

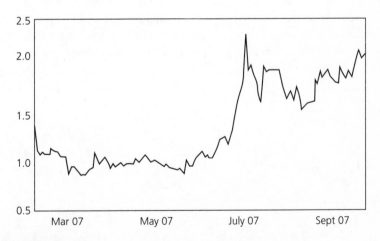

FIGURE 3.10 *Beacon Power Corporation*

with so much profit potential, it wasn't hard to see why investors loaded up on shares when the stock was trading at record lows.

### High Voltage!

As you read earlier in this chapter, wind is the fastest growing of all renewable power sources, increasing at the rate of about 25 percent per year. And because of this impressive growth rate, wind is quickly transitioning from a small niche market to a major status-quo power supply. However, this is also creating a new problem—and a new opportunity. You see, as the industry grows, it's going to be forced to solve voltage regulation and dynamic voltage stability problems.

We'll spare you the science lesson, but essentially, wind farms can consume a large amount of *volt ampere reactive power* (VAR). This uncompressed reactive power demand can cause large voltage drops at or near the interconnection point.

Who's responsible for fixing this? The U.S. government has stated that the wind farm owners are responsible for this issue as a condition of interconnection—although the responsibility could also get passed along to the turbine manufacturers that utilize certain technologies within their products. Either way, no one's ignoring the issue, as a solution benefits all parties involved. In fact, we've already seen one company capitalize on this in a major way.

A company called American Superconductor Corporation (NASDAQ: AMSC) has developed a system called D-VAR, which provides tight voltage regulation and power-factor correction to alleviate fluctuating voltage and VAR demands at wind farms.[55] Since developing this technology, the company has received contract after contract. And the company's stock performance reflects this success: From January 2006 to November 2007, its stock gained 313 percent. (See Figure 3.11.)

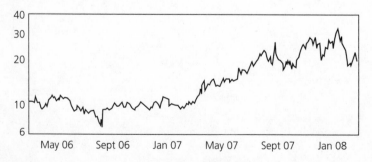

**FIGURE 3.11** *American Superconductor*

Of course, not all the company's success can be traced back to its D-VAR system. However, the company had a clear technological advantage in energy markets, and it also had a lot to gain from the wind energy sector.

In November 2006, American Superconductor acquired a company called Windtech. This company develops and licenses proprietary wind turbine system designs and sells wind turbine electrical systems. Within the first six months of 2007, through Windtech, American Superconductor landed more than $12 million in contracts, including one that has the potential to provide royalty payments of more than $30 million. Again, American Superconductor isn't necessarily a wind turbine developer, but its operations within the wind industry have made it—and its investors—a lot of money. This is a perfect example of how to play the "less-obvious" wind energy opportunities.

## Going Offshore

Wind farm developers are also continuing to seek out more consistent winds. And they're finding exactly that in the ocean. Because our oceans are, for the most part, consistently windy all over, they make excellent locations for turbines.

Most of the work being done today in the area of offshore wind development is happening overseas. Online, there are currently 16 offshore projects worldwide. (Although all 16 can be found in only four countries: Denmark, Holland, Sweden, and the United Kingdom.[56]) But there are plenty more on the way, and they're coming in many different varieties. In fact, international market analyst Sam Hopkins turned a few unsuspecting Green Chip investors on to an interesting, albeit surprising wind play in Scotland a couple of years ago.

After returning from a trip to Scotland, he wrote about a declining oil and gas platform that was about to get 70 percent of its power from two 5-megawatt wind turbines anchored in the bedrock of the UK continental shelf, about 50 meters under water.

A company called Talisman Energy (NYSE:TLM) was installing two heavy-duty turbines next to an existing oil and gas platform that would increase the efficiency of the original structure and maximize oil recovery from the field. Now while this would certainly give one of its older platforms a new lease on life, it also set the company up to lead the new power sector with up to 200 more turbines nearby. And it wasn't a difficult transition, because the company was already utilizing many of the project management, engineering, and fabrication skills developed in the UK's offshore oil and gas industry.

But here's the prize: Once fully installed, 200 of these massive turbines would be able to provide up to 20 percent of Scotland's energy needs. Again, not necessarily a pure play, or even a company that supplies nothing but clean energy, but definitely something to keep an eye on for the future.

Of course, most of the opportunities we're seeing for investors in offshore wind are once again coming from the likes of GE and Vestas. However, the future of U.S. offshore wind could create an avalanche of new opportunities here. In the United States, there's a region of the Atlantic Ocean that runs from Cape Cod, Massachusetts, to Cape Hatteras, North Carolina, known as the *Middle Atlantic Bight*. Due to its large area of shallow water, it makes a very good setting for wind turbines, because current technology allows these things to be built only to a depth of 20 to 30 meters.[57]

According to University of Delaware researcher Willett Kempton, there are experimental turbines being built to a depth of 50 meters in Scotland. And with reasonable additional costs, this researcher expects to see these turbines being built to a depth of 100 meters. And that's when it gets interesting, because, from these studies, the installation of approximately 160,000 turbines on the Middle Atlantic Bight could meet the energy needs of most of the East Coast.[58]

Also, the U.S. Department of Energy estimates that there's enough potential wind energy off the coast of the United States (most near population centers where energy costs are high and land-based wind development is limited) to cover nearly all the current installed U.S. electrical capacity.[59]

So what's the holdup? Cost is certainly an issue. But the regulatory hurdles are proving to be an even bigger headache for developers. Bottom line: No one seems to want a wind farm in his backyard or in the path of his ocean view. (Though we'd certainly rather look at a wind turbine than a coal-fired power plant any day.)

Probably one of the most well-publicized potential offshore wind farms in the United States is the Cape Wind project in Massachusetts. However, there's still a lively debate that essentially boils down to million-dollar ocean views versus soaring energy bills. At the time of this writing, even after an environmental impact report approval, there's still a holdup, as opponents continue to try to overturn the state's approval. Many in the industry are looking to the Cape Wind project as an indicator for future offshore development. The idea is that if this does happen, the floodgates will open and offshore development in the United States will really take off.

As investors, we have to watch to see how this pans out. If it goes through, the rush to develop new offshore sites should deliver a wealth of new opportunities. We suspect, however, that most of the turbine deals will be coming from GE, Vestas, and the companies developing the materials, components, and transmission-related technology, and even the companies that physically put these things in the water. This is also the kind of news you should be tracking. Certainly we'll continue to do so at *Green Chip Stocks*.

## Development Opportunities

Moving back onshore, one of the only true pure wind plays in North America that seems to have enough juice to provide consistent revenue and growth right now is a company called Western Wind Energy Corporation (TSX-V:WND). This is a company that's actually not new to the game. It currently produces 34.5 MW of wind power in California, and holds a power purchase agreement to expand its capacity by 120 MW. We suspect that to be a no-brainer, given California's demand for renewables, and the company's foothold in two of the hottest wind-generating regions in the nation—Palm Springs and Tehachapi. Both of these regions boast significant wind resources, and just as important, have established transmission already in place. Now there are other regions of the United States that hold enormous amounts of wind energy potential, too. But without transmission in place, it's of no immediate use.

That being said, we will continue to monitor new transmission projects in wind-rich areas. You can be certain that, whether it's Texas, North Dakota, or New York, if there's a strong wind resource and there's a new transmission project underway in those wind-rich areas, a wind farm will be soon to follow. And the companies developing those farms will be the next in line for significant, wind-generated profits.

# CHAPTER

4

# THE HEAT BELOW

Geothermal power—using the enormous heat generated in the Earth's core by the radioactive decay of unstable elements—could prove to be the cleanest, greenest, and most abundant source of energy we have ever used. Literally beneath our feet is a white-hot, seething mass of magma that generates temperatures of up to 9,000 degrees Fahrenheit. The heat is used to generate electricity or heat facilities.

Geothermal energy is so sustainable that the first modern site, established in Lardarello, Italy, in 1904, is still producing power.[1] The existing plant has been in operation since 1913, and was interrupted only once, by a World War II bomb.[2]

Although geothermal energy is experiencing a relatively recent resurgence, it's hardly new. It has been powering the United States since 1922,[3] and currently produces 65 percent more power in the United States than solar and wind *combined*.[4] Yet despite its commercial success since 1960,[5] geothermal's full potential is just starting to be tapped by a few visionary companies.

The reservoirs of steam and hot water that make large-scale geothermal generation possible are primarily located in the western states, Alaska, Hawaii, and other parts of the Pacific Rim's "Ring of Fire."[6] However, as we shall see later in this chapter, geothermal heat pumps and direct-use applications can tap the heat energy underground almost anywhere.

## WHAT IS GEOTHERMAL POWER?

In a traditional geothermal plant, steam or superheated water from deep inside the Earth is used to drive a turbine and generate electricity.

The designs typically come in two types: steam plants and binary plants.

1. **Steam plants:** Steam plants use steam or hot water resources (generally, hotter than 300° F). Either the steam comes directly from the source, or extremely hot, high-pressure water is injected into the well and then depressurized (flashed) to produce steam. The steam turns the turbines, which drive generators that produce electricity.

   In a traditional plant, a geothermal well is drilled, typically 5,000 to 10,000 feet deep, in order to access water that has trickled down through cracks in the Earth's crust and collected in subterranean reservoirs, where it is heated by magma from the Earth's core and becomes superheated steam (usually over 500° F).

   After the steam has spent its energy driving the turbines, it is reinjected into the geothermal reservoir to be reheated and used again. With proper management of a geothermal resource, it can be truly renewable.

2. **Binary cycle plants:** In a more modern binary cycle plant, a geothermal fluid is cycled through the production well and passed through a heat exchanger, which transfers the heat to a secondary "working fluid" that has a lower boiling point. This causes the working fluid to flash into vapor, which turns the turbines that drive the generators. The working fluid is then recycled through the system.[7]

   Due to the lower boiling point of the working fluid, binary cycle plants—so called because they use two different fluids—have the advantage of being able to harvest heat from a dry hole, or from a lower-temperature resource (between 100° F and 300° F).

### Geothermal Heat Pumps

The geothermal technologies we have discussed so far are suited to generating electricity at a commercial power plant scale, and should not be confused with the totally different technology used in so-called "geothermal" (or "ground source") heat pumps. These are essentially HVAC (heating, ventilation, and air-conditioning) units, which are commonly used for heating and cooling in residential or commercial buildings. They exchange heat with the Earth using pipes buried about five feet deep in the ground, where the temperature is stable year-round at about 55 degrees.[8]

By cycling a fluid through a heat exchanger, geothermal heat pumps can draw heat from the ground in the winter, and discharge heat underground in the summer. These units tend to be more efficient and cost-effective than their traditional counterparts, because the thermal energy they draw from the Earth is free (although they still use electricity to run the compressors, pumps, and fans).

## BENEFITS OF GEOTHERMAL POWER

Geothermal power holds several advantages over other forms of renewable energy, and many advantages over fossil fuels:

- It's one of the cheapest forms of energy, and the cheapest of all forms of renewable energy. At a typical cost of around 5 cents per kWh,[9] it's about half the price of grid utility power, on a par with the lowest-cost power sources available. (See Figure 4.1.)

- Geothermal energy produces nearly 50 times less carbon dioxide, nitric oxide, and sulfur emissions than traditional fossil-fuel power plants.

- Modern binary cycle geothermal generators have no emissions, not even steam. They make no smog, no toxic chemicals, and no waste. They're *clean.*

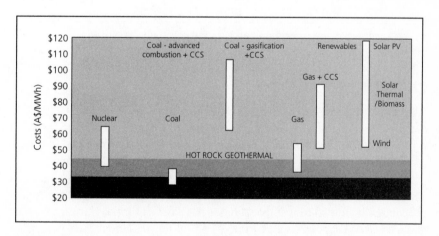

FIGURE 4.1 *Comparative Costs per Watt of Different Energy Sources*
Sources: "Power from the Earth," slide deck; "Geodynamics," presentation to the Society of Petroleum Engineers by Adrian Williams, http://victas.spe.org/images/victas/articles/74/Geodynamics.pdf.

■ Watt for watt, the geothermal plants are tiny compared to other power plants. The PureCycle® units made by United Technologies generate 225 kW of power in an 11- by 17-foot area—about one-tenth the footprint of solar PV for the same power output.

■ These power plants use no fuel because they provide all their own power. (Older plants, such as The Geysers in California, are starting to take a different approach, using solar PV to run their plants. An $8 million, 1 MW plant is being installed there to run the pumps that inject water into the wells.[10])

■ They require no power storage, unlike large-scale solar and wind plants. Simply shut down the cycle and the power stays underground.

■ They run at 89 to 97 percent uptime, making them perfect for *baseload utility generation*, or power generation that's on all the time. By comparison, coal- and nuclear-powered plants, which are normally used for baseload capacity because they're so hard to start up and shut down, average only 75 to 90 percent uptime. (Solar and natural gas–fired electrical plants are more suited to satisfying times of peak electricity demand.) This makes geothermal power the *most reliable* form of power we have.

■ Geothermal power plants have minimal aesthetic impact. Units that harvest heat from underground hot water sources, and reinject it back into the ground, can be very low-profile.

■ The supply of geothermal energy is virtually inexhaustible.

## CURRENT PRODUCTION

Worldwide, geothermal electrical generating capacity is about 9,732 MW, between 24 countries,[11] representing about 0.4 percent of the world total. An estimated 12,000 MW of additional geothermal power is employed in *direct-use* applications such as district heating and ground-source heat pumps.[12]

The United States is one of the world's largest producers of geothermal energy, with 209 plants in operation and more coming online soon. Currently, production is limited to just five states—Alaska, California, Hawaii, Nevada, and Utah—and supplies about 3,000 MW[13] of power, a mere 0.37 percent of the nation's electricity.[14] (In early 2008, U.S. Geothermal [OTCBB:UGTH] began production in Idaho.)

But the industry is only just getting started. In May 2007, Paul Thomsen of geothermal developer Ormat Technologies asked the House Science

Subcommittee on Energy and Environment, "Today, we are tapping only 3.5% of the estimated hydrothermal resource base. Is that acceptable when our country imports 10 million barrels of oil a day and is 60% dependent on net petroleum imports?" That's a good question! Thomsen sees an enormous economic opportunity in geothermal, stating, "Today, nearly 3,000 MW of new geothermal power are under development, which will create over 10,000 new jobs and new investment of over $7 billion, but much more is possible."[15]

Currently, California is the nation's largest producer of electricity from geothermal energy, contributing about 7 percent of the state's total power production in 2003, and 22 percent of the state's total renewable energy (second to hydropower). In fact, about 40 percent of the total *worldwide* geothermal power production takes place in California, much of which is produced at the massive, 30-square-mile, 750 MW facility at The Geysers, north of San Francisco. In total, California's 41 geothermal power plants have a production capacity of approximately 1,900 MWe (megawatts of electrical power)—enough to power nearly two million typical households.[16]

Overall, geothermal is the third largest source of renewable energy in the United States. Andy Karsner, Assistant Secretary for Energy Efficiency and Renewable Energy at the U.S. Department of Energy (DOE), understands the true potential of geothermal power, observing, "We spend a lot of time talking about the resource that beams down from space or blows over us. But we don't spend enough time looking at our very abundant terrestrial geothermal resources that will provide reliable, renewable baseload power."[17]

The geothermal renaissance isn't limited to the United States. Geothermal power plants are springing up all across the globe. While there were 24 countries identified as using geothermal in 2005, it is now estimated that the number of countries producing power from geothermal could hit 46 by 2010.[18] Of particular interest outside North America is the Philippines, where geothermal energy already provides 27 percent of the country's total electricity, and Australia, where the country has witnessed a 57 percent increase in geothermal license applications in 2007.[19]

One company that has already jumped headfirst into Australia's geothermal possibilities, the publicly traded Australian geothermal energy company Geodynamics (ASX:GDY), is now exploring in the Cooper Basin area of South Australia. This region, which palaeontologist and global warming activist Tim Flannery has dubbed *geothermia*, boasts some of the hottest rocks in the world, reaching temperatures of over 500° F. The ambitious Geodynamics project would use a closed-loop system cycling through fractured granite over 4 km below the surface. The company plans to start with a 1 MW plant in 2008, and then decide whether to proceed with a 50 MW demonstration plant.

If that is deemed successful, the company plans to expand to a 500 MW plant by 2015. They believe that the resource could ultimately support a whopping 10,000 MW of generation—over three times the entire current geothermal generation of the United States.[20] Neighboring New Zealand already has over 400 MW of geothermal generating capacity, and permits for another 130 MW have been granted.[21]

Of all the globe, however, Iceland uses the greatest proportion of geothermal energy, which constitutes about 72 percent of its total energy usage. Sitting atop the Middle Atlantic Ridge, Iceland enjoys easily accessible heat from the mountain's depths, and has made intensive use of the resource. The island nation is now entirely powered by renewable energy—principally geothermal and hydroelectric, but also thermoelectric—and nearly all buildings are heated geothermally. Even sidewalks are kept ice-free by their abundant geothermal heat. Not only has this strategy turned Iceland's air from filthy to virtually emissions-free, it has transformed the country from one that just 30 years ago was dependent on coal and oil and one of the poorest in the world, into one that is now energy independent and among the most affluent in the world. Their access to cheap electricity is attracting such industries as aluminum smelting, which requires large amounts of cheap electrical power.[22]

### Massive Potential

Today's 9,732 MW of installed worldwide geothermal capacity is but a tiny fraction of the power that's there, however.[23] The recoverable share of the heat energy found beneath American soil alone is about 14 million quads[24]—or about 140,000 times our current annual energy consumption.[25] It's just a matter of actually getting it.

One of the more interesting applications of geothermal technology is in co-production from oil and natural gas reservoirs that have trapped water, usually at a depth of two to four miles underground. This water ranges from 190 to 390 degrees Fahrenheit, and while a nuisance for the oil and gas industry, it offers good potential for modern binary geothermal plants. For example, in West Texas, nearly 100 barrels of hot water are co-produced along with every barrel of oil, which is then reinjected into the ground.

Significant hot water resources of this type have been found in at least 11 states, mostly in the West. It is often commingled with natural gas, which can also be produced profitably. The NREL estimates that such resources could produce between 400 and 2,200 MW of power in Texas alone, and as much as 70,000 MW (about 10 percent of the nation's electrical needs) nationwide over the next 20 years—a very significant part of the solution to our national energy challenges![26]

The greatest potential for geothermal development, however, may be found not just in specialized sites with particular geological characteristics, but literally anywhere. According to a 2006 study by the Massachusetts Institute of Technology (MIT), there are over 100 *million* quads of accessible geothermal energy worldwide—when the entire worldwide consumption of energy is only 400 quads. That's enough to meet the world's total current energy needs for 30,000 years.

The MIT scenario is based on the use of "enhanced geothermal systems" or "universal geothermal" technology, in which two holes are drilled at least 10 km down into hard rock, and the rock between them is fractured. Water is pumped down one hole and harvested as steam when it comes back up the other, which is then used to spin a turbine. Such facilities could be built almost anywhere in the world, since adequate heat is available at those depths worldwide.[27]

The report estimates that "a cumulative capacity of more than 100,000 MW from enhanced geothermal systems (EGS) can be achieved in the United States within 50 years with a modest, multiyear federal investment for R&D in several field projects in the United States."[28] With an investment of $800 million to $1 billion, the report estimates that the United States could produce more than 100 gigawatts of electricity by 2050, equal to the combined output of all of its nuclear power plants. And if EGS could tap just 40 percent of the heat under the United States, it would meet demand 56,000 times over.

## Explosive Growth

Utilities and independent developers have been researching and testing methods of producing electricity from geothermal energy for more than four decades at dozens of unique geothermal sites in California, Utah, and Nevada, but it's never been a big-money business. Now, however, after languishing for decades, geothermal power is once again catching fire, thanks to the twin challenges of peak oil and global warming.

A report on the international market by the Geothermal Energy Association (GEA) recognized 40 countries where geothermal power development is under way, and projected a 50 percent growth in geothermal power production worldwide by 2010, from 8,661 MW in 2000 to 13,500 MW or more in 46 countries.[29] "We have seen dramatic new interest in the geothermal industry," said Karl Gawell, executive director of the GEA. "That is translating into many new geothermal projects in the U.S. and around the world."

According to the GEA's May 2007 survey, the installed capacity of geothermal power in the United States is set to nearly double. In addition to the 2,851 MW of geothermal capacity we have today, another 2,500 to 2,900

MW of capacity is currently under consideration or development in 12 states: Alaska, Arizona, California, Hawaii, Idaho, Nevada, New Mexico, Oregon, Texas, Utah, Washington, and Wyoming. That would be enough to supply the needs of 6 million households.[30]

A large chunk of that increased production may come from Nevada. A January 2006 report from the Geothermal Taskforce of the Western Governor's Association (WGA) estimated that 1,488 MW of geothermal power could be deployed in Nevada by 2015, which could grow to 2,895 MW by 2025—all from identified resources.[31]

With all this growth under way, the big money has smelled the opportunity, and now they're jumping in. In May 2007, Merrill Lynch announced that it had made a $35 million investment in Vulcan Power Co., a private company and one of the largest geothermal property holders in the United States. "We believe that an investment in Vulcan is critical to accelerate development of geothermal resources that benefit the environment," said Rob Jones, the head of the Merrill global energy and power group.

But that's just the first round. In total, Vulcan intends to raise $150 million to develop some 900 MW worth of geothermal energy from its portfolio. Before even breaking ground, they had buyers for the power. The company has announced 20-year power purchase agreements with Nevada Power Co., Pacific Gas & Electric Co., and Southern California Edison Co. for the project.

### Geothermal Incentives

Like any new form of energy production, geothermal power is getting a boost from a combination of state and federal incentives to encourage investment in new power plants. The capital needed to build a new plant is significant, the time needed to build a plant is long, and the risks are extensive. So these incentives are essential for the growth of the industry.

"New federal and state initiatives to promote geothermal energy are paying off," commented Karl Gawell, GEA's Executive Director. "State renewable standards coupled with the federal production tax credit are creating a renaissance in U.S. geothermal power production," he added. Here is a sampling of some of the incentives available for geothermal development:

- Plants that came online before 2008 can earn a federal tax credit of $19 per MWh. For a 100 MW plant, this would mean $15.5 million per year for 10 years ($155 million). It is expected that Congress will extend this credit to plants coming online by the end of 2011.

- Because they produce clean power, without the emissions of carbon and sulfur typical of fossil-fueled power plants, geothermal plants earn emissions credits, also known as "green tags" and "renewable energy certificates" (RECs). These credits can be sold on the new "carbon trading" markets for an additional source of revenue, generating between $6 per MW and $50 per MW, depending on location. (The lower prices are typical of the still-developing, voluntary carbon market in the United States; the higher prices are typical in Europe, where cap-and-trade carbon markets are mandated by law.)

■ The State of Idaho offers a 100 percent rebate on Idaho's 5 percent sales tax for the construction of new renewable energy plants, and similar state subsidies are likely to be forthcoming in states that have renewable portfolio standards and decent geothermal potential.

Geothermal power is also enjoying renewed federal support. The Energy Policy Act of 2005 provided a full production tax credit. In addition, increased funding and support from federal agencies such as the Department of Energy (DoE) and the Bureau of Land Management (BLM) have been instrumental in clearing the way for new geothermal projects.

In 2007, various pieces of legislation to promote geothermal energy were kicked around in Congress, but did not survive the process to make it into law. But the effort has continued, and as of this writing (January 2008), an energy bill has passed the Senate that would direct the Department of Energy to spend $95 million annually to research and promote geothermal energy.[32]

We have no doubt that geothermal energy will be a major player in the renewable energy portfolio of tomorrow. With more than half of the United States having created *renewable portfolio standards* (RPS) that require a portion of electricity to be produced from renewable sources within the next 10 to 20 years, and the difficulty that many utilities have had in satisfying those requirements with wind and solar, geothermal power is the only obvious alternative that could fit the bill.

## Financing Challenges

Once a good site is found, the major challenge to starting up a traditional geothermal project is financing. The capital requirements are significant, the projects typically take a long time to build, and there is always the risk that once an expensive hole is drilled, the resource will not produce as hoped. Obtaining the up-front capital to begin, therefore, can be a challenge.

Additionally, geothermal projects rely on drilling technology from the oil and gas industry, where demand for drilling equipment is greater than ever. This can slow the progress of projects and inflate their ultimate costs. Consequently, a cottage industry in workshops and seminars on geothermal financing and regulatory hurdles has sprung up in recent years, and is attracting an eager and willing audience. We believe that within the next five years—by 2013 or so— many of these issues will have been worked out, and geothermal power will be the darling of Wall Street.

## INVESTING IN GEOTHERMAL

There can be no discussion about the geothermal industry without mentioning Ormat Technologies (NYSE:ORA), as this is one of the most successful and well-recognized names in the geothermal business. The company has been around for about 40 years, and is the third largest geothermal power producer in the United States. Simply put, Ormat Technologies is the best of breed among publicly traded geothermal companies. We recommended this stock to Green Chip subscribers back in 2005, when the stock was trading around $16.00 a share. (See Figure 4.2.)

Over the course of the next two years, the company landed contract after contract and the stock soared, getting as high as $57.93 a share in December 2007, and delivering our early investors gains of as much as 262 percent. Today, Ormat Technologies is still in our *Green Chip Stocks* portfolio, as we believe this stock represents a solid geothermal position that will continue to increase in value over the next few years as the demand for geothermal power continues to grow. And much like any solid, experienced company, Ormat doesn't have all its eggs in one basket, either.

While Ormat is clearly a leader in the geothermal game, it's also quickly becoming a leader in *recovered energy power generation* (REG). REG essentially involves capturing unused residual heat from industrial processes and converting it into electricity.

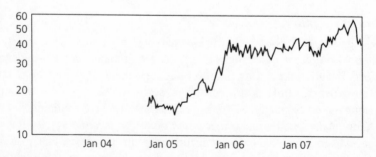

**FIGURE 4.2** *Ormat Technologies, Inc.*

Originally, it was their geothermal business that attracted us to Ormat. But after sitting down with Ormat VP Daniel Schochet back in 2006 to discuss the company's Ormat Energy Converter (OEC) that's used for REG plants, we quickly became convinced that Ormat's position in the REG industry wasn't to be taken lightly either. These REG plants not only generate power, but generate some serious money, too.

After our brief conversation with Mr. Schochet, we found that two of Ormat's wholly owned subsidiaries had received supply and construction orders worth about $29 million for three REG power plants from a power producer in Western Canada. Since then, the company has continued to line up new REG contracts.

Beyond the REG projects the company's been supplying since 1998, the company now has eight new REG projects under construction in Canada, Spain, India, Italy, and the United States. The company also continues to rack up recovered energy purchase agreements. One of the most recent was a 20-year deal with a consumer-owned cooperative in Colorado for the sale of electricity generated from a 4 MW REG plant being constructed along a natural gas compression station near Denver.

Of course, even with these very lucrative REG contracts, it's still Ormat's leadership in the geothermal sector that attracts investors. In fact, Ormat's so far ahead in the geothermal game that the company not only operates its own facilities, but actually helps smaller geothermal firms construct their own power plants. That's what Ormat Nevada (a subsidiary of Ormat Technologies) was brought on to do for a smaller geothermal firm called U.S. Geothermal, Inc. (AMEX:HTM).

U.S. Geothermal announced in 2006 that it was proceeding with the engineering, procurement, and construction of a 10 MW geothermal power plant in Idaho. And Ormat Nevada would be supplying this power plant. Interestingly, this was a company we were already considering as our second geothermal position.

You see, in the world of renewable energy, it doesn't take much to launch a company into the spotlight. Get yourself one decent contract or one long-term power purchase agreement with a major utility, and these lower-priced stocks soar. That's why we were so bullish on U.S. Geothermal in 2006.

Here was this little $0.80 stock that had a very lucrative feather in its geothermal cap: an Idaho-based geothermal project called Raft River. This one single project had a potential annual revenue of about $140 million. The best part was that hardly anyone realized the company was only months away from breaking ground at the Idaho site—thereby launching the state's only geothermal power plant.

Of course, U.S. Geothermal wasn't the first to dig around in Raft River. In 1974, the DoE spent eight years and over $40 million developing the reservoir, and constructing and operating a 7 MW binary cycle geothermal power plant.

After the energy crisis of the 1970s subsided, many renewable energy projects were quickly forgotten, including Raft River. Then, in 2002, right before the renewables industry really got its second wind, U.S. Geothermal acquired the project and quickly found itself in 100 percent control of the 8.2 square miles of geothermal rights. Moreover, it would be the only company building a power plant to tap a piece of Idaho's vast geothermal reservoirs, which, according to a document we dug up in some old DoE archives, had a projected capacity of as much as 5,100 MW (enough to provide for about 4 million households).[33]

Granted, U.S. Geothermal's 8.2 square miles hold only a fraction of the entire state's capacity. But it was certainly enough for a 10 MW deal with the Idaho Power Company. And once that agreement went through, the big money started paying attention. In fact, Green Chip investors thoroughly enjoyed watching the stock pop after it was announced that Goldman Sachs was pumping $27 million into the company. All in all, this was a great play, though, admittedly, we weren't able to recommend it as early as we had liked.

You see, while we can often do a lot of our research online, when it comes to power generation, we try to go to the source. Obviously, few people have the time or even the opportunity to do this. But before we make a recommendation, we like to see firsthand exactly how the company is operating. So, while we were ready to pull the trigger in early 2006, we waited until we could actually get out to Raft River. And let me tell you, it wasn't a quick trip.

After a long flight to Boise, a three-hour bus ride to Raft River, and a two-hour tour of the property, which was littered with construction equipment, rattlesnake holes, jackrabbit carcasses, and a boatload of potential, we were convinced that this would end up being a great play for us.

On July 25, we put out the recommendation on U.S. Geothermal. By October 2007 the stock had reached a new high of $4.78. (See Figure 4.3.)

And the best part is, they're still developing new geothermal sites. Over the next few years, this will be a company to follow closely.

### The Path to Profits

Ormat and U.S. Geothermal have certainly delivered for Green Chip investors. But they're not the only games in town. There are a handful of other publicly traded geothermal companies to watch, and if they perform even half as well as Ormat and U.S. Geothermal have, you'll have no complaints.

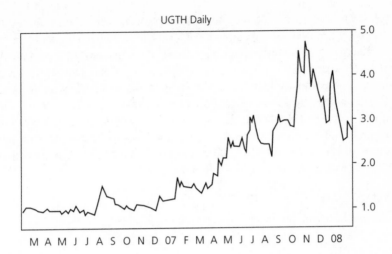

**FIGURE 4.3** *U.S. Geothermal*

So exactly what is it that you should be watching? With geothermal companies there are a number of things we look for, such as:

- Geothermal property with strong capacity projections

- Power purchase agreements

- Transmission agreements

- New capital flowing into the projects

- Power plant construction

All of this information can be easily found online through utility company and utility commission web sites. As well, a lot of this information is discussed quite openly at renewable energy conferences. All of this can also be found at *Green Chip Stocks.*

### A Touch of Geothermal

With geothermal energy offering such significant potential for investors, there are also companies that aren't considered pure geothermal companies but have seen their stock price spike after investing in this sector. Take Raser Technologies (NYSE:RZ), for example.

Raser Technologies manufactures high-performance electric motor and controller technology for electric vehicles. This is what originally got us interested in this company, and ultimately one of the reasons we recommended it as an alternative transportation play. However, in January 2007, we got word that the company had decided to get into the geothermal game. A few days later, a press release appeared announcing that Raser Technologies had secured geothermal rights to a few properties in Nevada. A few months later, more properties were announced. Then a few weeks later, another property was announced. It became a trend. In fact, from late March through October 2007, Raser announced all of the following:

- Five drilling targets in Nevada.

- Two additional geothermal leases in Nevada.

- A geothermal lease in Utah.

- A series of agreements with United Technologies Corporation's UTC power unit, for UTC to provide 135 *Pure Cycle* geothermal power systems for three Raser power plants.

- The securing of a project permit for the purpose of developing geothermal well fields in Nevada.

- A project alliance agreement with Cummins & Barnard to construct power plants.

- The securing of an option to develop geothermal properties in California.

- Three new drilling targets in Utah.

- The securing of an additional 3,972 acres of geothermal rights in Utah.

- The securing of yet another 11,294 acres of geothermal rights in Utah.

When we first jumped on Raser, back in November 2006, the stock was trading around $6.05 a share. But look at what happened to the stock, starting in January, after the company began its aggressive geothermal push. (See Figure 4.4.) Investors who picked up shares of Raser on our original recommendation picked up gains in excess of 200 percent in just over a year.

### A Twenty-First-Century Land Rush

Today, there's a kind of "gold rush" happening in certain parts of the United States, but this time it's for hot geothermal properties, and companies are buying them up left and right.

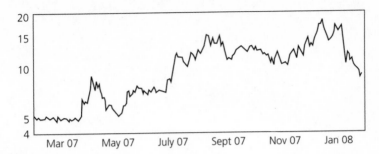

FIGURE 4.4 *Raser Technologies, Inc.*

The best geothermal resources can be found in the Western part of the country—Idaho, Nevada, Utah, Washington State, Oregon, California, Montana, and Wyoming. So if you see that a company is heavily acquiring geothermal leases in any of these states, *pay attention*. As investors, picking up on a little trend like this could make you a lot of money.

Continued investment opportunities should arise as some of the newer, younger geothermal firms start landing the necessary funding they need to develop their sites. They will be primarily long-term, giving early investors the opportunity to double or triple their money over the subsequent three to five years.

# CHAPTER

5

# WHAT MAY WASH UP
# IN THE TIDE

Next to solar energy, the largest source of energy on the planet is ocean energy—the motion of waves and tides. Both sources of energy are inexhaustible: Waves are caused by winds and the heating of water, which in turn are caused by the Sun; tides are caused by the gravitational attraction between the Earth, Sun, and Moon.

Essentially, because it derives from the Sun—as do wind and solar energy—marine energy is essentially concentrated *solar* energy. It's concentrated because water is dense, and so it absorbs and delivers a lot of energy.

Compare the amounts of energy delivered by sun, wind, and water per square meter by looking at Table 5.1. The density of the energy source has a huge effect on the power that can be generated from it. For example, because water is 850 times denser than air, tidal turbines can produce 40 times more power than windmills with similar gear, but with smaller equipment and lower costs per watt.[1]

## THE LARGEST UNTAPPED SOURCE OF ENERGY

Of all forms of energy we use today, marine energy is our largest untapped energy source. Compared to other renewable technologies, it is still very much in its infancy, having received minimal attention and development capital.

## TABLE 5.1 Energy Density of Renewable Energy Sources

| Energy Source | Energy Density |
|---|---|
| Solar | 100–200 W/m² typical |
| Wind | 400–600 W/m² for a good-to-excellent site, but ranges from 100 to 700 W/m² |
| Tidal | 2,000 W/m² typical, but ranges from 1,500 to 4,500 W/m² |
| Wave | 1,000,000 W/meter of wave crest length, or 20,000–70,000 W/m² for the best sites |

*Data sources:* Wave energy: World Energy Council, "Survey of Energy Resources 2007," http://www.worldenergy.org/publications/survey_of_energy_resources_2007/wave_energy/760. asp; Tidal energy: Electric Power Research Institute, "Overview: EPRI Ocean Energy Program," slide deck, Duke Global Change Center, September 14, 2006, http://archive.epri.com/oceanenergy/ attachments/ocean/briefing/Duke_Sep_14.pdf; "Marine Renewable Energy," British Wind Energy Association, http://www.bwea.com/marine/resource.html; Wind energy: National Renewable Energy Laboratory, as cited by RS/GIS Laboratory, Utah State University, "Western U.S. Wind Resource at 50 Meters Above Ground Level," February 2004, http://sagemap.wr.usgs.gov, http:// mercury.ornl.gov/metadata/nbii/html/gbip/jester.wr.usgs.gov_nbii_westus_50mwind_sgca.html.

The first major real-world trials of a new generation of commercial wave and tidal generating machines are just getting under way.

Ocean energy offers clean, green, and consistent power, all at a relatively low cost, with negligible environmental impact. And since the "fuel" of ocean generators—the movement of waves and tides—costs nothing, marine energy holds the promise of being able to generate electricity at highly competitive rates. In addition, they avoid the NIMBY (Not In My Backyard) resistance that has inhibited wind projects because tidal projects are underwater and most wave projects are very low profile and well out to sea.

### Types of Generators

Despite the immaturity of marine-energy technology, tidal-energy generators, which are similar to dams, have been around for centuries. The oldest tidal mill in England has been operating for over 900 years.

In recent decades, dozens of different designs have been offered and some prototype systems have been constructed, but the contest of technologies at commercial scale in the field has only begun. The main hindrance has been that the source of energy, while immense, has been too scattered to harvest economically. It simply takes so many devices spread out over so large an area that the capital costs, technical challenges, and environmental review considerations become onerous.

Of course, this technology is also still in its infancy. In a recent interview with *Scientific American*, a leading ocean-energy expert estimated that marine power is about 20 years behind wind power, "but it certainly isn't going to take 20 years to catch up."[2] Currently, at least four companies are testing wave-conversion devices worldwide.[3]

Constrained oil supplies and rising energy prices have finally prompted governments and private capital to take a fresh look at marine energy. This has generated a wave of investment capital for private/public research and demonstration projects. Now the conditions for advancement in this sector are ripe, and it seems assured that the hurdles of the past will be overcome by the sheer bulk of capital being thrown at marine energy today. We expect significant technical advances and efficiency gains to be made in short order.

There are now many different marine-energy systems in development, employing a variety of technologies using pumps, pistons, turbines, and hydraulics: wave energy, tidal energy, ocean current energy, offshore wind, salinity gradient energy, even ocean thermal gradient energy.

Of these, wave and tidal designs are emerging as the two main types of marine energy that are grabbing the lion's share of investment bucks. Because the energy available in the constant motion of waves is about an order of magnitude greater, and of a very different kind, than that of the twice-daily tides, the two types of energy require different technologies to capture it. Let's take a closer look at them.

### Tidal-Energy Devices

"Barrage generators" such as the Rance tidal-power plant in Bretagne, France, were among the earliest types of tidal generators. A barrage generator is essentially a dam across a body of water that traps water when the tide is high and then uses it to power turbines by letting the water out when the tide is low.

A very different approach to tidal energy uses the same principles as wind turbines, only underwater. These "tidal stream" or "marine current" generators are typically situated in a narrow strait such as the Golden Gate at the mouth of San Francisco Bay, or an oceanic current, where a large, consistent stream of water movement takes place with the tides. As the tide goes in and out, it forces the underwater turbines to spin. Tide farms, like those developed by Marine Current Turbines, resemble underwater windmills on steroids and are mounted on concrete pylons on the ocean floor.

## Wave-Energy Devices

Wave-energy devices typically use one of four principles to harvest energy: A *point absorber* captures the energy of a device bobbing on the surface as it pulls against its anchor on the ocean floor; an *attenuator* uses hydraulics to capture the sinuous flexing motion of a long snakelike device (like the Pelamis™, which we'll discuss a little later); a *terminator-oscillating water column* traps water within a cylindrical shaft onshore, using the air pressure caused by its rising and falling volume to power turbines; and an *overtopper* uses a ramp to channel water up into a raised reservoir, and then captures the energy with low-head turbines as the water falls back to the surface level.

# MASSIVE POTENTIAL

The amount of energy in ocean currents and tidal streams alone is estimated at about 5 terawatts (TW) continuous, theoretically enough to meet the entire world's electricity requirements.[4] The energy exerted by waves in a single day—72 trillion watt-hours (TWh)—could power more than half of all American households for an entire year.[5]

Put another way, the World Energy Council estimates that in theory, ocean energy could supply twice as much electricity as the entire world now consumes, which is about 14,000 TWh.[6] However, because most ocean energy is not located where we need it, the Council estimates that the economically exploitable wave resource is considerably more modest, at between 140 and 750 TWh/year in ocean depths of at least 100 meters, although it could be as much as 2,000 TWh/year with technological improvements. In 5 to 10 years, the Council believes that wave energy could be a significant part of the supply mix.[7]

A more liberal estimate was offered in a 2004 study prepared for the Scottish Parliament. This study found that the total practical worldwide potential for wave and tidal energy is between 8,000 TW and 80,000 TW, which is still within the same order of magnitude as world electric consumption, and estimated that the wave energy potential for Europe is around 320 GW, or about three times the current electrical generating capacity of the UK.[8] Even better, the study estimated that the power could be delivered for 4 to 7 p/KWh, which is on a par with the cost of grid power.

Another study, done in 2005 for the Electric Power Research Institute (EPRI) by Roger Bedard, estimated the incident wave energy along the U.S. coastlines at 2,100 TWh per year, or about half the country's total electricity consumption.[9] Just one quarter of this potential could produce as much energy as the entire U.S. hydropower system at rates competitive with contemporary grid power, and that's assuming that we use just 20 percent of the commercially viable offshore wave resources at only 50 percent efficiency![10] (See Figure 5.1.)

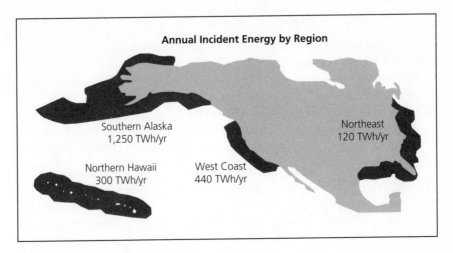

**FIGURE 5.1** *U.S. Wave-Energy Resources*
*Source:* "Wave & Tidal Energy Technology," Renewable Northwest Project, http://www
.rnp.org/RenewTech/tech_wave.html#_edn2.

According to the EPRI's analysis, the best wave resource in the U.S. Lower 48 is the West Coast, particularly Oregon (average 21 kW/m$^2$) and Washington (average 27 kW/m$^2$). Combined with the resources of the Northeast, they estimate that some 560 TWh/year could be generated in the U.S. Lower 48.[11]

The wave resources in Alaska and Hawaii are very significant, but they are too far away from the Lower 48 to help with those electrical loads, so those potential energy sources would mainly benefit Alaska and Hawaii. Still, the potential for wind and tidal energy is indeed enormous and cost-competitive.

## U.S. Projects
At least nine countries are already evaluating tidal- and wave-energy projects, although most of them are in pilot or development stage.[12] Among government initiatives is the Energy Policy Act of 2005, which requires the U.S. Department of Energy to consider ocean energy in its inventory of renewables, and makes it eligible for research and development monies.

And as of this writing, the Federal Energy Regulatory Commission (FERC) is considering an expedited licensing process for pilot projects involving wave- and tidal-energy technologies. The change would promote the rapid deployment of pilot projects, as long as they are five megawatts or smaller in capacity, located in waters that have no sensitive designations, and can be removed or shut down on relatively short notice.[13] Such expedited licensing should remove much of the regulatory risk that has so far inhibited investment.

New projects are starting up in several U.S. locations:

- **New York:** In June 2007, New York began generating power from the first-ever tidal turbine facility in North America, on the bed of the East River. The project uses six 35-kilowatt tidal current turbines made by Verdant Power LLC, which are now generating approximately 1,000 kWh per day for Roosevelt Island while a $1.5 million sonar system monitors effects on local fish populations. The project is in pilot phase now, but Verdant Power hopes to eventually expand it into a 10 MW tidal farm.[14]

- **San Francisco Bay:** California's Pacific Gas and Electric Company (PG&E) is working with local agencies to explore tidal power options in San Francisco Bay. A recent article in the *San Francisco Chronicle* estimated that the city could supply 100 percent of its electricity demand with marine energy.[15]

  Two major sites have been evaluated for the city by the Electric Power Research Institute. One wave-energy plant on Ocean Beach would require 152 Energetech devices, or 213 Pelamis devices, to produce approximately 300,000 MWh/year—enough to power 25,000 homes. Another in-stream tidal flow system at the Golden Gate, with about 16.5 MW of realistic generation capacity, would provide enough power for about 12,800 homes, using 80 underwater turbines of about 18 m in diameter.[16]

- **Washington State:** In Washington State, the Snohomish County Public Utility District (PUD) is looking at potential tidal energy sites along the coast.[17]

- **Rhode Island:** Prototype projects are starting up in Rhode Island as well.

## Europe Catches a $1 Trillion Wave

The world's first commercial wave farm is now being built in Portugal.[18] The €8 million, 2.25 MW project will meet the electricity demand of more than 1,500 households.[19] The initial phase will consist of three Pelamis converters located off the north coast. The Pelamis, developed by Pelamis Wave Power (formerly Ocean Power Delivery, Ltd.), is a snakelike machine about the same size as a freight train, consisting of a series of cylindrical hollow steel segments that are connected to each other by hinged joints. As it bobs on the surface of the water, the flexing motion of the segments drives hydraulic pistons inside, which pump oil into a hydraulic generator.[20]

An even bigger installation has been approved for a site 10 miles off the coast of Cornwall, in southwest England. The initial 5 MW wave power project, called WestWave and built by Oceanlinx, will consist of a mix of Pelamis converters and MRC1000 converters from ORECon, around a central "Wave Hub" which will function as a socket to connect them to the grid onshore. The project will initially generate enough electricity to power the equivalent of 3,000 households, or about 3 percent of Cornwall's needs.[21] At an estimated startup cost of £28 million, of which £21.5 million has been raised, the project is expected to save £76 million over the next 25 years and create 170 jobs for the local economy. Eventually, the Wave Hub could produce as much as 20 MW, powering 7,500 homes with an installation eight square kilometers in size.[22]

It seems a bit ironic that the Pelamis "wave-energy converters" are made by a Scottish company, but its initial commercial projects are elsewhere. Not to be outdone, Scotland awarded £13 million in grants in 2007 to develop marine energy technologies for operation in Scotland.[23] Enterprise Minister Nicol Stephen has strongly endorsed the effort, saying, "I am committed to supporting Scotland's huge wave and tidal energy resource. Scotland has a real opportunity to be a world leader in this field."[24]

Eventually, the British government hopes to supply one-fifth of its power needs with marine energy.[25] To this end, they have already spent more than £25 million ($46.7 million) on research and development, plus another £50 million to make marine energy a commercial reality.[26] The Cornwall plant should come online by 2009. If the plan works, Britain will be able to satisfy all of its obligations under the Kyoto Protocol using marine energy alone![27]

Elsewhere in Europe, global energy giants like General Electric, Norsk Hydro of Norway, and E.ON of Germany are betting that the ocean holds as much promise as the solar and wind industries. They've already poured more than $100 million of funding into tiny marine energy companies in 2006, and are pledging more for the future.[28]

Eventually, the marine energy industry in Europe alone could be worth at least $1 trillion, according to Benoit Dal Ferro of the energy consulting firm Douglas-Westwood: "The technologically recoverable natural resource presented by wave and tidal energy could be a long-term global business opportunity for European industry worth at least £600 billion (US$1 trillion)," he says. "This could be a commercial opportunity for Europe on the scale of the Airbus project."[29]

## COSTS FALLING

Like any new technology, the first wave and tidal energy devices will cost significantly more than the succeeding generations. And like any renewable energy technology, the costs are highest at first and decline over time, because the "fuel" is free and most of the costs owe to the equipment itself.

According to the World Energy Council's *Survey of Energy Resources 2007*, the power generating costs of the first wave-energy devices are around

$300/kWh, as compared to an average grid power cost of around $0.10/kWh. But the UK-based Carbon Trust (2006) estimates that the generating cost of typical commercial projects will range between $0.44 and $0.55/kWh, and in time will achieve cost parity with other renewable energy sources under a typical program of gradually declining incentives.[30]

Since nearly all of the costs of renewable power are up-front, one should compare them to traditional power sources on the basis of "levelized costs" which the Energy Information Administration defines as "the present value of the total cost of building and operating a generating plant over its economic life, converted to equal annual payments. Costs are levelized in real dollars (i.e., adjusted to remove the impact of inflation)."[31]

The Renewable Northwest Project has calculated the levelized costs of wave and tidal energy in the United States based on data from the EPRI, and determined that the current levelized cost of wave energy is between 10 and 30 cents per kWh, but in the future should drop to around 5 to 6 cents per kWh. (Again, this compares with an average price of about 10 cents per kWh for regular grid power today.) They found that the levelized cost of tidal energy was even lower, at between 8 and 12 cents per kWh today, dropping to 4 to 6 cents in the future.[32]

In sum, on a levelized cost basis, tidal energy is already competitive with grid power, and wave energy soon will be. In the future, when the prices of today's fossil fuels are skyrocketing, the cost of ocean energy will be falling to about half the price of today's grid power!

Where might the cost reductions be found? According to a 2006 study by the engineering, consulting, and construction company Black and Veatch, the best opportunities for cost reduction through R&D investment are in the components that comprise the largest part of the systems' costs. For wave energy devices, the best bang for the buck will be in improving the structural materials (such as the floats and device bodies), followed by the electrical generator unit, mooring systems, power converter, and offshore cabling and substations, respectively. For tidal current devices, the study found that the greatest cost reductions could be made in the gearbox assembly, followed by the rotors, structural materials, cabling, the electrical plant, the offshore substation, and finally the mooring systems. Further, crossover technologies such as mooring and cabling could help to reduce costs in both types of systems.[33]

## INVESTING IN MARINE ENERGY

When it comes to investing in renewable energy, we believe that the marine energy sector is probably the one that will require the most patience for long-term investors. In fact, searching for quality marine energy stocks now is roughly the equivalent of searching for solar stocks 10 to 20 years ago.

In other words, the potential for profits is there—but the big payoff in most cases is years away. The reason is that the industry is only just now really bringing renewable energy solutions to the market.

For investors, this presents both a benefit and a downfall. The downfall is simply the fact that marine energy generates only a tiny fraction of what other renewable industries generate at the moment, which itself is just a tiny fraction of what's generated from coal and natural gas. We're not talking about a small fish in a big pond; we're talking about small plankton in a big ocean.

However, it is such a young and small industry, the ground-floor opportunities tend to be a bit more plentiful. Over the next few years, we should begin to see quite a few ground-floor opportunities in this sector. Certainly there are larger corporations tapping this industry now for future profits. As mentioned earlier in this chapter, GE, Norsk Hydro, and E.ON have already poured more than $100 million of funding into small marine-energy companies. As the demand for renewable-energy options continues to increase, more and more individual investors will be looking for a way to play this sector as well.

## Permits and Power

Right now, there really are only a handful of domestic, publicly traded companies that operate in this industry. In fact, we just saw marine energy's first IPO in the United States in 2007 with Ocean Power Technologies (NASDAQ: OPTT). The company has been promoting its proprietary PowerBuoy™ technology since 1994. The PowerBuoy system is a point absorber type of generator, which captures wave energy using large floating buoys anchored to the seabed.

The company began ocean trials in 1997 off the coast of New Jersey. Seven years later, the company formed a joint venture with Iberdrola S.A. of Spain (which trades on the Madrid Stock Exchange) to build a wave farm on the north coast of Spain. Iberdrola is Europe's largest utility in renewable energy, with over $13 billion in annual revenues.

A year later, Ocean Power Technologies signed an agreement with Total S.A. of France (which trades on the New York and Paris stock exchanges) to develop a wave power station on the west coast of France. Total S.A. is the world's third largest publicly traded oil and gas company.

In 2006, the company:

■ Was awarded a contract from the U.S. Department of Homeland Security to provide remote, ocean-based power for vessel reconnaissance.

- Was selected to occupy a position at the South West Wave Hub project off the north coast of Cornwall, England, for the installation of a 5 MW wave power station.

- Signed an agreement with Iberdrola for the turnkey construction and installation of the subsea power transmission cable, underwater substation, grid connection, and the first PowerBuoy unit in connection with a 1.25 MW wave power station on the north coast of Spain.

- Signed a marketing cooperation agreement with Lockheed Martin.

By 2007, Ocean Power Technologies raised net proceeds of $90 million through its IPO, was awarded a $1.2 million grant through the Scottish Minister's Wave and Tidal Energy Support Scheme, and was awarded a $1.7 million contract from the U.S. Navy. During this year, they also filed applications for permits from the U.S. Federal Regulatory Commission (FERC) for two power-generation projects located at Coos Bay and Newport, Oregon.

That definitely got our attention, because an earlier press release had announced that the company had filed an application for a permit to FERC for a 50 MW wave-power generation project in Oregon. This was an application for the first utility-scale wave-power project in the United States. So we watched the FERC web site closely, following up to see if the permit would be received. Sure enough, on February 16, 2007, FERC issued the company a preliminary permit to study the site.

We regularly pull up FERC documents to monitor this kind of progress, because, as in the case of Ocean Power Technologies, a company must submit a report that describes, for that report period, its progress as a condition of the permit.

Obviously, this isn't something most people have the time or even patience to do. However, regulatory filings like these can clue you in as to just how far a certain company is progressing. This typically isn't the stuff you're going to find in random press releases.

Nonetheless, if you're willing to do the necessary digging, the benefit (i.e., moving on news before the rest of the trend chasers) can certainly be well worth the time. In fact, had you been sifting through these kinds of regulatory documents back in 2006, you might've come across an application for the construction of an offshore power plant in Washington state by a company called Finavera Renewables (TSX-V:FVR).

Finavera does operate in the wind sector, but also boasts a number of wave-energy projects using its wave-energy converter system, the AquaBuOY. With this technology, an energy transfer takes place by converting the vertical component of wave kinetic energy into pressurized seawater by means of two-stroke hose pumps. Pressurized seawater is directed into a conversion system consisting of a turbine driving an electrical generator. The power is then transmitted to shore by an undersea transmission line.[34]

Finavera currently has five wave power projects underway:

1. The Makah Bay Project—a 1 MW demonstration plant expected to generate 1,500 MWh/year, or enough energy to supply about 150 homes in Neah Bay each year.

2. The Coos County Project—currently planned as a 100 MW wave park.

3. The Figueira da Foz offshore pilot power plant—a 2 MW demonstration plant to be constructed with commercial expansion of the plant to 100 MW.

4. The Ucluelet, B.C. Project—a 5 MW facility that Finavera is now in the process of assessing with government agencies as to the provincial and federal permits required for the project.

5. The Western Cape, South Africa Project—a 20 MW facility that Finavera is now in the process of assessing with government agencies, to obtain the permits required for the project.

As you can clearly see, Finavera is still in the early stages, so investors looking for the big payday won't find it here in the short term. However, over the next few years, this company has an excellent opportunity to be one of the first on the wave energy scene, supplying juice to the grid. If that happens, those that got in early could benefit handsomely. So we'll be following Finavera closely over the next few years to see how this one turns out.

### Even in the East River

Investors looking for profits in this sector should also stay on top of a few companies that are not publicly traded, for the simple reason that their progress could dictate future IPOs, government funding, and even the reduction of regulatory hurdles. We definitely saw the latter happen when a company called Verdant Power came on the scene.

Verdant Power has developed a "kinetic hydropower system" (KHPS). This is basically dam-less hydropower converted from energy found in the flowing water currents of oceans, tides, rivers, and manmade channels or conduits.[35]

As mentioned earlier, in 2007, Verdant began generating power from the first-ever tidal turbine facility in North America, on the bed of the East River.

The project, dubbed the Roosevelt Island Tidal Energy (RITE) project, generates about 1,000 kWh per day. But this is just the beginning. The company has further phases of development planned, which will ultimately progress from six to as many as 300 tidal KHPS turbines running in rows beneath the waters of the East River. At full capacity, the project could provide 10 MW of local power, or enough to provide energy to nearly 8,000 homes in New York by 2010.

Verdant isn't publicly traded, but the company's effect on the industry cannot be ignored. In 2005, FERC decided to waive the licensing requirements for generating and delivering power during the testing phase of the RITE project. This order was actually entitled the *Verdant Ruling*. And in the future, we suspect that clean, efficient tidal projects such as this one will also get favorable treatment from regulators—as long as the companies can ensure their projects don't harm the environments above and below the water. Any action that expedites or waives licensing requirements gets these projects online faster.

It should also be noted, however, that New York has thoroughly embraced renewable energy projects. States less hospitable to renewable energy, or even hostile to their integration, will slow progress, and with projects similar to RITE, may not get the state and local support we see today in New York.

Verdant Power is pursuing other projects, such as the Cornwall Ontario River Energy (CORE) project. Initial plans for this one are to conduct it as a two-phase project over four years with the ultimate goal of developing 15 MW of power at Cornwall, Ontario.

The company is also pursuing projects with a number of water agencies and authorities focused on harnessing the kinetic hydropower potential of constructed waterways. As well, Verdant is in the early stages of assessing resources in the United Kingdom, South America, China, and India.

At this point, however, some of the most interesting progress in marine energy is actually being made in Scotland.

### Profits in the Highlands

Back in 2003, in an effort to stimulate and accelerate the development of marine power devices, Highlands and Islands Enterprise (which is the government's economic development agency for northern Scotland and its adjoining islands) launched the European Marine Energy Centre in Orkney, a group of islands a few miles from the northeast tip of mainland Scotland. Because of its exposed North Sea location, Orkney has one of the highest wave energy potentials in Europe, if not the world.

This state-of-the-art research facility boasts four test berths (with individual armored cables connected to the onshore substation) with a combined output of 30 MW, or enough to power as many as 20,000 homes.[36]

The first wave-energy converter used here was the Pelamis P-750. In August 2004, the P-750 was installed and immediately completed its first week of energy generation into the UK grid.

Nine months later, Pelamis Wave Power (formerly Ocean Power Delivery, Ltd.), the developer of the wave-energy converter, announced it had signed an order with a Portuguese consortium, led by Enersis (NYSE:ENI), to build the initial phase of the world's first commercial wave farm. The project would have a combined rating of 2.25 MW, and was expected to meet the average electricity demand of more than 1,500 Portuguese households. Norsk Hydro (a company mentioned at the beginning of this chapter) was also a major backer of this project through its venture capital arm, Hydro Technology Ventures.

According to Antonio Sarmento, the director of the Wave Energy Center, Portugal could ultimately win a 10 percent share of the world technology and equipment market for this type of wave farm, estimated at about $385 billion.[37]

## A PERFECT EXAMPLE

The South Koreans jumped on the marine energy bandwagon in 2005. During that time, developers claimed that the Sihwa Tidal Power Plant was the largest tidal energy plant in the world, projecting to generate 260 MW from the constant flow of water in and out of a seaside bay. Consisting of 10 turbines with direct-driven generators, the $250 million project was designed to allow up to 60 billion tons of seawater to be circulated annually.

Following the Sihwa announcement, equipment contracts were quickly awarded. For example, VA Tech Hydro, an international supplier of equipment and services for hydropower plants, received a $94 million order from Daewoo Engineering and Construction for the engineering and delivery of the electromechanical components for the Sihwa Plant.

(VA Tech Hydro was acquired by Austrian behemoth Andritz AG in June 2006. Andritz trades under the symbol ANDR on the Vienna Stock Exchange.)

As we see more and more tidal and wave energy plants move on to construction phases, the number of contracts for equipment such as turbines and generators will increase dramatically, providing investors with more opportunities within this sector.

As stated earlier, this is a very young industry. Over the next few years, we're going to see a lot of testing and a lot of regulatory hurdles. The few companies that are operating in this sector right now have a long uphill battle in front of them. But so did solar up until the late 1990s, and so did wind, and so did biofuels. And look how well these sectors have performed over the past few years.

If you're patient, and can stomach some risk, the marine energy sector could pay off quite well. But you really have to stay on top of it by constantly monitoring regulations, following technological advances closely, and just keeping track of every move the industry and supporting industries make along the way.

# CHAPTER

6

# WHAT'S THAT SMELL?

Its origins may not exude the sweetest smell, but biogas, which is the product of anaerobic digestion (decomposition without oxygen) of organic matter, such as sewage, animal waste, and municipal solid waste, serves as another energy source that can help offset the use of nonrenewable resources.[1] For the purposes of this chapter, however, we will focus on only two of the largest sources of biogas that are actively being used right now for power generation:

1. Landfill gas (LFG)

2. Agriculture/livestock manure

## LANDFILL GAS: WASTE OR WATTS?

Before we discuss how to make money by investing in biogas, we should quickly address the argument that using landfill gas for energy cannot be considered "green" for two reasons. First, it is suggested that if an energy source emits dioxin (LFG combustion can produce small quantities of dioxins), it's not really green. While we agree with this statement, it could be equally argued that it's still better than coal, and therefore should not be disregarded when discussing alternative forms of power generation.

The second reason is that LFG uses excessive amounts of waste that could otherwise be composted, or never generated to begin with. Certainly producing less waste would be the best bet, environmentally speaking. But as much as we advocate minimizing waste, it would be senseless for green investors to disregard the use of LFG for energy. Whether we like it or not, as a society, we waste a lot. And as our numbers grow, so will the amount of trash we produce. That's not to say that we should discourage the minimization of our waste streams. In fact, it should be encouraged through consumer education and more sustainable business practices. But in the meantime, we must be realistic. And that is why we see no problem investing in this sector.

Municipal solid waste found in landfills produces a number of gaseous products. In these oxygen-lacking environments anaerobic bacteria thrive, resulting in the decomposition of organic materials, and more importantly, the production of carbon dioxide and methane. The methane, which is a principal component of natural gas, and can migrate out of landfills because it is lighter than air and not very soluble in water, can be captured by LFG energy facilities, and burned to produce energy.[2]

For years, LFG was extracted from landfills and then directed to a central point where it was burned, or "flared," simply as a safety measure. (Landfills with over 2.5 million metric tons of waste in place are required by federal law to collect and either flare or utilize their gas.)[3] Basically, it was free energy being wasted nearly 24 hours a day, seven days a week.

Today, however, there are more than 1,200 landfills across the globe that extract LFG and use it to generate electricity, process it into alternative fuels, or send it into the gas pipeline network.[4] In 2005 alone, there were roughly 400 operational projects in the United States delivering 9 billion kilowatt hours of electricity—enough to power more than 725,000 homes, and heat close to 1.2 million homes.[5] Two years later, there were 427 operational projects in the United States delivering 1,275 megawatts, plus 550 candidate landfills identified by the EPA. These could deliver an additional 1,320 megawatts.[6] Combined, these projects amount to 2,595 megawatts, or enough to power more than 2.3 million homes.[7] To put that in perspective, based on the 2006 U.S. Census, which estimated housing units data, this is enough juice to power every housing unit in the states of Wyoming, Vermont, South Dakota, North Dakota, Montana, Delaware, and the District of Columbia, combined.[8] That's not bad for something that for years was just flared and wasted— especially when you consider the economics of using LFG.

In 2007, the UN's Economic and Social Commission for Asia and the Pacific (ESCAP) reported on the economic benefits of LFG. What they found validated what so many *LFG-to-energy* (LFGTE) advocates had been preaching for years. According to ESCAP's report, using LFG creates jobs associated with the design, construction, and operation of energy recovery systems for engineers, construction firms, equipment vendors, and utilities. As well, a significant portion of the cost is spent locally for drilling, piping, construction, and operational personnel, thereby assisting communities with increased employment and local sales. The report goes on to state that businesses using LFG (which is a local energy resource) as a replacement for more expensive fossil fuels realize additional cost savings. In addition, electric utilities that participate in LFGTE projects are able to broaden their resource base, as well as enhance customer relations.[9]

End-users can also realize significant operational cost savings when using LFG. For example, NASA's Goddard Space Flight Center is using LFG to fuel its boilers, expecting to save taxpayers around $3.5 million in fuel costs. Lucent Technologies estimates it will save $100,000 per year on fuel bills by using LFG for the company's boiler system at its Columbus facility, and General Motors is now using LFG at three of its assembly plants. At its truck assembly plant in Fort Wayne, Indiana, GM has estimated that using LFG will save the company as much as $500,000 a year.[10] Even biofuel producer Abengoa Bioenergy has used LFG to reduce its use of natural gas. That has provided the company with an estimated cost savings of $1.4 million per year.[11]

There are also economic benefits related to emission offsets. The Chicago Climate Exchange issues Carbon Financial Instrument (CFI) contracts on the basis of all methane collected and destroyed net of $CO_2$ released upon combustion. This is done at a rate of 18.25 metric tons of $CO_2$ for each ton of methane combustion. This is often referred to as *$CO_2$ equivalent* (CO2E). At anywhere between $1 and $5 per metric ton of CO2E, it wouldn't take long for an LFG project using a typical 1-, 5-, or 10-million-metric-ton landfill to generate a nice chunk of additional revenue. Incidentally, on a global scale, landfills account for over 223 million metric tons of CO2E.[12]

### But Is It Good for the Environment?

Of course, the environmental benefits of generating energy from LFG can't be ignored, either. This is especially true because methane, about 50 percent of LFG, is 23 times as potent as $CO_2$, and has more than doubled its atmospheric concentrations over the last two centuries. The EPA has stated that this is largely due to human-related activities. Today, China, India, the United States, Brazil, Russia, Mexico, Ukraine, and Australia are estimated to be responsible for about half of all global methane emissions stemming from agriculture, coal mines, landfills, and natural gas and oil systems.[13] The source of this methane varies depending on its country of origin. For example, in China, it is primarily from coal, and in Russia, it is primarily from natural gas.

Here in the United States, landfills are the largest source of methane emissions.[14] In fact, about 25 percent of human-related methane emissions in the United States are from municipal solid-waste landfills.[15] But it's now estimated that an LFG project can capture between 60 and 90 percent of the methane from a landfill (depending on the system), and then convert it to water or less potent $CO_2$ when it's burned to produce electricity.[16]

## AGRICULTURE/LIVESTOCK MANURE: FROM COW CHIPS TO GREEN CHIPS

Beyond landfills, we can also trace another 8 percent of U.S. methane emissions to livestock waste.[17] (The UN has actually stated that livestock are responsible for 18% of global greenhouse gas emissions.) Although this resource is not as large as landfill gas, it is a source that continues to grow at a rapid pace due to the fact that humans are consuming more meat and dairy products every year. In fact, from 1999/2001 to 2050, global milk output is set to increase from 580 to 1,043 million tons, and global meat production is set to more than double in the same time.[18] So unless the world's population converts its diet to one consisting of only fruits, grains, and vegetables, the international community should expect to see a significant increase in cows and cow manure. This forecast does not take into account poultry, pigs, and sheep, where production is also expected to increase significantly. So as we continue to witness these production increases, we also witness serious environmental impacts, especially when it comes to greenhouse gases. However, this also ushers in additional opportunities for those operating in the biogas sector.

The EPA has noted that anaerobic digesters (systems that break down biodegradable material in the absence of oxygen) can help reduce greenhouse gases produced by "factory farms," from which the world gets 74 percent of its poultry products, 50 percent of its pork, and 43 percent of its beef. Moreover, about 7,000 of those factory farms (or *concentrated animal feedlot operations* [CAFO], for those who are afraid to call out these farms for what they really are) operating in the United States could use anaerobic digestion cost-effectively and could reduce greenhouse gas emissions by an estimated 1.3 million metric tons.[19]

## A SIDE NOTE

Factory farming is probably one of the biggest contributors to global environmental destruction and resource depletion. While it isn't our intention to preach, the negative environmental, social, and economic issues associated with factory farming are proving to stimulate the demand for organic and local agriculture. This reinforces our bullish position on more sustainable agricultural practices. While we certainly are not advocating irresponsible factory farming, we will monitor the biogas sector as it relates to the reduction of greenhouse gas emissions, as well as the production of energy from livestock waste.

## INVESTING IN BIOGAS

As with most of the newer alternative power generation opportunities in the world, it's often the behemoth corporations that take the early lead. And this industry is no exception. In fact, one of the most successful publicly traded companies operating in this sector right now is General Electric (NYSE:GE). Utilizing its Jenbacher engine (an engine that combines high output density with low exhaust emissions and low cost construction), GE generates 11.1 million MWh of power per year from biogas.[20] From landfill gas alone, more than 1,100 Jenbacher engines generate enough power for 667,500 American homes, 2 million EU homes, or 4.4 million Chinese homes in one year.[21] And Waste Management, Inc. (NYSE:WMI), North America's leader in waste management services, is also bullish on LFG. This should not come as a surprise, considering the company maintains 283 active landfills. As of the writing of this book, Waste Management currently supplies enough LFG to generate more than 250 megawatts, or enough to power roughly 225,000 homes.[22] In 2007, the company announced that it could spend as much as $400 million over the next five years to develop 60 new LFG projects in the United States and Canada. Considering the EPA's Landfill Methane Outreach Program expects about 25 new landfill gas projects to come online every year, Waste Management's goal of 60 new projects is quite impressive. Once completed, those 60 projects are expected to create about 230 megawatts.[23]

## Diamonds in the Dung

While there's no denying that those are some pretty impressive numbers, let's face it: GE and Waste Management, Inc. aren't really the most direct ways to play this sector. There are, however, a few other options that are worth keeping an eye on, such as Environmental Power Corporation (NASDAQ:EPG). This is a company whose principal operating subsidiary, Microgy, develops biogas facilities that can produce renewable gas from agriculture and food industry wastes.

Microgy uses an anaerobic digester where, in a digestion tank, waste decomposes over time into a variety of products, including biogas rich in methane. This gas can then be used for a number of applications, including the direct sale of biogas or pipeline-grade methane either for thermal energy or for the generation of electricity.[24]

Currently the company has eight projects it is using as case studies:[25]

- Five Star Dairy in Elk Mound, Wisconsin, which generates 750 kilowatts per hour, powering 600 local homes.

- Four California locations, which, combined, can produce enough gas to power 50,000 homes. (These are currently under development.)

- Huckabay Ridge near Stephenville, Texas, which is expected to produce 635,000 MMbtu/year at full capacity.

- Norswiss Dairy in Stanfold Township, Wisconsin, which can generate 850 kilowatts per hour, powering 700 local homes.

- Wild Rose Dairy in Webster Township, Wisconsin, which can generate 750 kilowatts per hour, powering 600 local homes.

With a small company like Environmental Power Corporation, it doesn't take much in the way of positive news to push the stock up. In fact, back in October 2006, the company announced that it had formed a strategic alliance with Cargill to identify opportunities for farmers to turn their waste products into bio-based energy and carbon offset credits. The two would share in the resulting revenue streams.

Before this announcement was made, the stock was trading around $5.00 a share. Less than three months after the announcement, the stock hit a high of $8.85 a share, as shown in Figure 6.1. That's a 77 percent gain in less than three months.

There are now two facilities that Cargill and Environmental Power Corporation expect to have operational by 2009. These are expected to produce over 800,000 MMBtu/year of renewable natural gas.

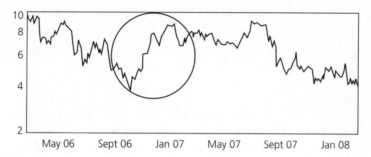

**FIGURE 6.1** *Chart of EPC*

Some of the most impressive technology in this sector is coming from private companies. Investors in biogas need to monitor these closely, because these private firms have the ability to offer up the kind of disruptive technology that could completely transform the marketplace. It doesn't take much more than a quick acquisition to put another publicly traded biogas firm at the head of the pack.

One type of potentially disruptive technology we're watching now is dry fermentation. One company that has already developed and is using this technology is Bekon Energy Technologies. Simply put, Bekon can take biowaste from the farming industry and turn it into biogas. But unlike traditional biogas plants that use liquid fermentation and require access to cheap water resources, Bekon's process requires limited water consumption, thereby translating into significant water cost advantages, particularly in locations where water shortages already exist.

Back in 2006, the Dubai investment company Tejoori Limited (which trades on the Alternative Investment Market [AIM] of the London Stock Exchange) recognized that Bekon's proprietary processes put its technology at the forefront of the industry. In an effort to capitalize on this sector, Tejoori agreed to invest 6 million euros to acquire a 16.7 percent interest in Bekon, thus giving it access to Bekon's "Circle-Fermentation," which focuses on agricultural waste and products to create biogas, as well as its "In-Box Fermentation," which derives biogas from organic material from municipal collection systems.

Just as there's opportunity in agricultural waste, there's even more opportunity in municipal waste and landfill gas.

## A LUCRATIVE INVESTMENT

"Biogas is one of the most efficient sources of renewable energy and Bekon has developed proprietary processes that put its technology at the forefront of this vital industry. With predictions from the German Biogas Association that global sales of biogas facilities will be between EUR 7.5 and 10 billion by 2010, our investment in Bekon is both relevant and timely."[26]

*Source:* Steffen Schubert, Managing Director of Tejoori.

Look at DTE Energy (NYSE:DTE), for instance. This company is one of the biggest players in landfill gas recovery. Through its DTE Biomass Energy Division, DTE has recovered more than 120 billion cubic feet of landfill gas to date. The company's Michigan facility alone recovers more than 4.3 million cubic feet of gas per day. Here, two solar gas turbines operate 24 hours a day to use the landfill gas and generate electricity for sale to Detroit Edison customers. This 6.6 MW facility produces enough electricity to continuously power more than 5,000 homes.[27]

### The Micro Angle

Another way to play this sector is through the companies that manufacture the actual equipment used to generate power. The most common include internal combustion engines and gas turbines, though organic Rankine cycle engines, Stirling external combustion engines, and microturbines are now starting to gain entrance into the sector. We're quite bullish on microturbines, as these can provide more economically viable solutions for smaller landfills. After all, more than half of the nation's operating LFG projects are small landfills.[28]

One company that's really taken the lead in microturbines is Capstone Turbine (NASDAQ:CPST). Capstone has developed a microturbine that burns waste gases to create renewable power and heat. The company has hundreds of biogas-fueled microturbines in operation all over the world. We mention Capstone specifically because their technology is much higher in efficiency and reliability compared to conventional technologies. It also boasts much lower emissions.[29] Such a technological advantage is what we'll be looking at in the years to come as we hone in on the equipment manufacturers that'll take the lead in turning biogas into real power.

While neither DTE nor Capstone are straight landfill gas plays, the fact is, there really are no pure-plays in this sector. This can be frustrating for some investors, but it allows us the opportunity to monitor private companies for new signs of acquisitions or IPOs.

For instance, take FirmGreen Energy. FirmGreen is not a publicly traded company, but it does represent a new trend in landfill gas conversion that we're now seeing as a potential opportunity for investors in the very near future.

To put it simply, a lot of companies that convert landfill gas focus primarily on providing power to the utilities. But the fact is, landfill gas really has the ability to extend far beyond just juicing up the grid. FirmGreen, for example, can process landfill gas into renewable fuels, methanol, and hydrogen.

In fact, one of the company's standard landfill gas plants can produce enough clean-burning alternative fuels to power more than 18,000 cars per year. And the annual environmental benefit to the community is equivalent to:

- Removing emissions equivalent to 22,900 vehicles

- Planting 32,615 acres of forest

- Preventing the use of 277,600 barrels of oil

- Displacing the use of 13 million gallons of gasoline[30]

## At the Cusp of Change

As energy prices continue to increase, the demand for biogas conversion will only continue to grow. Whether it's from landfills in the Northeast or dairy farms in the Midwest, the potential to convert massive amounts of biogas to useable energy is very real. Granted, the opportunities for investors right now are few and far between. But there was a time when there weren't a whole lot of solar stocks to choose from, either. Today, that's simply not the case. But those who followed the market back in the late eighties and early nineties were first to the party when solar began its ascent, right before the turn of the century.

Being among those at the cusp of change is what always separates the winners from the trend-chasers.

# CHAPTER

7

# THE EFFICIENCY ADVANTAGE

In the previous chapters, we have discussed a number of different renewable power generation technologies that will increasingly be used in an effort to get us off fossil fuels. Though one of the simplest and most cost-effective solutions in the short term is one that doesn't involve new power generation at all, but rather using the energy we generate now, more efficiently. So instead of increasing generation, we're talking about decreasing consumption.

Amory Lovins coined the term "negawatts" in 1989 to describe the concept of energy you *don't* have to generate. An accomplished author and Chief Scientist at the Rocky Mountain Institute, Lovins is perhaps one of the most influential voices when it comes to conservation and efficiency. Over the past few years, the emergence of the energy crisis has sparked renewed interest in negawatts among the world's most forward-thinking investors.

## NEGA-*WHAT?*

Negawatts not only can help to reduce greenhouse gas emissions (as well as other pollutants, such as mercury, sulfur dioxide, and nitrogen oxide), but also can increase energy supplies quickly and cost-effectively.

For example, a Natural Resources Defense Council (NRDC) report in 2007 concluded that if utility companies in Texas invested $11 billion in energy savings and incentives for consumers and businesses before investing in new power plants, the Lone Star State would yield close to $50 billion in savings and other economic benefits over a 15-year time span. As well, through enhanced energy-efficiency efforts, the state could prevent 52 million metric tons of $CO_2$ annually by 2021. That's roughly the total emissions from 10 million cars.[1]

California has adopted the most aggressive energy-conservation and -efficiency policies in the United States. Combined with robust investment, California saves enough electricity every year to avoid building 24 large power plants (i.e., 500 MW or more). In fact, according to a report issued by the California Public Utilities Commission, the average cost of energy-efficiency programs is roughly half the cost of baseload power generation. With these programs, the state has contributed to a 17 percent decrease in $CO_2$ emissions from the electricity sector.[2]

California also instituted Governor Arnold Schwarzenegger's Green Building Initiative in 2004, which mandates a 20 percent reduction in electricity consumption in state buildings by 2015. It is here, in buildings, where we'll see energy conservation and efficiency measures really take hold. As of October 2007, California had increased its number of buildings pursuing LEED certification from 9 in 2004 to 209.[3] California also maintains the nation's first statewide green building code.

## WHAT IS LEED CERTIFICATION?

LEED (Leadership in Energy and Environmental Design) certification is a building sustainability standard that is designed and maintained by the U.S. Green Building Council (USGBC). It is a voluntary system used to pinpoint the exact degree of sustainability of new construction and renovations. In other words, to be considered a "green building," the project must be approved by an agent of the USGBC's LEED certification program.

LEED certifications come in four degrees: Certified, Silver, Gold, or Platinum. Each rating is based on points awarded in a variety of categories that include:

- Sustainable Sites
- Water Efficiency
- Energy and Atmosphere
- Materials and Resources
- Indoor Environmental Quality
- Innovation in Design

The more sustainable and efficient a building is in each category, the more points it is awarded. There are more points available for energy and atmosphere than for anything else, so energy efficiency is important to obtaining a high certification.

Even without LEED certification, integrating energy efficiency and conservation into any building adds value and significant operational cost savings. Indeed, that's what will enable the continued momentum behind energy efficiency in today's and tomorrow's buildings.

## Build It Green

Commercial and residential buildings in the United States used 40 quadrillion Btus (quads) of energy in 2005, at a cost of $300 billion. That number is projected to increase to 50 quads at a cost of $430 billion by 2025.[4] That's more than 10 percent of total world energy consumption. Buildings are also responsible for 38 percent of the nation's $CO_2$ emissions—more than the industrial or transportation sectors.[5] But a burgeoning green building movement is looking to change all this.

Green building (or high-performance building), is about designing, building, renovating, or operating a building in an ecological and resource-efficient manner.[6] For our purposes here, we will focus primarily on the energy savings, which, compared to conventional buildings, amount to an average of 33 percent.

## Show Me the Green

Despite the numerous environmental benefits of green building, it is primarily the proven economic benefits that have started to move it from a niche market to the new status quo of building construction. Take, for instance, green schools.

The average school's energy costs run about $1.15 per square foot per year. That's $138,000 per year for an average 120,000 sq. ft. school. Whereas a green school of that size, with a 33 percent energy savings, will have energy costs of just $0.77/sq. ft. or $92,400. That's a savings of $45,600 annually, or nearly a million dollars over a 20-year life span.[7]

The green California EPA Headquarters Building in Sacramento is another great example. With systems calibration, monitoring, and maintenance for energy performance, the building delivers annual savings of nearly $200,000. After-hours heating and lighting controls as well as the building's exterior lighting systems add another $110,000 of yearly savings. Just these few efficiency upgrades resulted in a savings of more than a quarter of a million dollars per year for that building. And those don't even include the annual savings from grounds management, water-efficient landscaping, elimination of garbage can liners, collection of recyclables, occupant recycling, reduced landfill disposal costs, and entryway cleaning to prevent particle and dirt buildup. Overall, $500,000 was invested in efficiency upgrades, operations, and employee practices, which generated a total of $610,000 in annual savings. That initial investment was recovered in less than a year. And using an 8 percent capitalization rate, the annual cost savings increased the asset value by close to $12 million.[8]

Of course, there is still the issue of green buildings carrying a heftier price tag. After all, it is often expected that one will pay more up front to achieve significant cost savings down the road. And certainly this can be the case with green buildings.

In 2003, California's Sustainable Building Task Force reported on the costs associated with its green buildings. That report found the cost premium averaged less than 1 percent for basic LEED certification, 2.1 percent for Silver certification, 1.8 percent for Gold, and 6.5 percent for Platinum.[9]

But in 2007, consulting service Davis Langdon released a report that questioned the cost of incorporating sustainable design features into various building projects. It built on a previous report, "Costing Green: A Comprehensive Cost Database and Budget Methodology," which was published in 2004. Davis Langdon found that there was no significant difference in average costs for green buildings as compared to nongreen buildings.

It should be noted that while average construction costs rose between 25 percent and 30 percent from 2004 to 2007, the green building industry still had a large number of projects achieve their LEED certifications within budget.[10] Cost, of course, depends on a number of factors that include building type, climate, site conditions, location, level of sustainable design (advanced features can add significant costs), and so on.[11] Generally, though, energy savings produced through sustainable design and energy efficiency and conservation applications are significant, long term, and add to the overall value of the building. And the most basic kinds of energy efficiency and conservation can be incorporated into most buildings at little or no additional cost.

## INVESTING IN ENERGY CONSERVATION AND EFFICIENCY

At *Green Chip Stocks*, we see three ways to play the efficiency and conservation angle, all of which can be found in industries that manufacture products incorporated into the construction, operation, or maintenance of buildings—whether LEED certified or not.

## *Light It Up*

At a cost of more than $50 billion a year, 18 percent of the total energy use in the United States comes from lighting.[12] However, with the integration of new technologies, as well as basic education, this cost can be drastically reduced. Take, for instance, compact fluorescent lamps (CFLs). CFLs can use as little as 75 percent of the energy consumed by standard incandescent light bulbs, and last up to 10 times longer. If every home in the United States replaced just one incandescent light bulb with a CFL, the savings would add up to more than $600 million in annual energy costs.[13]

But the country will soon be doing much more than just replacing one bulb in every home. The Energy Independence and Security Act of 2007 calls for the phasing out of incandescent bulbs beginning in 2012. By 2014, for the most part, you'll be able to purchase only the compact fluorescent variety. The new standards will ultimately improve lighting efficiency by 70 percent by 2020, or the equivalent of closing 24 coal-fired power plants.[14]

Of course, playing the CFL angle is nearly impossible if you're looking for a pure play. There is TCP, Inc., the world's largest manufacturer of energy-saving light bulbs, which makes about 70 percent of the CFLs on the market.[15] But it's not a publicly traded company. Then there are companies like Siemens and GE—which again, are not pure plays. Fortunately, the CFL angle isn't the only efficient-lighting angle to play.

One area that really started to gain serious attention around 2006 and 2007 was that of light-emitting diodes (LEDs). LEDs can be 90 percent more efficient than incandescent bulbs.[16] So LED technology is quickly becoming the lighting of choice for industrial lighting consumers across the globe. LEDs boast:

- *Long life:* Some LEDs are projected to produce a long service life of about 100,000 hours, making them ideal for hard-to-reach fixtures, like exit sign lighting and pathway lighting.

- *No UV emissions:* LEDs produce no UV radiation and little heat, making them ideal for illuminating objects that are sensitive to UV light.

- *Durability:* LEDs are extremely rugged, as they feature no filament that can be damaged due to shock and vibrations.

- *Small size/design flexibility:* A single LED is quite small and produces little light overall, so LEDs are often combined in a number of different shapes to produce the desired output for various design and economic goals.

Today, LEDs are found in everything from architectural and vehicle lighting to remote controls, backlighting for LCD televisions, computers, and traffic lights. For example, a red traffic light that contains 196 LEDs draws only 10 W, compared to the 150 W that an incandescent light draws. Consequently, most new traffic lights today use LED lamps, and older traffic signals are being retro-fitted with LEDs.

Some LEDs are even solar-powered. One publicly traded company called Carmanah Technologies (TSX:CMH) specializes in solar-powered LEDs. The company manufactures solar-powered traffic signals, as well as solar-powered:

- Marine lights for the U.S. Coast Guard, the U.S. Navy, and the Canadian Navy.

- Railway and industrial lights for the Georgia Department of Transport, Wharf Rat Dock Systems, and Norfolk Southern Railway.

- Aviation lights (airfield lighting) for some of the largest airports in the world, as well as for all branches of the U.S. military.

LEDs can be found almost everywhere today. In green buildings, LEDs are regularly used for track lighting and motion-detection lights. Though cost can still be an issue, LEDs will continue to gain momentum in the coming years. In fact, the LED lighting market is expected to reach $1 billion in 2011, the largest application being for architectural lighting.[17]

Improvements in *high-brightness* LEDs (HB LEDs) are providing impressive growth predictions in the integrated circuit (IC) market, too. This is being driven by signs, displays, automotive applications, and general illumination. The total market for HB LED driver ICs is expected to come in at just under $2 billion in 2011. In 2005, the market was worth about $205 million.[18]

One company that got an early jump on LEDs is Cree, Inc. (NASDAQ: CREE). Cree manufactures blue and green LED chips, lighting LEDs, and LEDs for backlighting. Cree's most recent claim to fame came in September 2007, when company officials announced that they had achieved R&D results of 129 lumens per watt for a cool-white LED and 99 lumens per watt for a warm-white LED. These are the best results reported for any packaged, high-power LED.[19] The company has also demonstrated a light output of more than 1,000 lumens. This is the equivalent output level of a standard household light bulb. Granted, this may not sound like the most exciting stuff, but the reality is that Cree's aggressive R&D has made it one of the most technologically favorable LED companies out there. And the market has rewarded investors who banked on this one when the LED industry started heating up in early 2007.

As you can see in Figure 7.1, the stock soared from a low of $15.27 in January to as high as $34.87 in September 2007.

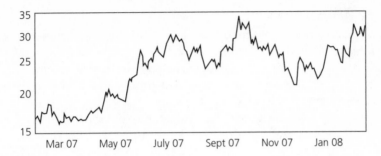

**FIGURE 7.1**  *Cree Research, Inc.*

But while Cree's technological prowess has made it a leader, it is also technological innovation that will provide competition for lighting in the green building space. This is why we're definitely looking to the future with *organic light-emitting diodes* (OLEDs). OLED manufacturing requires fewer chemicals and less waste than conventional LEDs. They are also flexible, as they can be produced in bendable layered sheets. This technology is excellent for monitor displays, but could also, one day, be used on entire walls—efficiently and cost-effectively generating light.

Green chip investors are also looking at fiber-optic lighting. This is not necessarily a new, groundbreaking technology that just came on the scene, but because fiber-optic lighting systems can significantly reduce energy consumption, they're quickly finding a home in green buildings.

Energy Focus, Inc. (NASDAQ:EFOI) is one company that grabbed a lot of investor attention in 2007 with its *efficient fiber optics* (EFO)—a technology that delivers light comparable to conventional lamps at a significant reduction in energy consumption. We're talking about a savings of as much as 80 percent over halogen and other incandescent lighting systems.

The company also manufactures a lighting system that illuminates frozen and refrigerated products in those freezer and refrigerator cases you see at the supermarket and convenience stores. Called EFO ICE, these systems save an average of $100 per door annually, simply by reducing electrical consumption for refrigeration and lighting, as well as simplifying maintenance. Typical LEDs and fluorescent lamps add heat to a case, thereby increasing the compressor load. But EFO ICE lights products without adding any heat to the case. Applying the benefits of optical fiber, EFO ICE removes all of the heat before routing the light into the case. One EFO ICE lamp replaces three to five fluorescent lamps, and contains no glass, thereby eliminating the possibility of shattering a lamp inside the case.

## Motor Management

Another major drain on electricity supplies can be found in motors operating in buildings. There are an estimated one billion motors in operation in the United States, which consume more than half of the country's electricity, with 20 percent of motor energy being consumed primarily from space conditioning and ventilation in the commercial sector.[20]

However, between new, more efficient technologies and a few design alterations, electricity consumption from motors can be drastically reduced. Take pumps, for instance, which make up the majority of motors. A low-friction redesign of a conventional industrial pumping loop can save 92 percent of its pumping power, simply by using fat, short straight pipes instead of long, skinny crooked pipes.[21]

Of course, integrating simple redesigns, like the one just mentioned, with more efficient motors could deliver the most bang for the operational buck. AC induction motors and other kinds of electric motors drive nearly all the motorized operations in industry. From hydraulic pumps to air-conditioning units, if it's operating in a commercial building, industrial complex, or warehouse, it's most likely an electric motor.[22] And with the bottom line at stake, it's no surprise that we're now starting to see sound motor management take center stage in energy efficiency. With case study after case study demonstrating how companies have reduced costs, improved productivity, and reduced downtime, it's clear that technologically inferior and inefficient motors are going the way of the typewriter. Just take a look at what some of the early adopters have already done:

- Eastman Kodak retrofitted about 600 motors with premium-efficiency models, saving the company $664,000 annually, reducing energy consumption by nearly 6 million kWh and realizing a payback of 2.3 years.[23]

- Woodgrain Millwork installed an efficient motor that will save 20,700 kWh per year, and deliver a $6,000 cost savings over the life of just that one motor.[24]

- Weyerhaeuser Engineering has saved an estimated $2.5 million in energy costs by using a motor management system that established consistent specifications for purchasing and repairing motors, focusing on maximum productivity and energy efficiency.[25]

AC motors are still available in various efficiency ranges, though it's the high-efficiency and premium-efficiency ones that are most common. Premium-efficiency motors provide the best energy savings, but do cost between 10 and

20 percent more than standard-efficiency models. However, under normal operations, a premium-efficiency model will typically pay for its premium price within one to two years, just from reduced energy bills.[26]

Most of the publicly traded companies manufacturing these premium-efficiency motors are member companies of the National Electrical Manufacturers Association's NEMA Premium® Energy Efficiency Motors Program. This program was designed to help consumers find and purchase motor systems that reduce electric consumption and costs. They estimate that the program could save 5,800 gigawatts; this is the equivalent of displacing 80 million metric tons of $CO_2$, or keeping 16 million cars off the road.

Some of the more common names in motors include GE, Siemens, and Toshiba. Again, as we've seen in other sectors, these are not necessarily the pure plays green chip investors are looking for. However, there are still a few smaller companies out there working on advanced technologies. They may not be able to compete with the likes of GE or Siemens right now, but they are definitely vying for a piece of the action.

Take Raser Technologies (NYSE:RZ), for instance. The company is in the process of applying a new technology to industrial motors. It's called the Symetron™, and the company hopes to prove that by using the Symetron, building operators will be able to realize significant cost savings. Early calculations indicate that large industrial operations could save as much as $20,000 a month in energy costs—with just a 1 to 2 percent gain in efficiency.

### Energy Intelligence

According to the North American Electric Reliability Corporation, electricity demand is projected to grow 19 percent nationwide over the next decade, but transmission capacity is expected to grow by only 6 percent.[27] And while increasing transmission is certainly one way to reduce strain on overworked grids, improving overall efficiency is proving to be an even more attractive solution for the short term.

It's not surprising, then, that investment in this category grew from $192 million in 2004 to $476 million in 2006.[28] According to Clean Edge, one of the top research and publishing firms in the clean energy sector, energy intelligence was the second most heavily venture-invested sustainable industry in 2006. Clean Edge also noted that "with energy efficiency and demand response high on the list of many utilities as a 'new' source of power, energy-intelligence companies may be the new darlings of energy tech."[29] We couldn't agree more. In fact, we suspect that demand management will be one of the hottest investment opportunities over the next couple of years.

Demand management is really about utilizing strategies that enable the maximization of efficiency and the reduction of loads to avoid or postpone the construction of new power plants.[30] And in 2007, we saw this sector pick up a lot of investor attention after two companies, Comverge, Inc. (NASDAQ: COMV) and EnerNoc, Inc. (NASDAQ:ENOC), went public.

Comverge and EnerNoc provide demand-response and energy-management systems. When they went public, alternative-energy investors jumped all over them. Of course, as the following list shows, it didn't hurt that both were landing deal after deal following their IPOs:

- May 3, 2007—Comverge announced 126 Megawatt Clean Energy Program with Nevada Power.

- May 9, 2007—Comverge announced that the California Public Utilities Commission approved its Demand Response Purchase Agreement with Pacific Gas & Electric Company.

- May 24, 2007—EnerNoc announced that it had expanded its Clean Gen demand-reduction program with San Diego Gas & Electric from 25 MW to 50 MW.

- June 7, 2007—Comverge announced that the California Public Utilities Commission had approved the expansion of its Demand Response Capacity Delivery Agreement for an additional 30 megawatts with San Diego Gas & Electric.

- July 23, 2007—Comverge announced that it successfully completed its acquisition of Enerwise Global Technologies, thereby making it the largest demand-response company.

- September 6, 2007—EnerNoc announced that it entered into an agreement with Tampa Electric Company to deliver 25 MW of demand-response capacity.

- October 1, 2007—Comverge announced that it acquired Public Energy Solutions.

- October 2, 2007—EnerNoc announced that it signed a new demand-response capacity agreement with Southern California Edison.

- October 8, 2007—Comverge announced that it had executed a 10-year Virtual Peaking Capacity contract with the Connecticut Light & Power Company.

- October 18, 2007—Comverge announced that it entered into an agreement with Southern California Edison to implement a Virtual Peaking Capacity program of up to 50 megawatts.

■ November 2, 2007—Comverge announced that it entered into a multiyear agreement with Tampa Electric Company for the company's two-way communication technology for demand-response and automated meter-reading capabilities.

Some investors also found themselves lured to this sector after an auto-mation systems company called Echelon (NASDAQ:ELON) announced on July 10, 2007 that McDonald's Corporation had chosen its technology to net-work its restaurant kitchen equipment, in order to lower energy consumption and increase operational efficiency. Figure 7.2 shows what happened to the stock following this announcement.

Investors who knew these kinds of systems would soon be integrated on a major commercial scale had waited for such an announcement. Their forward thinking, coupled with a little patience, certainly paid off. And that's how we're looking at the future of the energy-conservation and -efficiency market now.

Certainly companies like Comverge, EnerNoc, and Echelon will continue to attract energy investors as world energy supplies continue to fall short of demand. But there will also be another round of conservation and efficiency companies coming in 2009 and 2010, and these will be much more segmented and niche oriented. In other words, we'll soon see a number of companies concentrating on specific consumer and industrial needs.

For example, we're now starting to see a number of companies popping up that audit energy consumption for industrial facilities and offer engineering, equipment, and design solutions that enable customers to reduce their energy consumption, and ultimately save money. There are also companies that develop and market energy-saving technologies for electric motors found in escalators, elevators, and industrial grinders. We're even seeing companies developing sys-tems for consumers that eliminate "phantom loads"—electricity consumed by a device when it's turned off but still plugged in.[31]

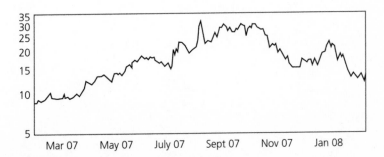

**FIGURE 7.2**  *Echelon Corporation*

Now, on an individual level, this may sound a bit far-fetched. But according to the DoE, in the average home, *75 percent of the electricity used to power home electronics is consumed while the products are turned off.*[32]

We're also starting to see some changes in our electricity infrastructure that enable more efficient transmission. One company, Composite Technology Corporation (OTCBB:CPTC), has developed a power transmission and distribution cable that boasts a higher operating efficiency and which can help decrease power-generation costs.

## A One–Two Punch

Overall, investors looking for the shortest route to gains in energy may find them in this sector. But it is the combination of energy efficiency and renewable energy integration that packs a one–two punch for the new-energy economy— and for those smart enough to ride this one for the long term. Staking your claim now and riding it over the next few years will bring the greatest rewards.

# PART

# THE END OF OIL

*"We are not good at recognizing distant threats even if their probability is 100%. Society ignoring [peak oil] is like the people of Pompeii ignoring the rumblings below Vesuvius."*

—JAMES SCHLESINGER, FORMER U.S. ENERGY SECRETARY

# CHAPTER

## 8

# FOREIGN OIL

## THE PATH TO SUICIDE

Of all forms of energy in use today, oil has the lion's share. It accounts for 40 percent of our overall energy consumption, and over 90 percent of the energy we use for transportation.

Essentially everything in our modern lives is made with some contribution from oil. For example, oil and gas are embedded into every aspect of making a common shirt: from the feedstock to making nylon or rayon, to running the looms, to transporting the shirt to a store, to the transportation used to take the shopper to and from the store.

Further, our whole civilization is heavily dependent on it—as George W. Bush has famously said, "America is addicted to oil." Liquid fuels made from petroleum are incredibly convenient, dense in energy, and easy and cheap to produce. And they are not easily replaced with something else.

But we are now facing a serious and imminent problem with oil production. As mentioned in Chapter 1, this problem is known as *peak oil*.

Peak oil presents us with an enormous challenge, because all economies depend on constant growth, which in turn depends on constantly increasing the rate of energy production. After we pass the peak rate of production, we have to live with less and less oil each year, rather than more and more.

This is a difficult realization, for we have generally managed to increase oil production continuously since the birth of the oil industry, long before any of us were born. The assumptions and theory upon which we have built our economies are about to be shaken to the core.

## WHAT IS PEAK OIL?

Peak oil is a theory that explains how, for a given oil-producing region, oil production tends to increase for some time, reach a peak right around the half-way point, and then taper off, in an irregular bell curve shape.

What the bell curve describes is the *rate of production*, not the volume of oil produced. This is an important concept because peak oil theory is often mischaracterized as a "running out of oil" problem, when it's really about the *flow rate* of the oil. As Dr. Jean-Marie Bourdaire, a sometime director of the International Energy Agency and the World Energy Council put it, "It's not the size of the tank which matters, but the size of the tap." If you had a bottomless well of oil, but you could have only as much of it as you could suck through a straw, then your use of it would be necessarily limited, forever.

The peak oil theory was originally proposed by a geologist and physicist named M. King Hubbert (1903–1989), who worked for Shell Oil and the U.S. Geological Survey (USGS), and who held professorial positions in geology at UC Berkeley and Stanford University. His bell curve model came to be known as "Hubbert's Peak."

Hubbert's insight was simple: The production curve of a given oil region is very similar to its discovery curve, just delayed some years later. (See Figure 8.1.) He used the model to correctly predict in 1956 that the United States would reach its oil production peak in 1970. His prediction was scoffed at by his peers, but it proved to be spot-on.

Contemporary geologists have applied Hubbert's model, with some modern refinements, to the global outlook for oil production. The results of these studies have been quite startling, as shown in Figure 8.2.

The world passed the peak of oil discovery between 1962 and 1964 (depending on whose numbers you use).[1] In recent years, we have been finding only one barrel of oil for every three we produce,[2] which is now approaching one out of four. And the fields we are discovering now are progressively smaller, in more remote and geographically challenging locations, often with hostile host governments.

That means that the production peak is somewhere dead ahead. The question is: When?

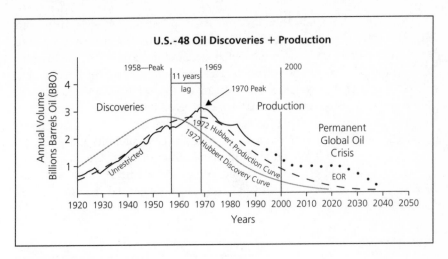

**FIGURE 8.1** *U.S.-48 Hubbert Curves*
*Source:* "Hubbert Center Newsletter # 97/1," http://www.hubbertpeak.com/hubbert/
centerNL971/mkh-new2.html.

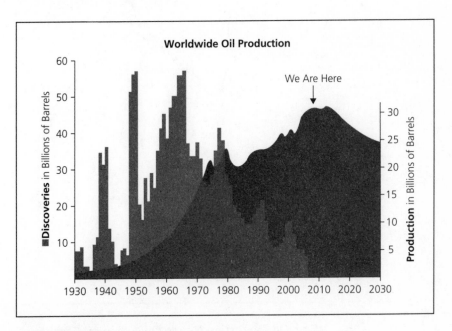

**FIGURE 8.2** *World Hubbert Curves*
*Source:* "The Oil Age Poster," http://www.oilposter.org as quoted in http://www
.aspo-global.org/newsletter/ASPOGlobal_Newsletter77.pdf.

Although the application of enhanced oil recovery techniques and advanced seismic modeling and drilling techniques have managed to squeeze a bit more oil from places previously considered uneconomical, the big picture in oil discovery and production is clear and remorseless: Seventy percent of our daily oil supply comes from oil fields that were discovered prior to 1970, and there is no turning back the clock on oil discovery.[3]

The past few years have seen an intensified interest in the peak oil problem, and many observers have done their own calculations on when the global peak of oil production will occur. Interestingly, the majority of informed, respected projections (aside from a few politically motivated outlier models) have a distinct locus of consensus right around 2011 to 2012, as depicted in Figure 8.3.

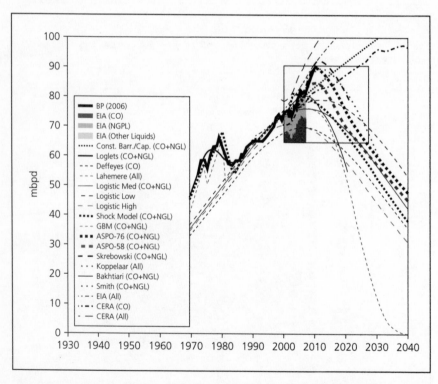

**FIGURE 8.3** *World Oil Production (Crude Oil + Natural Gas Liquids) and Various Forecasts, 1940–2050*

Source: Samuel Foucher, http://www.theoildrum.com/node/2620.

For our money, the most rigorous (and therefore likely to be accurate) model is that of the Association for the Study of Peak Oil and Gas (ASPO), headed by retired petroleum geologist Dr. Colin Campbell. As of September 2007, their model puts the global total of all oil that will ever be produced at around 1,900 billion barrels of regular conventional oil, where 1,001 billion barrels has already been produced and there are 899 billion barrels to go.

They put the peak date of conventional oil production at 2005, so it's already in the past. The production increases we have now are from unconventional forms of oil, such as heavy oil, tar sands, polar, deepwater, and natural gas liquids. The ASPO estimates that the total for "all liquids," or both conventional and unconventional oil, is 2,500 billion barrels, with a peak date at 2010, 1,102 billion barrels produced to date, and 1,398 billion barrels to go.[4]

Figure 8.4 shows their model, accounting for all liquids.

Now, projecting global oil production is part art, and part science, as much of the available data is dubious, having been influenced in many cases by politics and OPEC quotas. This is particularly true for the Middle Eastern

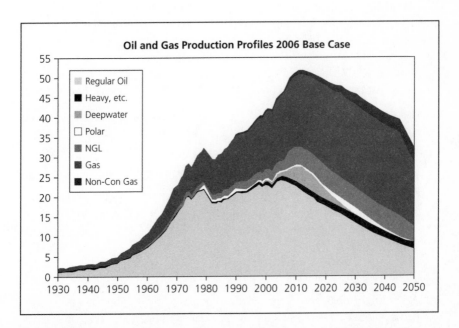

**FIGURE 8.4** *World Oil Production (All Liquids)—ASPO 2006 Base Case*
*Source:* Association for the Study of Peak Oil and Gas (ASPO), Newsletter No. 82, October 2007, https://aspo-ireland.org/newsletter/en/pdf/newsletter82_200706.pdf.

countries, which hold the vast majority (about 61%) of the world's remaining oil. So in peak oil circles, the debates continue over when the peak will be (or was), and many clever mathematical models have been offered.

But in general, as the chart in Figure 8.3 shows, the variance between estimates is negligible enough that we can call the date of the peak "soon enough." Peak oil is such an enormous turning point for the world that it doesn't matter whether the peak is plus or minus five years from a given date—our call to action will be the same, albeit perhaps slightly more or less urgent. As Campbell puts it: "Arguing endlessly over the precise date of peak also rather misses the point, when what matters is the vision of the long slope that comes into sight on the other side of it."[5]

## Exports

Being a net importer, what we in the United States care about most is not the global production peak, but the availability of the two-thirds of our lifeblood that is imported. If we can't get it, it doesn't really matter how much of it there is out there.

Worldwide, exports in 2007 were running at 47 million barrels per day,[6] or a little more than half the total production of 85 mbpd. But the major exporters are concentrated: The top 15 exporters account for fully 84 percent of the total oil exported worldwide, and oil production in half of them is either flat or in decline.[7]

A June 2007 study by Rembrandt Koppelaar of ASPO-Netherlands looked at just the global oil exports from 2002 to 2007.[8] He concluded:

1. Total world exports of all fuel liquids have been on a plateau since the end of 2004, and declined slightly in the last year, despite production increases.

2. Liquids exports from non-OPEC countries as a whole have declined since the beginning of 2004.

3. OPEC liquids exports increased until the end of 2005, followed by a short plateau after which a slow decline set in, mainly due to declining production in Saudi Arabia.

Figure 8.5 shows his chart of global exports.

So, while global liquids production increased by 1 mbpd from 2005 to 2006, the amount exported was flat. Koppelaar explains: "This plateau implies that all liquids production growth in producer countries has been absorbed by internal markets in recent years."

In other words, as producer countries grow up and continue to industrialize, they consume more of their own production and are unable to increase exports.

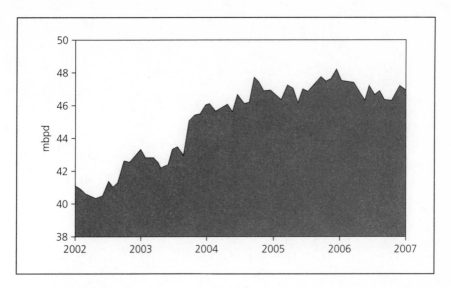

**FIGURE 8.5** *World Liquids Exports, January 2002–February 2007*
*Source: Oilwatch Monthly*, ASPO Netherlands, June 11, 2007, http://www.peakoil
.nl/wp-content/uploads/2007/06/oilwatch_monthly_june_2007.pdf. Alternative charts
at http://europe.theoildrum.com/node/2651.

*The Export Land Model* The impact on exports of rising consumption in oil-producing countries is the subject of an elegant *Export Land Model* (ELM) developed by Dallas-based independent petroleum geologist Jeffrey Brown and physicist and mathematician Dr. Samuel Foucher.[9] This model takes a hypothetical net-exporter oil-producing country, and makes the following assumptions:

- Ultimately recoverable resources (URR)[10] of 38 billion barrels.

- The peak occurs when 55 percent of the URR has been produced, and then production declines at the rate of 5 percent post-peak. (This is a reasonable assumption based on the historical example of Texas, which had a 4 percent depletion rate. In depletion analysis, Texas is frequently used as an example because it was a well-known, well-exploited oil province where the data was transparent and trusted, and the fields were well-managed.)

- Domestic consumption rises at the rate of 2.5 percent per year—a reasonable assumption for a growing economy, as all net oil exporters are. (See Figure 8.6.)

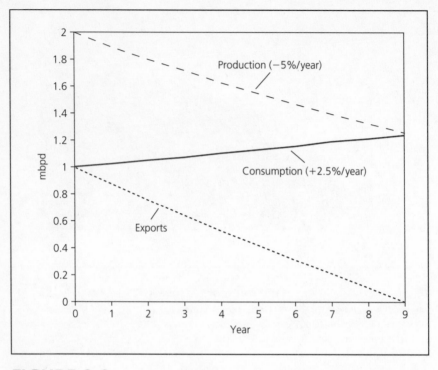

## FIGURE 8.6 *Export Land Model*

*Source:* Jeffrey J. Brown and Samuel Foucher, "Commentary: Declining Net Oil Exports—A Temporary Decline or a Long Term Trend?" *Peak Oil Review*, September 24, 2007 (pdf), http://www.aspo-usa.com/index.php?option=com_docman&task=doc_download&gid=465&Itemid=66.

The results of the model are pretty startling:

- Assuming that the peak occurs at the 55 percent point (which is typical), only 17 Gb (Gb = billion barrels) will remain to be produced.

- Ultimately, only about 10 percent of those 17 Gb would be exported—and exports would cease entirely after just eight years!

- The rate of decline in exports would be about *29 percent per year*, far steeper than the production decline rate of 5 percent per year, as they are squeezed from below by rising demand and squeezed from above by declining production.

■  The rate of decline in exports actually *accelerates with time*, going from 12.5 percent in the first year to 47.6 percent in the last.

Comparing the model to two actual post-peak net exporters, the United Kingdom and Indonesia, Brown and Foucher note that those countries' net export curves were actually worse than predicted by the ELM model. (See Figure 8.7.)

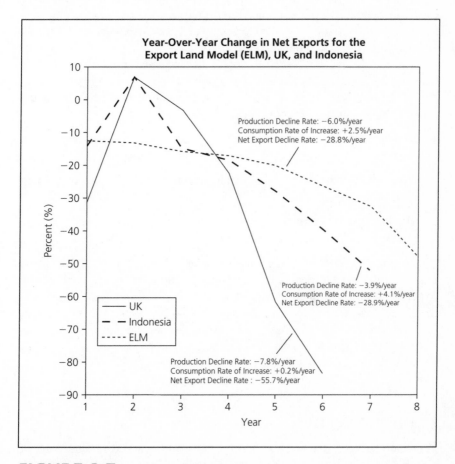

**FIGURE 8.7**  *Change in Net Exports*

*Source:* Jeffrey J. Brown and Samuel Foucher, "Commentary: Declining Net Oil Exports— A Temporary Decline or a Long Term Trend?" *Peak Oil Review,* September 24, 2007 (pdf), http://www.aspo-usa.com/index.php?option=com_docman&task=doc_download&gid =465&Itemid=66.

This is because the rate of a given exporter's decline in net exports after the peak is a function of three factors:

1. The consumption as a percentage of the peak production rate.

2. The rate of change of production.

3. The rate of change in consumption.

The UK and Indonesia had rapid net export declines because they were consuming about half of their production at the peak. Mexico's export decline will likely follow a similar pattern, reaching zero net oil exports by 2014, only 10 years after its 2004 production peak.

We believe that the ELM's assumptions are actually more conservative than the apparent reality for the world's top five net oil exporters—Saudi Arabia, Russia, Norway, Iran, and the United Arab Emirates—which account for about half of world net oil exports:

- Together, these five exporters have a combined 3.7 percent per year increase in consumption (vs. 2.5 percent in the model).

- From 2005 to 2006, their combined consumption accelerated by 5.3 percent per year.

- From 2005 to 2006, their exports declined at the rate of about 3.3 percent per year, and should accelerate from there.

In sum, the authors issued a stark warning: "In our opinion, we should base our plans on the very real possibility of a rapid decline in world net oil exports." *This means that all imports to the United States could potentially dry up over the next decade, at increasingly high prices.*

And that, my friend, makes our current dependence on imports—two-thirds of the oil we use—a suicide mission.

Let's take a closer look at it.

## COUNTING ON OPEC

As mentioned previously, about half of the world's largest producers are in decline. The United States, the United Kingdom, Norway, and Indonesia are all past their geological peaks, and China will soon be past hers. Mexico, Kuwait, and Russia are past their peaks due to a host of political and geological factors, from a lack of sustained investment to resource mismanagement. And major OPEC producers including Iran, Iraq, and Venezuela have passed their peaks as well, albeit due more to political factors than anything else. Russia, Iran, Venezuela, and Mexico may soon cease to be net exporters, again, due to their growing domestic needs. Supply from all non-OPEC producers has been stagnant for about six years now, and current projections say that it will likely reach its absolute peak some time between now (2007) and 2010,[11] although it will likely be a production plateau until roughly 2012.[12]

This means that the burden of any increased production—or exports—will fall squarely on OPEC.[13]

Figure 8.8 shows the EIA's projection, from their 2007 *International Energy Outlook*.

The ASPO projects that the supply from OPEC producers will increase through 2011, but other observers say it will peak much later, perhaps as late as 2025 or even 2050. However, the data is opaque and so it is very difficult to predict. The supply outlook for the OPEC states that are not located in the

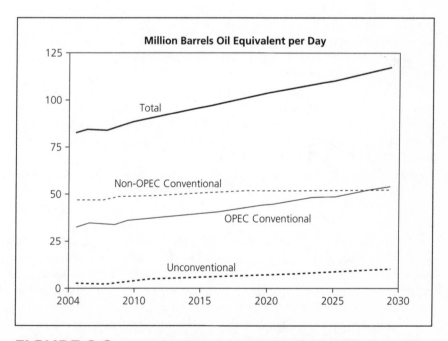

**FIGURE 8.8**  *EIA World Liquids Production, 2004–2030*
*Source:* "International Energy Outlook 2007," Energy Information Administration, May 2007, http://www.eia.doe.gov/oiaf/ieo/pdf/0484(2007).pdf.

Persian Gulf, especially Nigeria, Venezuela, and Indonesia, is uncertain, but it's clear that they won't be able to make up for depletion of non-OPEC producers.

In any case, it seems clear that by 2010 to 2012, if not sooner, the world will be looking to Saudi Arabia for all increases (if any) in global oil production. If demand remains strong, and they are unable or unwilling to significantly increase production, then it seems likely that we will see the global peak in oil production in that timeframe, right around 2011 as the ASPO has predicted.[14]

### OPEC: Unable or Unwilling?

Despite the world's reliance on OPEC supplies, OPEC certainly has been reluctant to increase production for the last two years, calling the markets "well supplied" with crude, and pointing to bottlenecks elsewhere, such as the refining sector.

When OPEC did announce a 500,000-barrel-per-day increase on September 11, 2007, oil immediately shot through its previous trading ceiling of $77 and headed for record territory, closing at $83.90 on September 20—precisely the opposite of the intended effect. Why? *Because traders thought that was insufficient—and they were right.*

On current trends, non-OPEC producers are producing about 100,000 bpd less than expected, while at the same time, demand is 100,000 bpd or more higher.[15] When crude oil inventories should be building, they are falling, likely because production has failed to live up to expectations. For example, the IEA reported that in the third quarter of 2007, OECD stockpiles fell by 33 million barrels or 360,000 bpd when they normally would increase by 280,000 bpd.[16] Barring some totally unexpected jump in supply, or a slashing of demand, we are entering a shortage scenario that can be resolved only by higher oil prices.

As for the 11 OPEC nations (prior to Angola's joining, just recently), as of 2007 only one had increased its production since September 2005, and that was a tiny 30,000-barrel-per-day bump for Libya. All the others declined, for a total decline of 2 million barrels per day.[17] That may be due to voluntary production cuts in accordance with OPEC's agreements—or it may be involuntary.

Figure 8.9 shows a chart of OPEC exports in aggregate. Based on the information presented in the figure, it looks as though the prospects for increased exports from OPEC are dim indeed.

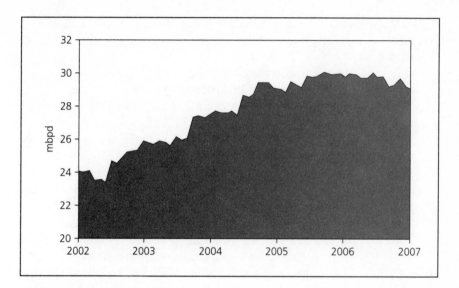

FIGURE 8.9 *OPEC Liquids Exports, January 2002–February 2007*
*Source:* "Peak Oil Monthly," ASPO Netherlands, June 11, 2007, http://www.peakoil
.nl/wp-content/uploads/2007/06/oilwatch_monthly_june_2007.pdf.

## THE BOTTOM LINE ON OIL

Here's the bottom line on oil: Global oil production has been basically flat for the last two years. But demand continues to rise at the rate of about 1.5 mbpd each year, and there are no expectations for any great new discoveries or techniques that might let oil production continue to increase.

Indeed, it looks like we'll be lucky to merely maintain the current level of global production, given the depletion of the largest and most productive fields. The average worldwide rate of oil field depletion has been assumed to be around 2.5 percent per year,[18] but now some worry it could be as high as 5 percent per year.

The outlook for our top suppliers is dim and dimmer. Rapidly increasing domestic consumption in Saudi Arabia, crashing production in Mexico, conventional oil production decline in Canada, and hostilities with Venezuela's Hugo Chavez all spell declining supplies. So, for net importers like the United States, peak oil is effectively already here.

We are clearly entering an era of an extremely tight balance between supply and demand. That means that the price will have to go up until demand is significantly curtailed, because there is no way that all the other alternative liquid fuels (such as biofuels, coal-to-liquids, gas-to-liquids, etc.) can make up such a volume of fuel.

This threat to the economy has expanded the discussion of peak oil beyond geological circles, and into the realm of investing. One of the first to recognize the importance of peaking exports was Jeffrey Rubin, the chief economist of the Canadian investment bank CIBC.

In a presentation to the Sixth Annual ASPO conference in September 2007, Rubin predicted that exports from OPEC, Russia, and Mexico will drop by 3 million barrels per day over the next five years, because of rising domestic demand and a sharp dropoff in production from Mexico due to the crashing of its supergiant field, Cantarell.[19] Of that 3 mbpd loss, Rubin expects 2 mbpd will come out of U.S. imports. That's 10 percent of our current usage!

Therefore, the United States will be forced to invest even more heavily in exotic and expensive unconventional oil production from sources such as the Alberta tar sands, and ultra-deep-water drilling. This, said Rubin, would send oil to $100 a barrel by the end of 2008, and oil prices would remain over $100 thereafter. (Although no one in the financial markets said so at the time, Rubin was apparently optimistic!)

### The Oil Junkie's Last Fix

Unfortunately, the prospects for future investment are limited. The remaining regions with significant reserves—such as Venezuela, Nigeria, and Kazakhstan—are increasingly hostile to foreign investment. This leaves Canada as one of the few remaining investment-friendly producers in the world, with its tar sands accounting for 50 to 70 percent of the total world reserves still open to private investment.[20]

Regardless of the level of enthusiasm for investing in the Canadian tar sands, however, there is a firm ceiling on their potential production. Natural gas, water, human resources, pipeline capacity, and other critical infrastructure will all limit the rate of production.

One of the most authoritative analyses on the tar sands is a comprehensive June 2006 paper, "A Crash Program Scenario for the Canadian Oil Sands Industry," by Prof. Kjell Aleklett of Uppsala University in Sweden, who is also the president of the ASPO.[21] Under a short-term crash-program scenario, he believes that the Canadian tar sands could grow from their current production rate of around 1 mbpd to a plateau of 3.6 mbpd around 2018[22] and stay flat until it drops off around 2040. (This projection is more or less in line with that of the IEA.) Production is currently increasing at the rate of about 8 percent per year.[23]

Under a long-term crash-program scenario, he determined that production could reach a maximum of 5 mbpd by 2030, but that a shortage of natural gas would limit it. Most other forecasts tend to center on a maximum production rate of 3.5 mbpd by 2025 to 2030.

But even at that maximum, the tar sands would account for a mere 4 percent of current global oil consumption, or about 2.5 percent of the IEA's forecast of 120 mbpd by 2025. That's about the same amount of oil that will be lost due to oil field depletion less than two years after the global peak. Indeed, it wouldn't even be enough to offset the combined decline of conventional crude oil production from the North Sea and Canada.

Nor is the outlook for other, more exotic oil field discoveries and methods any better. According to the respected energy research firm Platts, the world needed to invest $350 billion in 2006 just to ensure adequate oil production in 2010, but the IEA says that only $250 billion was actually spent.[24]

Indeed, for the major integrated oil companies, the trend in recent years has been toward prospecting on Wall Street (by buying out smaller companies and rivals) rather than prospecting in the field, and large dividend payouts. Why? Because they know that the remaining available prospects are very limited.

This is, most emphatically, not a growth scenario.

## THE PARTY'S OVER

The outlook for oil is clear: As noted peak oil author Richard Heinberg titled his seminal book on the subject, *The Party's Over*.

There is simply no way to continue the oil game. Supply is falling relentlessly, demand is still increasing, prices are going up steadily, and the only thing we can do about that is to stop using so much of it.

As mentioned in Chapter 1, the global supply stories on natural gas, coal, and even uranium are similar to that of oil: Every year we're needing more, but getting flat or declining amounts, and paying more for them. And these trends show no signs of abating, because we can increase neither domestic production nor imports. In fact it appears that we may reach the peak of *all traditional forms of energy* by 2025!

But the first to peak—and the most significant—will be oil. For net-oil-importing countries like the United States, the yawning 2-percent-per-year gap that is opening between production and demand is a grave cause for concern, and not just for financial reasons.

## Food

One of the most serious, and difficult to mitigate, risks of our dependence on oil is in the production of food.

Oil and natural gas are embedded into every aspect of the food we eat, from the field to the table. Oil not only powers the tractors, combines, and other machines of commercial agribusiness, but it's also the feedstock for making pesticides and herbicides. Commercial fertilizers are made from ammonia, which is synthesized from natural gas using the Haber-Bosch process.[25] Then there is the fuel to transport and process the goods, deliver them to your grocery store, and keep them cold. And that doesn't even count the energy needed to transport you to the store, and you and your groceries back home, or the energy used to cook the meal.

In fact, on average, every calorie of food we consume in the United States requires 10 calories of fossil-fuel energy to create and bring to our tables.[26] Given the outlook for oil and natural gas, this is a dangerous dependence. Given their intimate connection, then, it should be no surprise that as the prices of oil and gas have shot up over the last few years, so have the prices for grain, as shown in Figures 8.10 and 8.11.

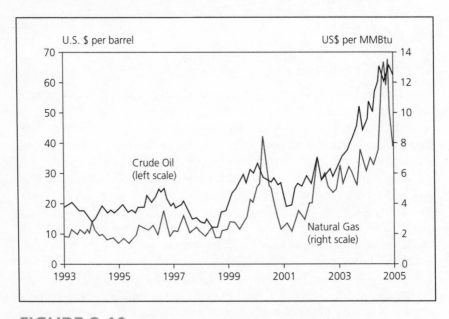

FIGURE 8.10   *Crude Oil vis-à-vis Natural Gas Prices*

*Source:* TD Bank Financial Group, TD Economics Special Report, February 20, 2006, http://www.td.com/economics/special/db0206_natgas.pdf.

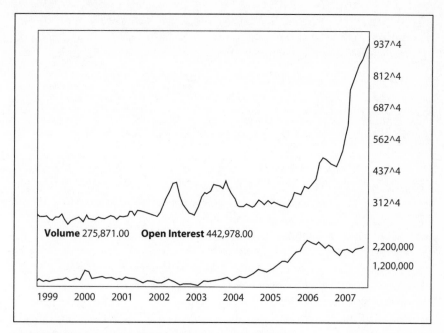

937^4

812^4

687^4

562^4

437^4

312^4

**Volume** 275,871.00    **Open Interest** 442,978.00

2,200,000

1,200,000

1999    2000    2001    2002    2003    2004    2005    2006    2007

**FIGURE 8.11**  *Wheat Futures, 1999–2007*
*Source:* Wheat Monthly Price Chart, TFC Commodity Reports, http://www
.tfc-charts.w2d.com/chart/CW/M.

In a very straightforward way, food *is* oil and gas. According to noted
peak oil author Richard Heinberg, food travels an average of 1,300 miles from
the farm to the plate in North America, leading critics such as James Howard
Kunstler to decry the "3,000-mile Caesar Salad" that travels from California's
breadbasket, the San Joaquin Valley, to his table in Scranton, Pennsylvania.

Paradoxically, part of what has caused grain prices to spike up is that we
are shifting part of the fuel burden away from petroleum and over to domestic
biofuels. That sudden, recent spike in wheat prices in Figure 8.11 is over the
same period of time that subsidies for biofuels were implemented, causing
many farmers to switch over to the market-ready biofuel crops of corn and
soybeans. Consequently, less wheat and other grains were planted, which
drove up their prices.

This suggests two important points:

1. There is no easy or scalable way to substitute biofuels for 85 million
   barrels per day of liquid fuels from petroleum.

2. Biofuels that compete with food crops are necessarily limited, and probably a bad idea in the long run. Only biofuels made from nonfood feedstocks—such as cellulosic ethanol—have a sustainable future.

But peak oil challenges more than our ability to feed ourselves.

## Security

Security issues surround the global oil trade, and the cost of securing oil imports is enormous.

The security costs alone of having the U.S. military protect the oil supplies of the Persian Gulf were estimated at around $44 billion per year in 2007,[27] but those are just the security costs, so it's a very conservative estimate.

According to Milton Copulos, the head of the National Defense Council Foundation, the oil supply disruptions of the 1970s cost the U.S. economy between $2.3 and $2.5 trillion, but the cost of such an event today could be as high as $8 trillion—63 percent of our annual GDP, or nearly $27,000 for every man, woman, and child living in the United States.

In fact, an in-depth analysis of the true total economic cost of the nation's growing dependence on imported oil is estimated at $825.1 billion—almost twice the President's $419.3 billion defense budget request. And much of that goes into the pockets of people who hate us.

That would be equivalent to $5.04 for every gallon of gasoline from all imports, or $8.35 for every Persian Gulf gallon, bringing the "true" cost of a gallon of gasoline refined from Persian Gulf oil to $11.06. (This figure adds $8.35 to the price of gasoline that Copulus saw from the day before he posted these numbers.) That would make the *real* cost of filling up a family sedan about $220, and filling up a large SUV about $325, and that's based on 2007 gas prices![28]

After taking into account all the hidden costs, he says, a $75 barrel of oil really costs us about $480.[29] And even then, we have secured only today's supply. In order to secure tomorrow's, we'll need to keep pouring money and blood on the oil fields of the Middle East for as long as we still need the stuff.

This is hardly a productive or wise way for the country to invest its blood and treasure.

## Transportation

Perhaps the most immediate threat that oil peaking presents to us is in the area of transportation.

Oil accounts for 90 percent of our transportation energy. The convenience, ease, power density, and relatively low cost and high abundance of petroleum-based fuels has made them the fuel of choice for moving heavy vehicles around.

What will happen to our transportation infrastructure when we are beginning the descent down the other side of Hubbert's Peak? Can we switch to something else?

*A Liquid Fuels Problem* Our transportation infrastructure is almost entirely dependent on *liquid* fuels. Very little in the way of non-liquid-fueled transportation exists, outside of a few inner-city transportation systems. And it's just not practical to burn other fuels at today's scale. With 230 million cars in the United States, imagine any significant percentage of them burning, say, coal or wood.

That means that our choices are to either use liquid fuel substitutes, or switch to an electric infrastructure. Obviously, the latter isn't going to happen overnight. For at least the next decade or so, our transportation fuel likely will be constrained to whatever petroleum products we can get, plus a small amount of other alternative fuels.

Unfortunately, the available liquid fuel substitutes all have undesirable side effects: Coal-to-liquids (CTL) technology still produces an unacceptably high level of $CO_2$ emissions, and incredible environmental destruction. Gas-to-liquids (GTL) requires abundant supplies of natural gas and low-cost production, which don't exist. Biodiesel, which is typically made from vegetable oils, can quickly come into competition with food production as it is scaled up, although there are some promising developments in the world of algae and jatropha-based biodiesel, as we'll discuss in Chapter 9. And ethanol from corn (which is currently the main feedstock for ethanol in the United States) is extremely energy intensive to produce. All of the above will be necessarily limited in scope, due to their respective technical and economic challenges.

Only commercial-scale cellulosic ethanol—ethanol made from woody fibers such as agricultural waste and woodchips—has the potential to offset a significant portion of the nation's current 21-million-barrel-per-day appetite for oil without competing with food.

Some critics, such as Dr. Tad Patzek of the University of California at Berkeley, doubt that the United States could even achieve a 10 percent offset—about 2 mbpd of biofuels—without running into other biological and environmental limits.

In any case, although there are some exciting investment opportunities in cellulosic ethanol, the industry is still in its infancy and there are no commercial-scale production facilities at this time. A liquid fuel regime, given today's technology and demand, is simply not tenable without oil.

The game is most definitely up for oil. The unavoidable end of our current liquid-fueled infrastructure is already in sight. We simply cannot continue to drive 230 million cars and a massive fleet of heavy trucks on petroleum. It's over. *Finis.*

## THE FUTURE IS ELECTRIC

That leaves us with electricity. Electric power is the future for transportation, for three main reasons:

1. Electricity can be generated from any renewable or nonrenewable source. It is not bound to fossil fuels.

2. It can be generated almost anywhere. The shorter the distance between the point of energy generation and the point of use, the more efficient and robust your infrastructure is.

3. It can be emissions-free. If we could massively exploit the world's geothermal potential, for example, we could be running a good deal of our infrastructure on it, without contributing to global warming or otherwise contaminating the environment.

Short of everyone taking up the energy lifestyle of the Amish, electricity must be the energy of the future. This is particularly true 80 to 100 years from now, when there will be very little production of today's most dominant fuels. So an immediate transition strategy is paramount, as our century-old transportation infrastructure cannot be transformed overnight.

Plug-in hybrid electric vehicles (PHEVs) can serve as a transitional technology to the all-electric cars of the future, by supplanting some of their liquid fuel needs with grid electricity. Even better, electric trains offer a huge opportunity to offset an enormous portion of our fuel demand.

Engineer Alan Drake, who has done extensive research on the potential of rail, and electrified rail in particular, believes that it can significantly reduce our consumption of diesel fuel. He claims that two million barrels a day of diesel fuel (about 10% of our total oil usage) could be supplanted using just 1.4 percent of U.S. electrical production, and that switching half of our current truck freight to electric rail could save 6.3 percent of U.S. oil consumption.[30] With modern hybrid locomotives, Drake calculates that the savings realized by switching freight loads from diesel-powered trucks to modern electric rail is 20 to 1.

In all, Drake believes that with a supportive public policy, a crash urban rail building program could save 9 percent of our current transportation fuel consumption by 2020, with a corresponding 15 percent reduction in private auto travel—the same level of offsets that the entire petroleum and biofuels industries are now struggling to achieve.

## THE GAME IS COMING TO US

In sum, for those of us who invest in renewable energy, the game is coming to us. Peak oil, and the lack of viable alternative liquid fuels (other than cellulosic ethanol, which isn't quite yet ready for prime time), means that the enormous demand we have for energy must increasingly be satisfied by electricity. And climate change and other environmental issues mean that the new demand for electricity will favor renewable sources.

Since two-thirds of our petroleum use—about 7 mbpd of oil—goes to transportation, offsetting that enormous load will ensure a virtually permanent bull market for Green Chip investors.

There are simply no two ways about it!

# CHAPTER

# BIOFUELS

## MORE THAN JUST CORN

As we discussed in Chapters 1 and 8, peak oil is a *liquid fuels* problem. Renewably generated electricity is definitely the future, but until we build a new electrically powered infrastructure, we're still going to need liquid fuels for transportation.

The obvious best liquid fuel alternatives are biofuels, which are liquid fuels that are made from plants. There are other alternatives, such as turning coal and natural gas into liquid fuels, but at this point in time, none are scaled up to any significant level, and the economics of them remains to be seen. Since these liquid fuels made from coal and natural gas are based on fossil fuels and are not renewable, they are also outside the scope of this book.[1]

More than two-thirds of our petroleum use goes to transportation, so by switching to biofuels (in combination with higher-efficiency and plug-in vehicles) we can make a significant dent in our consumption. Plus every gallon of fuel we can grow domestically instead of importing it from a foreign supplier is a win on all levels—economically, politically, and environmentally.

## THE COMPLEXITIES OF BIOFUELS

The issues surrounding biofuels are complex, and the opinions on them are widely varied, so we'll start with a brief overview of biofuels, and then explore some of the important questions.

There are two main types of biofuel in use today: ethanol and biodiesel. Figure 9.1 summarizes their production methods.

### Ethanol

Ethanol is simply alcohol—the same stuff you drink in an alcoholic beverage. Alcohol for human consumption is tightly regulated, though, and industrial alcohol contains impurities that will make you sick if you drink it.

Making ethanol is a lot like making whiskey. Sugar is dissolved out of sugarcane or sugar beets, or converted from starchy crops like corn, wheat, and barley. The sugar is then fermented with yeast, which produces ethanol and carbon dioxide. (An alternative to fermentation is gasification, which we will discuss later in this chapter.) The resulting "beer" is then distilled to concentrate the ethanol from its original 16 percent or so into the 99.7 percent purity needed to run an engine.[2]

In the United States, corn is by far the dominant crop, and nearly all ethanol produced in the United States has been made from it. Other sugar-bearing

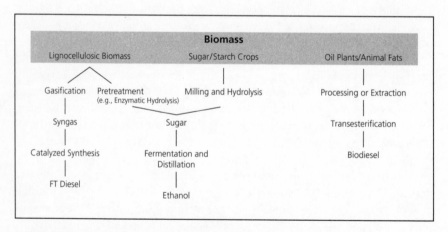

## FIGURE 9.1  *Biofuel Production Pathways*

*Source:* Organisation for Economic Co-operation and Development (OECD), "Biofuels: Is the Cure Worse than the Disease?" September 2007, http://media.ft.com/cms/fb8b5078-5fdb-11dc-b0fe-0000779fd2ac.pdf.

crops, such as sugar beets and sugarcane, are even more productive feedstocks than corn, but they don't grow everywhere.

An oft-cited ethanol success story is that of Brazil, which has been said to obtain as much as 48 percent of its passenger-vehicle fuel from domestically produced ethanol.[3] However, fuel engineer and energy analyst Robert Rapier contends that on a Btu basis, Brazil really only produces 10 percent of its fuel from sugarcane, and the other 90 percent is still domestic crude oil.[4] In any case, Brazil's success is due to its extraordinarily productive sugarcane crop, which is not something the rest of the world can replicate.

This is an important point, because ethanol is mostly a domestic business. Producers must use materials that are as local as possible, because the cost of energy required to move around large amounts of bulky feedstock is so high. Usually an ethanol refinery will be located right next to, even on the same site as, the fields where the feedstock is grown. Likewise, the finished product must be used as locally as possible, because its water content corrodes existing pipes, making long-distance pipelines impractical. (With the correct metallurgy, ethanol can be transported by pipeline, but the amount of ethanol we might expect to produce wouldn't be sufficient to justify the cost of building it.) About 99 percent of all ethanol used in the United States is blended into gasoline at a nearby refinery to make E10 fuel, which we'll discuss momentarily.

Therefore the crops that grow best locally are the crops that must be used for biofuels. For the United States, corn is the primary feedstock; for Brazil, sugarcane; and for Japan, rice.

Ethanol hits the road in three different concentrations today:

- Pure ethanol, usable only in specially modified engines.

- E10, an octane-boosting mix of 10 percent ethanol with regular gasoline. This combination is usable in any gas-powered vehicle and is already in wide distribution as an oxygenate substitute for MTBE, which was phased out in 2006 by federal mandate.[5]

- E85, a combination of 85 percent ethanol and 15 percent gasoline. A standard engine can be modified to run on either regular gasoline or E85 for about $35.[6] About 5 million of these "flex-fuel" vehicles are already on the road in the United States, but automakers have announced many new models of E85 vehicles that are headed for their production lines in the next three years.

Although automakers and ethanol proponents have made much of E85 fuel, as yet it is not widely deployed. Today, only about 1,400 out of the

170,000 gas stations in the United States offer E85, or less than 1 percent.[7] Experts believe that E85 would have to be available at around 10 percent of all stations before it will be eagerly adopted by the public,[8] so there is still about a factor of 10 in growth needed on the supply side. For example, California has 257,318 flex-fuel vehicles but only three public stations with E85, and New Jersey has 116,512 flex-fuel vehicles without a single station selling E85.[9] Consequently, "more than 99 percent of the flex-fuel cars run on regular gasoline because E85 is rarely available to the everyday driving public."[10]

For its part, Big Oil has actively resisted the expansion of the E85 market. According to the *Wall Street Journal*, oil companies make it difficult to deploy E85 pumps at gas stations. For instance, franchises may be required to purchase all the fuel they sell from the oil company, but if the oil company doesn't sell E85, which is most often the case, then the stations can't either without obtaining an exception from the oil company. There are other restrictions as well, such as prohibiting payment by credit card.[11]

Another reason E85 pumps have not proliferated is that the volume of ethanol produced really doesn't justify it. According to Robert Rapier, if all of the 7 billion gallons of ethanol supply we produced were blended to make E85, it would only provide about 6 percent (4 percent on an energy equivalent basis) of our gasoline supply. Consequently, the vast majority of ethanol produced is blended into E10, which can be used in a standard gasoline engine.

Still, the number of E85 pumps increased 500 percent in three years and is on track to continue its rapid expansion, thanks to government and ethanol industry grants that each provide up to $30,000 to install them.[12] We note that it is a significant departure from their historic lockstep relationship with Big Oil for automakers to embrace E85 as enthusiastically as they have.

Displacing petroleum usage is but one of the benefits of a domestic ethanol industry:[13]

- In 2006 alone, the value of the reduced oil imports kept $11 billion at home, rather than sending it to foreign oil producers. Not only does this help the domestic economy, it also deprives hostile countries of income.

- When blended with gasoline, ethanol's high oxygen content (35%) aids more complete combustion, resulting in lowered carbon emissions.

- Ethanol is biodegradable, so fuel spills do not threaten the environment like petroleum does.

- According to expert consulting firm LECG, a typical 100 million gallons per year (mgy) ethanol plant also brings a significant benefit to the local economy, adding 1,600 new jobs and $406 million in gross output.

There's still quite a bit more to discuss in regard to the advantages and disadvantages of biofuels, but first, let's get into the specifics of the various biofuel options.

**Corn Ethanol** Corn ethanol utterly dominates total U.S. ethanol production, at just over 7 billion gallons per year.[14] But it may already be approaching what some believe is its tolerable limit of its production, which has been estimated at perhaps 12 billion gallons per year[15] because of competition for arable land with food production. (HR 6, which mandates expanded biofuel production and was passed into law in December 2007, caps corn ethanol production at 15 billion gallons per year.[16])

The sudden 40 percent growth in corn ethanol capacity in 2007 did not come without a cost. With more land producing corn, less was producing animal feed, soy, and other grains and food crops, all of which contributed to a jump in food and beverage prices (with higher transportation costs adding significantly to the price jump, too).

For example, it has been estimated that corn ethanol consumed about 27 percent[17] of the U.S. 2007 corn crop to make about 5.9 billion[18] gallons of ethanol, but that is only 4 percent of the 145 billion[19] gallons of gasoline we consumed in the same year. The U.S. Department of Agriculture further projects that in five years, ethanol production will consume almost a third of the U.S. corn crop.[20]

Consider this: A federal law passed in 2007 mandates a quintupling of domestic ethanol production, to 36 billion gallons per year by 2022.[21] If we scaled that linearly, and continued to produce almost all of the ethanol from corn, as we do now, then we would need 162 percent of the 2007 corn crop to meet that 36-billion-gallon-per-year target, which would still offset only one-quarter of our current gasoline usage.

Clearly, we cannot scale up corn ethanol production enough to make a meaningful dent in our consumption of petroleum without running into some competition with food. The next best liquid fuel alternative is cellulosic ethanol.

**Cellulosic Ethanol** Ethanol can be produced not only from plant sugars, but from organic matter that contains cellulose, the basic building material of all woody plant fibers. The cellulose is either gasified, or broken down in a pretreatment process to free the starches within, which are then fermented. Feedstocks for cellulosic ethanol include certain grasses, woodchips, corncobs and stalks, sorghum, rice and wheat straw, and other waste materials that farmers normally might have to plow back into the ground, or dispose of at significant cost and effort.

This gives cellulosic ethanol several important advantages over other forms of ethanol:

- It can make use of unwanted biomass from agricultural and wood operations, turning a cost into a benefit.

- It can be produced without competing with food crops for land and water, and with less fertilizer and pesticides than are used in commercial food farming. In time, cellulosic feedstocks should become more abundant and much cheaper than food grains.

- It can reduce greenhouse gas emissions. Cellulosic ethanol may contribute 80 percent less net $CO_2$ than regular gasoline, as compared to only 20 percent less for corn ethanol, because most of the carbon was taken from the air when the plant grew.[22] One recent study from the U.S. Department of Agriculture found that emissions from cellulosic ethanol made from switchgrass were 94 percent lower than emissions from gasoline.[23] However, the definitive word on emissions from cellulosic ethanol is yet to be said, because no commercial facilities yet exist.

The cellulosic feedstocks with the largest potential may be switchgrass, a perennial grass native to the United States, and miscanthus, a grass native to Europe that can grow to 14 feet tall.[24] Such grasses can grow on marginally arable land, and can actually improve the environment in which they are grown by reducing soil erosion and chemical and water use, while at the same time providing habitat for wildlife. And because they can be grown with very little in the way of fossil-fuel inputs, taking all of their carbon from $CO_2$ in the air, they can produce a nearly carbon-neutral biofuel.

A recent University of Minnesota study found that high-diversity grasslands can even remove carbon from the atmosphere and sequester it in soils and roots, while at the same time producing 238 percent more energy than monoculture crops![25] However, the subject deserves intensive further study.

One of the major hurdles to large-scale production of cellulosic ethanol is the fact that nature designed cellulose *not* to break down easily. Several approaches to the problem are being attempted.

The most common technique is using high-tech, chemically engineered enzymes, which can break the cellulose down chemically into fermentable sugars. Unfortunately, high-tech chemical engineering also means high-priced, small-batch enzymes, which has limited the growth of the industry thus far. But as we discuss later in this chapter, several companies are tackling that problem.

Another way to make cellulosic ethanol is by steam heating the feedstock under pressure to gasify the cellulose, producing carbon monoxide and hydrogen. The resulting gas is then hydrogenated to turn it into synfuels such as ethanol, synthetic gasoline, or diesel. This process is not a fermentation, but rather a thermochemical process, and so it does not require specialized enzymes.

## Biodiesel

While biofuels are a "new" development in modern times, the reality is that they predated fuel made from petroleum. Rudolf Diesel designed his engine in 1897 to run on peanut oil, because he was a champion of the "common man." He wanted a fuel that could be grown locally, giving smaller industries, farmers, and average folk a chance to compete with the big industries that had monopolized energy production.

Biodiesel has similar properties to diesel from petroleum (or "dino diesel"), and is typically made from vegetable oils or animal fats. Biodiesel is produced via a process called transesterification, which is the reaction of a triglyceride (fat/oil) with an alcohol to form esters and glycerol.[26] The resulting fuel is just as effective as diesel, and can be used in a standard diesel engine without modification, either as a 100 percent biodiesel fuel (called *B100*) or blended in some proportion with dino diesel (a mix of 20 percent biodiesel would be called *B20*). In cold climates, biodiesel is usually blended with dino diesel at a 20 percent or less concentration, because it gels at low temperatures (technically speaking, it has higher pour and cloud points).

Biodiesel has a number of advantages over dino diesel and ethanol:

- It is 100 percent biodegradable.

- It reduces carbon emissions by 75 percent and produces less particulate matter, carbon monoxide, and sulfur dioxide emissions than dino diesel. It's also safer to store and transport.[27]

- Unlike ethanol, biodiesel is compatible with the existing infrastructure to deliver, store, and sell it.[28]

Soybean oil is currently the most economical base for biodiesel production, but it can be made from any oilseed crop, such as rapeseed, canola, mustard, jatropha, palm, and even algae.[29]

Jatropha may become a frontrunner in biodiesel feedstocks, because it offers some advantages over traditional biodiesel feedstocks like soy and palm: It's not a food crop; indeed, it's poisonous. It grows extremely fast and can be grown on virtually barren land with little rainfall, so it won't compete with food for arable land. It can survive through up to three years of consecutive drought,[30] and live for up to 50 years. And it can be planted next to other crops without significantly reducing the yield of the fields.[31]

**Biodiesel from Algae** One of the most promising sources of biodiesel feedstock isn't a plant at all, but rather the simple aquatic organisms called *algae*—the same organisms, ironically, that much of the crude oil we produce today was made from.

Algae can capture light energy through photosynthesis and create something like vegetable oil. Certain species of algae have a high oil content—some over 50 percent—and very high growth rates, and so are ideal for biodiesel production.

Algae has several advantages over oilseed crops:

- It can be grown almost anywhere with sunlight, in closed tubes or open ponds, because it's grown in water, so it doesn't need soil.

- The only inputs it needs are sunlight, water, a little power to run the operation, and carbon dioxide, which it takes from the atmosphere.

- Algae consumes $CO_2$, so it could be used to capture the $CO_2$ emissions of power plants that burn fossil fuels. One company, Israel's Alga Technologies (Algatech), is doing just that, by locating their algae-growing units alongside the smokestacks of power plants. Not only could this capture all the emissions of the power plant, but it could also provide a fuel source for the power plant, making the whole operation self-contained. And the resulting fuel would be carbon neutral.

- Algae produces far more oil per acre than traditional oilseed crops; for example, a yield of 4,000 gallons of oil per acre per year is claimed for algae, as compared with only 50 gallons per acre for soy.[32] On an energetic basis, the yield of algal biodiesel is estimated at 30 times more energy per acre than soybeans.[33]

How much biodiesel can we make from algae? According to Solix Biofuels, an aspiring producer of algae-based biodiesel, replacing all of the petroleum-based transportation fuel in the United States would require about 140 billion gallons of biodiesel a year, and could be done on just 95 million acres of infertile land.[34] Producing that much biodiesel from soybeans has been variously estimated at three billion acres of fertile land,[35] half the landmass of the United States,[36] and 15,000 square miles.[37] To produce it from canola, you'd need more than one billion acres, more than double the existing amount of cropland in the United States.[38] However, replacing all transportation fuel (or even all dino diesel) isn't really the objective; the point is to get an idea of how much of it we might reasonably grow economically.

## IMPORTANT QUESTIONS

The United States only began to scale up its use of biofuels around 2000[39] (see Figure 9.3), so data is scant on how well they can satisfy our need for transportation fuel. At this point, we are mainly relying on studies and models to discover our best options for moving forward. These studies are divided on several important questions, which we will explore in this section.

### The Potential: How Much Can We Really Make?

The first important question is obvious: How much biofuel can we make?

Estimating the potential for biofuels requires making a set of assumptions, including the amount of available land for cultivation, the yields per acre of various crops, and the value of residues from processing. All of these factors have been the subject of numerous studies and spirited debate, which is far from concluded. For example, estimates for the potential worldwide yields of biofuel feedstock vary from 54 gigajoules (GJ) to 330 GJ per hectare per year![40]

As an example of an optimistic study on biofuel potential, a policy paper from 2005 by ex-CIA chief James Woolsey and former Secretary of State George Shultz entitled "Oil and Security" projected that at least half of the U.S. oil demand could be displaced by cellulosic ethanol from switchgrass grown on unused land in the Conservation Reserve Program soil bank, and that the fuel could be produced for as little as 67 to 77 cents a gallon when the industry is mature.[41]

As an example of a pessimistic study, a 2000 estimate by Fisher et al. cited in a 2007 OECD study[42] on biofuels calculated that less than one-quarter of the world's land was suitable for rain-fed cultivation, because the rest lacked the right temperature, humidity, topography, or soil conditions. After excluding land needed for forests, housing, and infrastructure, and enough agriculture to feed 9 billion people by 2050, the worldwide potential is estimated at roughly 700 million hectares, most of it grassland, of which nearly two-thirds is in Africa, one-third in South and Central America, and zero in North America. For reference, only about 10 million hectares were under biofuels cultivation in 2004. After accounting for other factors, the authors' "back-of-the-envelope analysis" is that only about 440 million hectares could be used for biofuels crop production in 2050, which could satisfy perhaps 11 percent of total demand for liquid transport fuels. This sort of study demonstrates how little "extra" land will be available for cultivation after allowing for population growth; as the authors state, "Currently, virtually all of the Earth's land surface is already in use."

In 2007, the European Commission evaluated the effects of its mandate to obtain 10 percent of the EU's fuel from biofuels by 2020, and found that it would require 15 percent of the agricultural land already in use to meet the goal, assuming that 20 percent of the biofuel need would be met by imports. The Commission predicted price increases for oilseed and cereal crops as a consequence.[43]

But political and business decisions are rarely made solely on the basis of academic modeling. Biofuel cultivation is something we are doing, and we have decided to do a great deal more of it. It is not our role to arbitrate the best uses of land; we merely observe the markets and their investing potential. And we do see a great deal of that.

### The Greenhouse Effect: Will Biofuels Effectively Reduce Greenhouse Gas Emissions?

Another important question surrounding biofuels is their potential to reduce greenhouse gas emissions. Earlier in this chapter, we cited a Department of Agriculture report that claimed that ethanol based on switchgrass produced 94 percent less emissions than gasoline.[44] But on the other side of the debate, an oft-cited study on the subject published in April 2007 by Dr. Mark Jacobson of Stanford University asserted that the emissions from ethanol might be worse than gasoline.[45]

Naturally, the emissions-reduction potential varies widely with the type of feedstock used, as shown in Figure 9.2. One of the key reasons why estimates on biofuel emissions vary so widely is the boundary problem: At what point do you draw the line between what is counted and what is left out? Do you count only the emissions from the fuel used to run the machinery to cultivate, harvest, and process the feedstock into fuel, or do you also include the emissions from the making of the machinery? What about the emissions from mining the ores to make the steel that goes into the machines?—and so on.

At this point, we are cautiously optimistic that the emissions of biofuels are lower than those of petroleum fuels when all inputs are considered, but the jury is still officially out on the question.

### Net Energy: Will It Be Enough?

Perhaps the most contentious question about biofuels is the net energy, variously referred to as the *energy returned on investment* (EROI) or *energy*

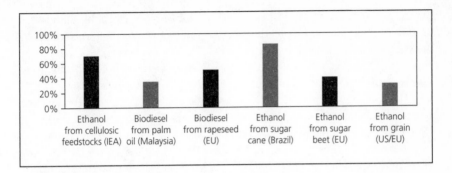

**FIGURE 9.2** *Range of Estimated GHG Reductions from Biofuels Compared with Gasoline*
*Source:* Organisation for Economic Co-operation and Development (OECD), "Biofuels: Is the Cure Worse than the Disease?" September 2007, http://media.ft.com/cms/fb8b5078-5fdb-11dc-b0fe-0000779fd2ac.pdf.

*returned on energy invested* (EROEI). Obviously, if you don't get significantly more energy from the fuel than you used to produce it, then it's not worth making.

In a 2003 article for the scientific journal *Nature* by five of the world's top academic authorities on EROI calculations, the authors explain the problem this way: "An EROI of much greater than 1 to 1 is needed to run a society, because energy is also required to make the machines that use the energy, feed, house, train and provide health care for necessary workers and so on."[46]

In fact, recent preliminary results from studies by Dr. Charles Hall—who is credited with originally developing the concept of EROI—and his colleagues suggest that if the EROI of an energy project isn't at least 5, it may not be a net source of energy at all, once the production and maintenance of the infrastructure to use the fuel are taken into account.[47] This is another example of the boundary problem.

Even when the boundaries are narrowly defined, however, EROI is one of the principal arguments against corn ethanol. Variously estimated between 1.2 and less than 1, it's just not high enough to make corn ethanol a viable substitute for petroleum-based fuels at any real scale—although this doesn't seem to be a consideration in setting federal incentives for ethanol.

Cellulosic ethanol, however, may be viable on a net-energy basis. According to a recent study for the U.S. Department of Agriculture, the EROI of cellulosic ethanol from switchgrass is 5.4, including "the energy used to make the tractors, the energy used to make the seed to plant the field, the energy used to produce the herbicide, the energy used to produce the fertilizer, [and] the energy used in the harvesting process." The results came out of a five-year study, where the switchgrass was grown in 3- to 9-hectare plots of marginal cropland in the U.S. midcontinent.[48]

Then again, other noted biofuels experts, such as Dr. David Pimentel of Cornell University, Dr. Tad Patzek of the University of California at Berkeley, Dr. Charles Hall of the State University of New York College of Environmental Science and Forestry, and fuel engineer Robert Rapier, have sharply criticized the assumptions of that report,[49] and have published numerous critiques of other similar biofuels studies. Patzek, for example, doubts that the United States could even achieve a 10 percent offset—about 2 mbpd of biofuels— without running into other biological and environmental limits.[50]

Again, like the other important questions about biofuels, the net-energy debate is far from over. In the meantime, significant subsidies exist for biofuels, and the biofuel industry is growing rapidly in response.

## THE MARKET: GROWING LIKE A WEED

According to the International Energy Agency's World Energy Outlook 2006, global production of biofuels was about 643,000 bpd (20 million tons of oil equivalent[51]) in 2005, or roughly 1 percent of total road transport fuel consumption. About 85 percent of that was from ethanol, and the remainder from biodiesel.[52]

The worldwide production of ethanol in 2006 stood at 13.5 billion gallons per year (bgy). The world's largest producers were the United States at 4.9 bgy; Brazil, at 4.5 bgy; and China at 1 bgy. All the rest produced 0.5 bgy or less.[53]

According to Clean Edge research, the global markets for biofuels (global production and wholesale pricing of ethanol and biodiesel) are set to grow from $20.5 billion in 2006 to $80.9 billion by 2016.[54]

In the United States, the ethanol production capacity stood at 7.2 bgy as of January 2008, having grown 440 percent since 2000.[55] That capacity comprises approximately 4 percent of our total vehicle fuel usage of 182 bgy in 2005.[56] This amazing growth story is vividly depicted in Figure 9.3.

By comparison, biodiesel production in the United States is a tiny market, about 1 percent the size of the ethanol market. As of 2006, U.S. production of biodiesel was 75 million gallons per year (mgy), only about 0.2 percent of the 38 bgy of the diesel used for transportation.[57] Accordingly, most of the incentives and investment in biofuels are directed toward ethanol.

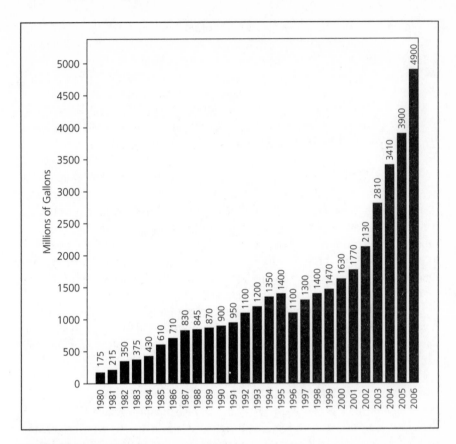

**FIGURE 9.3** *Historic U.S. Fuel Ethanol Production*
*Source:* EIA/RFA, *RFA Ethanol Industry Outlook 2007*, February 2007, http://www
.ethanolrfa.org/objects/pdf/outlook/RFA_Outlook_2007.pdf.

### The Ethanol Market

Driven by government subsides, the U.S. corn ethanol industry has exploded
in the last few years. But according to Lester Brown of the Earth Policy Institute, the growth spurt is increasingly due to its profitability:

"Investment in crop-based fuel production, once dependent on government subsidies, is now driven by the price of oil," Brown writes. "With the
current price of ethanol double its cost of production, the conversion of agricultural commodities into fuel for cars has become hugely profitable. In the
United States, this means that investment in fuel distilleries is controlled by
the market, not by the government."[58]

Indeed, the productive capacity for biofuels in the United States will easily shoot past the federal Renewable Fuels Standard for 7.5 billion gallons per year (bgy) by 2012. The Renewable Fuels Association projects that the 85 new ethanol projects under construction in 2007 would bring ethanol production to 12 bgy by the end of 2008,[59] and A.G. Edwards projects U.S. ethanol capacity will be around 13 to 14 bgy by 2009.[60]

The growth in domestic biofuels has been impressive, but like other renewables, it's still just getting started. According to the *2007 Joint Outlook on Renewable Energy in America* from the American Council on Renewable Energy (ACORE), renewable fuels could supply 30 percent of motor fuels produced in the United States by 2025.[61]

Although intensive study and pilot projects in recent years have reduced the cost of producing cellulosic ethanol from $5.66 a gallon in 2001 to $2.26 in 2005, conventional ethanol from corn still costs anywhere from one-third to one-half less, according to the U.S. Department of Energy (DoE). So further research and government support are still crucial to developing a truly viable, commercial-scale cellulosic ethanol industry.[62]

The DoE has been instrumental in encouraging the cellulosic ethanol industry, and in 2007 awarded grants totaling up to $385 million to six companies to build commercial plants for its production. In total, the plants are expected to produce more than 130 mgy of the fuel.[63]

The first of the projects to break ground was Range Fuels, Inc., who in November 2007 began construction of the nation's first commercial cellulosic ethanol plant in Georgia. The plant will use a gasification process, rather than the enzymatic process, which should make it easier to scale up production without the constraint of expensive enzymes. Beginning with 20 mgy of ethanol starting in 2008, the plant should eventually have the capacity to produce over 100 mgy.[64]

The DoE awarded $40 million for another partnership with BlueFire Ethanol Fuels (OTCBB:BFRE) to build California's first two commercial cellulosic ethanol plants, which will be sited next to existing landfills. Green waste and other cellulosic material will be diverted from the landfills and made into ethanol and butanol (another type of alcohol) via a proprietary "Concentrated Acid Hydrolysis Technology Process," which uses recycled water. Together, the two plants should produce around 20 million gallons of fuel per year and be operational by 2010. The company hopes to replicate the design at the majority of an estimated 1,600 landfill sites nationwide.[65]

Pacific Ethanol (NASDAQ:PEIX) received a $24 million award from the DoE for the first cellulosic ethanol demonstration plant in the Northwest, which will use wheat straw, woodchips, and corn stover as feedstocks.

The plant is scheduled for completion by the end of 2009, and will have a capacity of 2.7 mgy.[66]

Another commercial plant that will make the fuel from woodchips and other nonfood agricultural products is planned for Michigan, to be built by the Mascoma Corporation.[67] The company also hopes to build the nation's first facility to produce cellulosic ethanol from switchgrass, in partnership with the University of Tennessee, which should produce 5 mgy starting in 2009.[68]

The first commercial wood-to-ethanol plant in the world was unveiled in 2007 in Osaka, Japan. The plant is expected to produce 370,000 gallons of ethanol per year, using fermentation technology developed by Verenium Corporation (NASDAQ:VRNM). Verenium, which already operates a pilot plant in Louisiana, is also building a demonstration-scale plant that will produce 1.4 mgy.[69] Interestingly, Verenium is also in the process of trying to identify new, more efficient enzymes by probing the digestive system of termites. After termites ingest wood, it's then converted to fermentable sugars. The microbes living symbiotically in the termites can achieve a 95 percent conversion in less than 24 hours.[70]

Imagine being able to apply this natural, biological system to a system that can be adapted to process biomass into sugars. The Department of Energy and the California Institute of Technology have partnered with Verenium to move this project forward.

Novozymes (which trades in Copenhagen under the symbol NZYM) was one of the earlier players in this market, producing enzymes that optimize the conversion of corn and barley into ethanol. Back in 2005, the company and the National Renewable Energy Laboratory completed a four-year initiative to reduce the cost of enzymes needed to produce ethanol from biomass waste. They took the cost from more than $5.00 a gallon in 2001 to between $0.10 and $0.18 per gallon in 2005.[71] This was one of the biggest leaps forward for commercializing biomass-to-ethanol production on a large scale. And today, Novozymes is one of the key players in enzyme development. Since 2003, the stock has delivered gains in excess of 460 percent.

SunOpta (NASDAQ:STKL), which is actually known primarily as an organic and natural foods play, operates a Bioprocess Group that designs and builds biomass conversion equipment that is used to produce cellulosic ethanol. Back in 2006, the company announced that it had shipped a pretreatment system for Abengoa's Bioenergy Research and Development pilot plant. Abengoa (which trades on the Madrid stock exchange under the symbol ABG) is the largest ethanol producer in Europe. When the announcement was made, the stock was trading around $5.30 a share. By October 2007, the stock hit a new high of $15.50—giving some Green Chip investors a gain of nearly 200 percent in less than two years.

Taking a different approach, ethanol developers Citrus Energy LLC and FPL Energy LLC (a subsidiary of FPL Group [NYSE:FPL]) are now planning to build a commercial-scale cellulosic ethanol facility on the grounds of a Florida citrus processor, which will convert citrus peels into ethanol. The plant is expected to produce 4 mgy.[72]

Several companies are looking at ways to turn corncobs—currently a waste product—into cellulosic ethanol. POET, the largest ethanol producer in the United States at over 1 bgy, expects to have a commercial product ready by 2013.[73] (POET is a privately held company, the current incarnation of the venerable Broin family company that first began experimenting with home-grown ethanol back in 1986.[74])

### The Biodiesel Market

Biodiesel production is taking off in the United States. The EIA projects that it is headed for a 16-fold increase, from 25 million gallons in 2005 to 400 million gallons in 2030. Biodiesel production tripled between 2004 and 2005, and again between 2005 and 2006, to 75 mgy.[75]

The number of biodiesel refineries more than tripled from 2004 to 2006. At the same time, the typical plant size also roughly tripled, from 30 mgy capacity to 100 mgy.[76]

The algae-to-biodiesel business is still in its infancy. Only demonstration plants have been built thus far, but the results have been promising enough that several trial commercial facilities are expected to be built between now and 2010. For example, the biodiesel producer Green Star Products, Inc. is building on the success of its first 40,000-liter demonstration plant and will break ground on its first commercial plant, a 100-acre facility, in 2008. If that project performs as expected, the company plans to move on to several 1,000-acre plants.[77]

Not to overstate the case for biodiesel, as we noted earlier, biodiesel is still only about 0.2 percent of the 38 bgy of all diesel used for transportation. For an utterly frivolous comparison, consider this: A Norwegian businessman in Miami has reportedly signed an agreement with a local hospital to take 3,000 gallons per week of human fat from liposuction, and process it into 2,600 gallons of biodiesel.[78] There are over 1,200 lipo surgeons in the United States,[79] so if there are three per clinic, and each clinic could provide the same volume of fat per week, that would make 54 mgy right there, or about three-quarters of the total 2006 biodiesel market!

India is set to become the world's biggest producer of biodiesel from jatropha. About 11 million hectares of land have been identified as potential jatropha plantation, and planting has already begun. According to the CEO of British jatropha fuel developer Helius Energy (which trades on the London Stock Exchange under the symbol HEGY), "Every hectare can produce 2.7 tonnes of oil and about 4 tonnes of biomass. Every 8,000 hectares of the plant can run a 1.5 megawatt station, enough to power 2,500 homes."[80] By our calculations, if all 11 million hectares of jatropha-growing land in India produced at the stated level, India could generate 2,063 MW of power from jatropha, enough for 3.4 million homes, or about 1.5 percent of India's total electricity-generating capacity.[81]

European and Indian firms have also begun buying land for potential jatropha cultivation in Africa. Among other large investors, oil company BP has announced its entry into the field, with a £32 million investment in a jatropha joint venture in India, southern Africa, and Southeast Asia. The venture hopes to plant one million hectares in China by 2011. By 2010, Swaziland expects to start up its first jatropha-fueled power station.[82]

## INCENTIVES

Every renewable-energy technology needs a boost at first to bring it up to a level where economies of scale and innovation can reduce costs, and biofuels are no exception.

Matt Hartwig, communications director at the Renewable Fuels Association, views the incentives as a temporary need. "I equate the government support of ethanol to the government electrifying rural America or helping build the transcontinental railroads," he said. "The government helped set it up, and once it was there, the private sector took it over."[83]

In late 2007, the United States passed a law that mandates blending 36 bgy of domestic alternative fuels like ethanol into motor fuels by 2022—a fivefold increase. Of that amount, the portion derived from cellulosic ethanol must be at least 3 percent by 2012, and 44 percent by 2022, or about 21 bgy. The contribution of cellulosic ethanol could drive the percentage of all transportation fuels from 3 percent ethanol today to 16 percent.[84] (To keep that 36 bgy target in perspective, it would displace only about 24 bgy—about 17 percent—of our 142 bgy consumption of gasoline in 2006 due to the lower energy content of ethanol.[85])

As we discussed in Chapter 2, the European Commission has presented draft laws setting a 20:20:20 target (20 percent of energy from renewables by 2020, plus a 20 percent reduction in carbon emissions). It also set a target to obtain 10 percent of all vehicle fuel from biofuels by 2020.[86] These goals raised the target from a previous EU mandate, calling for 5.75 percent of fuel consumption to come from biofuels by 2010.[87] According to recent Frost and

Sullivan research, approximately 224 mgy of biodiesel would have been needed to meet that target.[88]

Japan has set its own target to produce 500,000 kiloliters per year (about 132 mgy) of biofuels in fiscal 2010/11.[89] In pursuit of that goal, Japan is now building its first commercial ethanol plant, using non-food varieties of rice as the feedstock. It is expected to produce about 264,000 gallons per year by March 2009.[90]

These are just a few notable examples of some of the incentives that are on offer for biofuels worldwide. A database search of the U.S. Department of Agriculture's Foreign Agricultural Service Attaché Reports turned up articles from the past year on efforts in 30 different countries to research and demonstrate local biofuel potential, and incentives to encourage their deployment.[91]

From an investing perspective, then, biofuels have guaranteed demand far above current levels of production, and large research and development grants in the offing. It's hard to ask for a better investing scenario than that.

## THE FUTURE OF TRANSPORTATION

After all the data and models and projections on biofuels, what one really wants to know is: What is the future of transportation?

Our long-term view, given the decline in petroleum and the limits of growing biofuel feedstock for fuel, is that the future of transportation must be electric. Plug-in cars, inner-city and long-distance rail, electric buses, even electric and wind-assisted boats can meet nearly all of our transportation needs (except for air travel). And we believe it's feasible that all of that electricity could be produced from renewable sources.

Switching over to an all-electric transportation regime will take many decades. For as long as we have relatively available fossil fuels—assuming we are in fact about 17 years away from peak energy in 2025—we believe we can still build new electric infrastructure fairly rapidly. After that, it's going to get progressively harder and more expensive, and require alternative sources of energy.

This is where we believe the role of biofuels lies: not as a total replacement for petroleum, which is clearly beyond its capacity given the enormous amount of liquid fuels we consume, but as a transitional strategy to get us from the liquid fuel-dependent infrastructure that we have now to one that runs on renewably generated electricity. It's one of those "silver BBs" that can offset some portion of our petroleum demand, along with plug-in cars and rail and other strategies, giving us some time to adapt to a new transportation regime. And looking far into the future, say 100 years, biofuels will likely be the one source of liquid fuels we can still expect to produce in any significant quantity. Accordingly, we believe that biofuels have a very long future indeed.

# CHAPTER

## 10

# PLUGGED-IN PROFITS

Almost immediately following President Bush's famous "addicted to oil" speech in 2006, we saw a massive run on renewable energy stocks. We were also inundated with armchair analysts and know-it-all talk show hosts belly-aching about our addiction to oil. But the fact that so many were quick to jump on this addicted-to-oil bandwagon made the contrarian in us question that very idea.

Are we really addicted to oil? *Addiction* is a strong word. Having volunteered at a rehab clinic during my college years, I can assure you that watching a heroin addict detox and watching city-dwelling consumers roll their eyes while shelling out $100 to fill their SUVs are two entirely different situations.

Still, there's no denying the fact that oil is the slippery glue that holds our increasingly fragile infrastructure together. However, the word "addiction" indicates that we, as a society, have a compulsive physiological and psychological need for oil, as if oil were cigarettes or caffeine. So the question is, when you wake up in the morning, do you crave oil? Do you need it to get through the day?

On instinct, most would say yes. You do need it, because without oil, you don't have gas, and without gas, how the heck are you supposed to get to work, school, or even the grocery store? As much as we all want a clean environment in which to live, cars don't run on good intentions, and many Americans don't live within walking distance of their workplaces, shopping districts, and

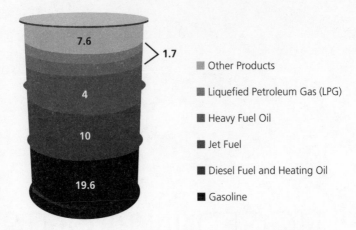

7.6

1.7

■ Other Products

■ Liquefied Petroleum Gas (LPG)

■ Heavy Fuel Oil

■ Jet Fuel

■ Diesel Fuel and Heating Oil

■ Gasoline

**FIGURE 10.1** *Products Made from a Barrel of Crude Oil (in Gallons)*

schools. So yes, assuming your car runs on gas (a safe assumption to make), your oil requirement is a real one.

Beyond our daily commutes, we also can't ignore the role oil plays within the shipping and distribution industries as well. Without diesel fuel, daily logistical operations would come to a standstill. So yes, we have a very strong reliance upon oil —especially when it comes to our transportation needs. As such, it's no surprise that more than half of every 42-gallon barrel of crude oil is used for gasoline and diesel fuel. (See Figure 10.1.)

But again, are we talking about an actual oil addiction here? Or is this merely a case of having a lack of options? In other words, if your car ran on something other than gasoline or diesel—something that was actually cheaper and more fuel efficient—would you still pay to fill your car with 87 octane because you're supposedly addicted? Of course not! And that's exactly why the concept of the United States having an addiction to oil must be examined. We do have options. It's just a matter of utilizing them.

## A DISCLAIMER

Before we go any further, we should preface the rest of this chapter by stating that what you're about to read is not an attack on Big Oil or the major automakers. Rather, it is simply an observation and an embracement of the responsible capitalist spirit.

For years, it has been suspected that Big Oil and the major automakers have launched numerous, strategic suppression and misinformation campaigns regarding alternatives to gas and the internal combustion engine. And who can blame them? If you ran a company that relied on a technology that you knew was antiquated, inefficient, and could easily be proven as such—would you invite any type of competition that could profit from that? Or would you do everything in your power to squash it?

Sure, one could assume that it would make sense to embrace new technologies and new options. But when you already have a trillion-dollar infrastructure in place that reliably (and consistently) supports a system that enables tremendous profits (as long as gas prices stay in check), good luck convincing millions of shareholders of anything but maintaining that revenue stream.

Call it what you want—conspiratorial nonsense or good business. But as oil prices remain above $100 a barrel and the reality of peak oil looms over our heads like an ominous black cloud, the truth about alternatives to oil and the conventional internal combustion engine are now surfacing. And the reason is simple. There's finally a market for this stuff!

And just like so many investors made fortunes in oil and auto manufacturing, we're going to do the same with the first alternative transportation market that will force auto manufacturers to embrace the future—or fall victim to it.

## OPEC'S BIGGEST FEAR

It wasn't long ago when OPEC President Edmund Daukoru stated that he was concerned about high oil prices, "because at a certain psychological level, alternative competing fuels would start to divert investment that should otherwise come to the oil sector."[1] And he was right. Homegrown renewable fuels like ethanol and biodiesel, while shaving only a very small percentage off our oil imports, still put a burn in OPEC's belly.

According to the National Commission on Energy Policy, with the new Renewable Fuels Standard and the increased fuel-efficiency standards in the Energy Independence and Security Act (HR 6), we will see the reduction of domestic oil use by 5 million barrels per day by 2030.[2] At $100 a barrel (and who knows what the price per barrel will be by 2030), that's $182.5 billion annually. Of course, that's just a drop in the bucket compared to the trillions of dollars of oil traded every year. But with each barrel consumed and each war fought over the stuff, the demand for alternatives to oil will continue to rise.

While we're only starting to see a glimmer of it now, when oil blows past $150 a barrel (and it will), all those who invested wisely in the right alternatives today are going to make a lot of money both in the short-term and well into the next decade. And when it comes to transportation, the most immediate solution that we believe will usher in a wave of opportunity will be found primarily in the plug-in hybrid electric vehicle (PHEV) sector.

## *Plugging In*

General Motors (GM) took a shot with the electric vehicle in the 1990s with its EV1, after the California Air Resources Board (CARB) adopted a zero-emission vehicle (ZEV) mandate. That mandate required that automakers' California market share include 2 percent ZEVs in 1998, 5 percent in 2001, and 10 percent in 2003.

Of course, this was not something the oil companies nor auto manufacturers were eager to embrace. Sure enough, a couple of years later, after an impressive manipulation of CARB's mandate by automakers, GM began strategically dismantling the EV1 altogether, halting production, laying off sales staff, and quietly removing the vehicles from the nation's highways. (For more on the EV1, we strongly recommend checking out the documentary *Who Killed the Electric Car?* at www.whokilledtheelectriccar.com.)

Earlier statements from GM regarding the demise of the EV1 seemed to have centered on the idea that there was a lack of demand. However, demand was actually quite robust, especially considering the obstacles the vehicle faced from the outset. At the time, the EV1 was available at only two locations; it was available only for lease (you could not actually buy one); an income of over $100,000 was required to qualify for the lease; you had to pass a written test to qualify for the lease; and you had to live within 50 miles of one of the two dealerships.[3]

Regardless, demand for PHEVs existed then and exists now—perhaps even more so today, now that the depletion of cheap oil resources is a very real threat, and has been validated as such. If this weren't the case, how else could you possibly explain the popularity of hybrid vehicles on the market today? You'd better believe these vehicles wouldn't exist without a robust demand for more fuel-efficient vehicles. Certainly Toyota has benefitted; by September 2007, the company had sold 1,188,255 hybrids worldwide.[4]

Of course, the hybrids on the market today also require gas—even if you're driving only a few miles. In our opinion, this gently appeases those who want fuel-efficiency, but allows Big Oil to maintain the status quo of oil necessity. PHEVs, on the other hand, require absolutely no gas at all. (Many of the PHEVs are also now being developed with flex-fuel engines. This way, some form of biofuel can kick in after the vehicle has gone beyond its all-electric mode.)

With the price of gas creeping up every day, loads of pollution being spewed into the air by conventional vehicles, and a continued reliance on foreign oil, do you honestly believe an alternative that could single-handedly change all of this wouldn't command interest from the car-buying public?

As for the cost factor, after accounting for carbon, natural capital, and security costs directly and indirectly connected to oil production and distribution, the PHEV is already cost-competitive, especially after stripping out the subsidies the oil industry receives under business as usual.

We believe we are at the dawn of a new age, and more importantly, a new industry that couldn't be in a more perfect position to exploit the coming oil implosion, and hand over significant gains for investors who are smart enough to tap this opportunity now.

### Never Buy Gasoline Again

Today's PHEVs are not inefficient bubble-car prototypes, as some would lead you to believe. In fact, many look and are operated just like the cars you and I drive today, only they're much more efficient. They can be charged in a standard home outlet, and some battery packs that are being used in today's PHEV conversions can power the vehicles for 30 miles on electric power alone. Since the average U.S. driver drives 29 miles per day, that 30-mile range is more than sufficient.[5]

Think about that for a second. Imagine being able to drive to and from work every day without using a single drop of gasoline. Better yet, imagine the effect that would have on the entire U.S. commuting population.

According to the U.S. Census Bureau, there are 105,046,395 commuters in the United States who drive to work, alone, in their cars, vans, or trucks. Assuming all the commuters drove 29 miles per day at 27.5 miles per gallon (which is an extremely generous figure), each commuter would burn through 1.05 gallons of gas per day.

## NOTE

Our figure of 27.5 miles per gallon is based on the National Highway Traffic Safety Administration's corporate average fuel economy standard (CAFE) for passenger cars as of December 18, 2007. On December 19, 2007, HR 6 was signed into law. That law mandates the raising of the fuel-efficiency standard to 35 miles per gallon by 2020. In comparison, Japan's fleet fuel economy averages for new vehicles in 2002 was 46.3 miles per gallon, with a 48 mpg goal for 2010.[6]

Based on our 105,046,395 commuters, you're looking at a consumption rate of 110,298,714.75 gallons of gasoline per day. At an average of $3.50 a gallon (the average cost at the time this was written), that's $386,045,501.62 hard-working Americans are paying every day—when they don't have to!

## SOMETHING TO
# THINK ABOUT

According to the Set America Free Coalition (organized by the Institute for the Analysis of Global Security), if all cars on the road were hybrids, and half were PHEVs by 2025, U.S. oil imports would be reduced by 8 million barrels per day.[7]

Of course, how long do you really think the national average for gasoline will hover around a $3.50 range? Even with temporary dips along the way, gas prices are sure to maintain a steady rise as oil demand continues to outpace supplies. Every time gas prices go up, so does the demand for alternatives, especially PHEVs, since they are the most efficient and cost-effective solution right now.

There are still some who will argue that the U.S. electric grid couldn't possibly handle all of these cars being plugged in, primarily because, in many areas of the country, the grid is already stressed on a regular basis. However, according to a report released in December 2006 by the DoE's Pacific Northwest National Laboratory, off-peak electricity production and transmission capacity could fuel 84 percent of the country's 220 million vehicles if they were PHEVs. And since most commuters would plug in at night, during off-peak hours, the utilities actually end up getting a new market for their product.

Another question posed by PHEV opponents has been the environmental impact of charging up these vehicles on a grid that relies primarily on coal and natural gas. But in the DoE's report, researchers noted that "even with today's power plants emitting greenhouse gases, the overall levels would be reduced because the entire process of moving a car one mile is more efficient using electricity than producing gasoline and burning it in a car's engine." And, of course, as many of the older coal-fired plants retire, newer solar and wind farms and geothermal plants will move in as replacements, thereby increasing the amount of clean energy being sent to the grid.

Even if you're not concerned with high gas prices or the environmental issues that surround the continued use of conventional internal combustion engines, perhaps the following quote from a jihadist web site will be the clincher:

*The killing of 10 American soldiers is nothing compared to the impact of the rise in oil prices on America and the disruption that it causes in the international economy.*

The greatest investment opportunities are often spawned from extreme crisis. Our reliance on oil, coupled with decades of complacency and special-interest influence, has put the world in an extremely vulnerable position. Moreover, it has become increasingly clear over the past few decades that relying on our elected officials to make the tough decisions that need to be made when it comes to curtailing our reliance on imported oil will amount to little more than election-time promises and bipartisan bickering, neither of which seem to ever accomplish a damn thing. That is why we're convinced that it is capitalism, not bureaucracy, that will dictate the future of transportation. It will reward real solutions in fuel efficiency, energy security, and good-old-fashioned ingenuity. In contrast, it will penalize the business-as-usual mentality that got us into this mess to begin with.

## INVESTMENT OPPORTUNITIES: PHEVs

When it comes to PHEVs, we're often asked which major automaker is the one that's going to take the lead, and more importantly, deliver for investors. But the fact is that we have no idea which major automaker will take the lead here, assuming any choose to do so. Moreover, even if they do come around (which is probably inevitable to some degree), you're definitely going to get a lot more bang for your buck with the companies developing the high-performance batteries that are needed to run PHEVs.

Lightweight and powerful—the high-performance-battery companies that can meet this requirement at a competitive cost will grab us and take us for one of the most profitable rides we'll see in this industry.

According to the Electronic Power Research Institute (EPRI), the performance and practicality of PHEVs depend on the weight of the battery in relation to the amount of energy it can store and the power it can produce.[8] The lighter and more compact the battery, the more efficient and practical the vehicle. The more energy the battery stores, the longer the vehicle's driving range.

Electric vehicles of the past used mostly lead-acid batteries, and had a very limited range. The considerable battery weight actually compromised vehicles' performance and efficiency. And lead-acid batteries also had a relatively short life, which meant several replacements over the life of a vehicle.

Today's advanced batteries, principally the nickel–metal hydride (NiMH) and the lithium-ion (Li-Ion) types, have demonstrated not only much higher energy storage and power delivery capabilities, but also far longer life in the deep-discharge cycling required for electric vehicle and PHEV propulsion. Specifically, for a given amount of energy storage, the NiMH battery weighs half as much as a lead-acid battery and produces two to four times the power. The Li-Ion battery weighs half as much as a NiMH battery and provides up to 100 percent more power than NiMH. Being the lightest and most powerful, the Li-Ion battery has a fundamental advantage.[9]

Also, unlike the lead-acid battery, both NiMH and Li-Ion batteries have the potential for very long life. NiMH batteries have been demonstrated to sustain more than 2,000 deep-discharge cycles—that is, cycles that nearly deplete the battery of its stored energy. The Li-Ion battery has sustained more than 3,000 deep-discharge cycles. These numbers correspond with the number of cycles a PHEV battery is expected to deliver over its 10-to-15-year life. NiMH and Li-Ion batteries can also be recycled to recover and reuse their valuable metal content and don't use any toxic materials.[10]

Of course, there's still one major hurdle for both NiMH and Li-Ion battery manufacturers to overcome: their high cost. Both NiMH and Li-Ion are more expensive to produce today than lead-acid batteries. The materials are more expensive, and the manufacturing methods are substantially more sophisticated. But just as the cost of the small NiMH and Li-Ion batteries used in cell phones has dropped dramatically, the cost of PHEV batteries is expected to drop as they go into mass production and as global competition for the market heats up.

The ultimate cost is likely to determine which applications develop first and to what degree PHEVs of extended electric range will penetrate the market. So it's no surprise that we pay close attention to developments in cost reduction from *any* high-performance battery company. Likewise, we consistently monitor technological developments and changes in market conditions that will ultimately favor quicker market penetration. In other words, we watch every high-performance battery company, every day, in an effort to capitalize on this stuff early.

In 2006, the PHEV industry picked up a lot of momentum. Whether it was because of high oil prices, global warming issues, or even the public attention drawn to the industry from the 2006 documentary *Who Killed the Electric Car?*, the attention this industry captured was not monopolized merely by consumers. Forward-thinking energy investors were also quickly ushered

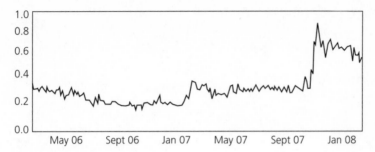

FIGURE 10.2 *Electrovaya*

into the fold after it was apparent that the potential growth could lead to some serious profits.

In fact, in late 2006, we actually wrote a special report about the future of the PHEV market, and identified three companies operating in the high-performance battery sector that, despite an enormous amount of speculation, saw their share prices rise significantly throughout 2007:

1. *Electrovaya (TSX:EFL):* While this company's SuperPolymer technology (a technology based on lithium-ion polymer battery technology) has primarily been used in batteries that provide longer runtimes for portable computers, mobile telephones, and other wireless devices, it was also used in the company's "Maya-100"—a zero-emission vehicle. (See Figure 10.2.)

   The Maya-100 delivered a 230-mile range with a top speed of 80 mpg. Its battery sported five times the energy density of lead-acid batteries, at less than one-third the weight.[11]

2. *Ener1 (AMEX:HEV):* This company develops lithium-ion battery systems for automakers that improve the performance, fuel-efficiency, and cost of hybrid electric vehicles. Their batteries are designed to be lighter in weight, occupy less space, provide more power and more energy, and have a longer life than the NiMH batteries found in today's hybrid vehicles.[12] (See Figure 10.3.)

3. *Altair Nanotechnologies, Inc. (NASDAQ:ALTI):* This company is actually a nanotech materials player, but it focuses a lot of attention on advanced materials for high-performance batteries. The company claims that its batteries offer three times the power of existing batteries, a high cycle life (10,000 to 15,000 charges versus 750 for existing batteries), and an extremely fast recharge time. This is also the company that's providing the battery packs for Phoenix Motorcars' all-electric sport utility truck.

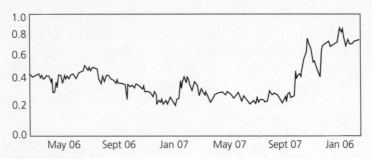

**FIGURE 10.3** *Ener1*

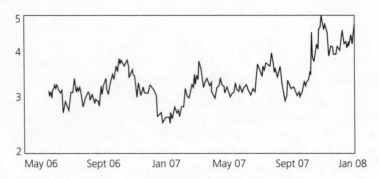

**FIGURE 10.4** *Altair Nanotechnologies, Inc.*

That vehicle gets more than 100 miles on one charge, has a top speed of 95 mph, and can run from 0 to 60 in 10 seconds. Again, this isn't some tinker-toy vehicle. It's an impressive sport utility truck that boasts 400 foot pounds of torque while still providing the standard features you'd expect on any vehicle these days, like power locks and air-conditioning.[13] (See Figure 10.4.)

Of course, this is a highly speculative market, and anything could have changed since the time we wrote this book. That's why it's imperative that you either follow these companies on a daily basis or follow the updates we send out from *Green Chip Stocks*. True, it does seem like an awful lot of work for just one market sector, but the preceding charts are just a sampling of what's to come.

Over the next few years, we expect Li-Ion battery companies to take the lead in the PHEV sector, as they are already displaying a technological superiority to both lead-acid and NiMH. During this time we expect to see an increase in investor attention and a significant rise in valuation of many of these stocks.

On the other hand, we also believe that lithium-ion's advantage could be disrupted in a few decades, due to potential supply issues. This doesn't mean the opportunities will disappear. In fact, we suspect they'll be around for some time. But as savvy investors, we always need to keep our eyes peeled for any new potential disruptions, no matter how far off they seem to be.

But before we get to that, let's take a closer look at what lithium is and where it comes from. After all, if we're investing in a sector that relies on a specific resource, shouldn't we know as much as we can about it?

## LITHIUM NIRVANA

Lithium is a metal that's extracted from only a few specific sources. It can come from the ore of a mineral called spodumene as lithium silicate—a type of glass. Or it can come from brine lakes and salt pans in the form of lithium carbonate and lithium chloride. Lithium-ion batteries can be made only from lithium that comes from brine lakes and salt pans, in the form of lithium carbonate.

In 2005, the world produced 23,589 tons of lithium. Of this, about 15,432 tons, or 65 percent, was lithium carbonate. Most of it (about 50%) came from Chile. There are deposits in Nevada, but those are in decline.

Bolivia holds one of the last and biggest untapped reserves in the world. But its attempts to exploit these reserves have been unsuccessful thus far. Political instability continues to act as a strong disincentive for western mining companies to operate there, not to mention the fact that the Bolivian government may never again permit the wholesale industrialization of their salt flats.[14]

We also can't ignore the fact that it takes 3.3 pounds of lithium carbonate per kWh of battery capacity. To be even moderately worthwhile, new hybrid-electric vehicles require a battery with at least an 8 kWh capacity. At that rate, it will require 26.4 pounds of lithium carbonate per battery.[15]

Collectively, the automobile industry is expected to sell nearly two million hybrids in 2010. However, we suspect that number will be significantly higher. At 26.4 pounds of lithium carbonate per vehicle, that's 52,800,000 pounds (or 26,400 tons). As mentioned earlier, the world produced only 15,432 tons in 2005—the same year that prices of lithium carbonate rose by 20 percent.[16]

## *The Zinc Solution?*

Of course, all this could change with technological advances in mining and production, new market conditions that could make the exploitation of these reserves worthwhile, and advances in nanotechnology that could enable increased efficiency but require less lithium carbonate. But as investors, we have to keep our options open. And for us, that often means sniffing out new technologies that, while they may not be making waves now, could offer significant growth opportunities in the future.

One area that we're watching for future growth is zinc, or more specifically, zinc-air fuel cells that could one day be used to power a new generation of zero-emission vehicles. Zinc-air cells have some pretty significant advantages.

For one, just 1.3 pounds of zinc can provide one kWh, while it takes 3.3 pounds of lithium carbonate to provide the same power. For another, there is about 35 times more zinc in the world than lithium.[17] At current production levels, it would take less than one year's supply of zinc to make 1 billion fuel cells—enough to power every car in the world. To do the same with lithium, it would take 75 years.[18]

The only disadvantage zinc has right now is the fact that lithium technology hit first. Zinc-air technology for vehicle applications is only now starting to gain some attention. But this technology is already quite common in the electronics industry. Zinc-air batteries can be found today in anything from hearing aids to calculators to watches.

The primary attraction for potential vehicle applications, however, is the simple fact that zinc maintains a significant cost advantage. Li-Ion batteries have end-user costs around $350/kWh, making the cost of an 8 kWh battery $2,800. But zinc-air fuel cells can cost less than $100/kWh, or $800 for an 8 kWh model.[19]

The zinc-air fuel cell has an energy density that's much greater than lithium-ion, too. (Energy density is the amount of energy stored in a given system per unit mass.) A lithium-ion battery has an energy density of 120 Wh/kg, so an 8 kWh battery would weigh in the neighborhood of 145 pounds. A zinc-air battery of the same power would weigh about 88 pounds. And with vehicles, lighter is always better![20]

The cost and functionality advantages alone could make the zinc-air fuel cell a top contender down the road. And the companies operating in the zinc-air arena right now could be some heavy hitters in the future.

Currently, there are only a few microcaps working primarily on zinc-air fuel cells. But since they're so small, and so speculative, not to mention the fact that the technology is in the earliest stages of development right now, it would be irresponsible to highlight them in this book. However, as these companies continue to develop, we'll monitor and report on them at *Green Chip Stocks*.

## GET YOUR MOTOR RUNNING

Beyond that which powers our next generation of PHEVs, we also need to pay close attention to the actual motors used in these low- and zero-emission vehicles. Because as we've seen in the past, it doesn't take much more than one significant deal to push some of these stocks into double-digit gain territory—almost overnight.

Take UQM Technologies (AMEX:UQM), for instance. UQM is a small, Colorado-based firm that develops electric power systems for electric vehicles. In November 2006, UQM announced that a young EV company called Phoenix Motorcars would be exhibiting its all-electric sport utility truck (SUT), powered by UQM's propulsion system, at the San Francisco International Auto Show. This was the first time we had an opportunity to see this thing in real life. But we weren't the only analysts checking out the SUT, and for good reason. Just two months later, UQM announced that it had received a $9.25 million production order from Phoenix. Those who picked up shares of UQM in November, after the auto show, witnessed a 64 percent gain in less than four months, as seen in Figure 10.5.

One can often find a host of analysts and researchers snooping around these auto shows. If there's a publicly traded company making some noise at such events, a quick pop in share price usually follows, assuming the company is actually worth anything.

We must reiterate though that this is still a highly speculative market sector in the short term. Although we're now witnessing the beginning of a social,

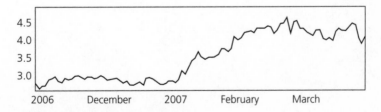

FIGURE 10.5 *UQM Technologies*

economic, and technological shift in the auto markets, placing bets on which company will lead the way in PHEVs is risky. That's why, instead of declaring a leader this early in the game, we simply monitor these motor companies, just like we monitor the battery companies, and report our findings along the way.

Ultimately, investors will benefit more from basing their decisions on the logical evolution of this market than picking a single stock right now.

PART

# THE SCIENCE AND PROFITABILITY OF CLIMATE CHANGE

*"You are here today because you recognize climate change as an opportunity as well as a threat. You understand that the shift to a low-carbon economy opens new revenue streams and creates new markets. You see the chance to usher in a new age of green economics and truly sustainable development. And you seek to address climate change in ways that are both affordable and promote prosperity."*

—From a speech given by UN Secretary Ban-Ki Moon at the Investor Summit for Climate Risk (2/13/2008)

# CHAPTER

## 11

# GLOBAL WARMING

## THE NOT-SO-GREAT DEBATE

More than a decade ago, in December 1997, the Kyoto Protocol was opened for ratification. It was the world's first major integrated attempt to take action on carbon emissions, in an effort to do something about global warming.

Since then, 174 nations have signed on, and 35 have agreed to firm caps on their emissions. In fact, the United States is the only developed nation in the world that continues to refuse to ratify the Kyoto Protocol, citing concerns about the economic cost, and rationalizing inaction by pointing to uncertainty in the data and theory. The media in the United States have been highly supportive of the government's resistance as well, continually referring to the global warming "debate."

Yet, the debate has been over for more than a decade. Only the countries who refuse to pay any cost to stop poisoning the world's atmosphere still call it a "debate." But that seems to be changing now. Over the course of George W. Bush's administration alone, their stance has gone from one of denying that global warming exists, to admitting that it exists but casting doubt on the causes of it, to admitting that human activity is at least partially to blame but still insisting that only nonbinding, voluntary reductions are palatable.

Hey, it's a start.

*Source:* TOLES © 2006, *Washington Post.* Reprinted with permission of Universal Press Syndicate. All rights reserved.

## THE CANARIES OF CLIMATE DOOM

Rather than embarking on a study of the science of climate change—a topic that would be far too large and complex for this single chapter—we simply refer the reader to the many studies that have already been done, and that continue to come out with increasing rapidity.

Just consider this small sample of recent headlines:[1]

- The Earth Today Stands in Imminent Peril

- Record 22°C Temperature in Arctic

- Arctic Melt Unnerves Scientists

- Billions Invested in 150 New Coal Powered Plants

- NASA Finds Greenland Ice Sheet Melting 150% More than Average
- Giant Ayles Ice Island Breaks in Two
- Europeans Angry after Bush Climate "Charade"
- Soil Erosion Danger
- Hunger Lurks as African Floods Recede
- Zimbabwe Harvests Only ⅓ of the Wheat It Needs
- Wheat Futures Rise for Eight Straight Days
- Global Food Shock Real
- Price of Eggs Set to Soar

Who can read these and not wonder why we aren't already taking aggressive action to counter global warming? Indeed, we have already had ample warnings from some major world authorities. Let's look at some of them.

## The Supreme Court and a Dozen States

In April 2007, the Supreme Court ruled that the EPA could no longer resist the demands of a dozen states and many environmental groups that it begin serious efforts to regulate greenhouse gases. "Under the clear terms of the Clean Air Act, EPA can avoid taking further action only if it determines that greenhouse gases do not contribute to climate change or if it provides some reasonable explanation," wrote Justice John Paul Stevens for the majority, putting the onus back on the global warming deniers to prove their position.

In short, the Supreme Court told the Bush administration to stop playing politics with global warming science, and get down to the dirty work of doing something about the problem. But, at the behest of the Bush administration, the EPA has continued to resist regulating CO2, forcing California and a dozen other states to move ahead with a lawsuit against the EPA that will grant them a waiver to set their own, higher standard. If the U.S. government is going to dig their heels in, the states reason, then they will have to take the lead.

A spokesman for California Governor Arnold Schwarzenegger was clear: "It's a priority for Californians to protect our environment, and if the federal government fails to act to protect our environment, we will take steps to do so ourselves."[2] The Governator himself, a Republican, said, "California is moving the United States beyond debate and doubt to action. What we are doing is changing the dynamic."[3]

"I believe that states have to step into a void created by a failure of federal action," said then New York Governor Eliot Spitzer. "The global warming issue is one where the current administration has first denied the scientific evidence and only recently begun to discuss the matter in a serious way."[4]

New York Attorney General Andrew M. Cuomo concurred: "New York State is moving forward on all cylinders to take aggressive action to curb global warming from both power plants and cars."

### *The United Nations*

Next to Al Gore's blockbuster 2006 documentary, *An Inconvenient Truth,* probably the biggest turning point in the public debate on global warming was prompted by four reports in 2007 by the IPCC: the UN's Intergovernmental Panel on Climate Change: "Climate Change 2007," the IPCC Fourth Assessment Report; "The Physical Science Basis" (February 2007); "Impacts, Adaptation and Vulnerability" (April 2007); and "Mitigation of Climate Change" (May 2007).[5]

The reports aroused a global response, by stating that greenhouse gas emissions from human activity were "very likely" to blame for causing global warming.

Three years in the making, these reports are the most comprehensive, global, and peer-reviewed studies on climate change ever written, bringing together the work of more than 800 scientists, more than 450 lead authors from more than 130 countries, and more than 2,500 expert reviewers. In short, the effort has been humanity's best attempt to date at getting the science right.

According to the IPCC, greenhouse gas emissions will continue to change the climate over the next 100 years, causing sea levels to rise by a half-meter. In turn, millions will be displaced from their coastal and low-lying communities, causing waves of environmental refugees. Snow in the mountains will disappear, desertification will intensify, oceans will die, and so will people, due to deadly heat waves, as world temps rise by some 3 to 5.8 degrees Celsius. Here are a few choice quotes from their reports:

- "Climate change could threaten the lives of hundreds of millions of people in the decades to come."

- "Even the most optimistic forecasts say the climate will continue to change and the planet will be irrevocably damaged. . . . In the absence of action to curb emissions of carbon dioxide and other heat-trapping gases, the future looks bleak."

- "Within two or three decades, there could be 1.5 billion people without enough water," creating "refugee crises like we've never seen."

- [Although some cold climates would enjoy warmer weather] "clearly there would be no winners left anywhere."

## THE EMPIRE STRIKES BACK

Big Oil wasn't about to take the IPCC's salvo lying down. On the very same day that the first IPCC report came out (on February 2, 2007), another story broke: The American Enterprise Institute (AEI) had sent letters out to scientists around the world, offering $10,000 to anyone who could undermine the IPCC's report, asking for essays that "thoughtfully explore the limitations of climate model outputs."[6]

Who is the AEI? It's a think tank that has received more than $1.6 million from ExxonMobil, with 20-plus staffers who have also worked as consultants to the Bush administration. Lee Raymond, former ExxonMobil CEO, is their board's vice chairman.

But Exxon's efforts go far beyond that. The month before, the Union of Concerned Scientists issued a report, showing that Exxon had spent some $16 million since 1998 to "seek to confuse the public on global warming science."[7]

Maybe the best summation of the Bush administration's denial of climate change came in the form of a letter to clients sent by the manager of Vice President Cheney's own personal investments, Jeremy Grantham. You read that right. (As far as we know, Mr. Cheney has not issued a response.) In the *GMO Quarterly Letter 2007*, he had a sharply worded essay entitled "While America Slept, 1982–2006: A Rant on Oil Dependency, Global Warming, and a Love of Feel-Good Data."[8] He wrote:

> Successive U.S. administrations have taken little interest in either oil substitution or climate change, and the current one has even seemed to have a vested interest in the idea that the science of climate change is uncertain. In fact, we have spent the last large chunk of time in this country with a strong bias to feel-good data at the expense of accurate, hard data in this field. This attitude seems to be reflected in the spin on U.S. economic success, which we've commented on several times, exaggerating, sometimes substantially, the absolute and relative performance of the U.S. economy. It has certainly been reflected in the general desire for environmental issues to be benign and optimistic or to simply go away.

> The U.S. policy approach to climate change (and other environmental issues) has been similarly casual in its unwillingness to plan for the long term. There is now nearly universal scientific agreement that fossil fuel use is causing a rise in global temperatures[. . .]. Yet the U.S. is the only country in which environmental data is steadily attacked in a well funded campaign of disinformation (funded mainly by one large oil company). This campaign has

*used and reused the solitary, plausible academic they can dig up, out of hundreds working in the field, plus one famous novelist—without qualifications in the field, but, still, for heaven's sake, widely quoted by the administration—and one Danish economist who really doesn't get Pascal's Paradox, but does seem to have shares in the Wall Street Journal.*

*Is it any wonder that the Bush team is now desperately trying to seem like it's on the right side of the climate change issue?*

Finally, in October 2007, the United Nations Environment Programme released its broadest and deepest assessment of the environment yet, in a major, 572-page report titled "Global Environment Outlook 4," which was prepared by 388 experts and scientists.[9] Its message was clear: "Climate change has become the greatest challenge facing humanity today."

Secretary-General Ban Ki-moon was unsparing in his foreword:

*Energy, climate change, industrial development and air pollution are critical items on the international agenda. Addressing them in unison creates many win-win opportunities and is crucial for sustainable development. We need to take joint action on a global scale to address climate change. There are many policy and technological options available to address the impending crisis, but we need the political will to seize them. I ask you to join the fight against climate change. If we do not act, the true cost of our failure will be borne by succeeding generations, starting with yours. That would be an unconscionable legacy; one which we must all join hands to avert.*

It's hard to be any clearer than that.

### The Pentagon

In 2004, a leaked report[10] from the Pentagon—not exactly a bastion of tree-huggers—predicted that rapid climate change may well set off global competition for food and water supplies and, in the worst scenarios, spark nuclear war. "Because of the potentially dire consequences, the risk of abrupt climate change . . . should be elevated beyond a scientific debate to a U.S. national security concern," it said.

In April 2007, a top panel of 11 retired military brass from all branches of the military, including five admirals and four generals, released a report that came to similar conclusions. Entitled "National Security and the Threat of Climate Change," it was commissioned by the Center for Naval Analyses, a nonprofit government-funded think tank.[11] Though initially several of the authors were skeptical of the topic, they spent months meeting with climate scientists, business leaders, and other experts, and found the experience "very sobering." Their conclusion was, "Climate change is a national security issue."

They said that the security consequences of climate change should be fully integrated into national defense strategies, and "the intelligence community should incorporate climate consequences into its National Intelligence Estimate." In other words, they insist that we stop pretending that climate change and defense are separate issues, and start working on them together. (To that list, we would also add peak oil.)

In March 2007, the U.S. Army War College sponsored a two-day conference on the subject, entitled "The National Security Implications of Global Climate Change." This marked the first time that we have ever heard a military expert connect global warming with the so-called global war on terror: "Climate change can provide the conditions that will extend the war on terror," said retired Admiral T. Joseph Lopez, former commander-in-chief of U.S. Naval Forces Europe and of Allied Forces, Southern Europe.

Why is this so? Because it's a "threat multiplier," exacerbating the conditions that tend to breed terrorist groups in volatile parts of the world, such as water and food shortages. For example, the report notes, nearly half the world gets about half of its drinking water from melting snow and glaciers that are quickly disappearing. The authors note that migrations of environmental refugees, strained border relations, and resource conflicts will make it hard for states to meet the basic needs of their residents, which will lead in turn to security problems.

But the climate change threat affects us all, as report author Vice Admiral Richard Truly admits: "It's going to happen to every country and every person in the whole world at the same time."

The report also showed that the commanders were wisely taking a long-term view of the problem. Said retired Marine Corps General Anthony C. Zinni, former commander of U.S. forces in the Middle East: "We will pay for this one way or another. We will pay to reduce greenhouse gas emissions today, and we'll have to take an economic hit of some kind. Or, we will pay the price later in military terms. And that will involve human lives. There will be a human toll."

## A CATASTROPHIC THREAT

All of the above studies have been based in large part on computer models, which must make assumptions about each of the modeled factors. Most of these models have predicted relatively slow, gradual changes: a few inches' rise in sea level over the next hundred years or so.

But we don't actually know all the factors yet, such that we can make reliable models. Nor can we say with any great certainty that our assumptions about those factors are good ones. In fact, recent observations from the real world are showing that the climate is changing much more quickly than even the more pessimistic models had projected.

Consider the analysis of scientist James Lovelock, who originally proposed the *Gaia hypothesis* (a view of the world as an intelligent self-regulating organism). He believes that the changes that we have put in motion by our emissions of carbon dioxide are now beyond our control, and we will have to live with some very hard consequences.

Lovelock believes that by the end of this century, the world's temperate zones (including North America and Europe) will warm up a full 14 degrees Fahrenheit—nearly double the most likely scenario presented in 2007 by the IPCC. Droughts and extreme weather will gradually become commonplace over the next decade, and by 2040, Europe will become a desert. The warm southern and southwestern states of the United States will become uninhabitable, along with many of the world's large coastal cities. And by 2100, epidemics, starvation, migration, and other afflictions will drive down the world's population from around 6.7 billion today to perhaps as little as half a billion, who will be living in the northernmost reaches of the planet.[12]

Now, Lovelock is the first to admit that all of the models are suspect and incomplete, and that he could be wrong. But there should be no doubt that the threat is so enormous, even a slight possibility is something we should be taking very seriously.

Moving beyond the models, though, aren't we already seeing the effects of climate change?

In October 2007, UN emergency relief coordinator Sir John Holmes warned that the unprecedented flooding, storms, and droughts the world has already experienced amounted to a climate change mega-disaster. "We are seeing the effects of climate change," he claimed. "Any year can be a freak but the pattern looks pretty clear to be honest. That's why we're trying . . . to say, of course you've got to deal with mitigation of emissions, but this is here and now, this is with us already."[13]

Another densely referenced scientific paper by the world's leading climate researchers, entitled "Climate Change and Trace Gases," has called climate change the "gravest threat" facing humanity.[14] "Recent greenhouse gas emissions place the Earth perilously close to dramatic climate change that could run out of control, with great dangers for humans and other creatures," the scientists said, calling for immediate and intense efforts to curb greenhouse gas emissions within just 10 years.

## Feedback Loops

Much of the newly heightened concern about climate change revolves around the problem of positive feedback loops—changes that fuel themselves. These little-understood phenomena could make even the most severe climate-change models look hopelessly conservative.

For example, over the past few years, the Arctic ice cap has been melting much more quickly than previously observed, and some scientists worry that it could disappear in the summer altogether by 2013. This opens a dangerous feedback loop: As the ice over the North Pole recedes, it leaves more open water, which absorbs more heat from the sun than ice does (ice reflects it back into space), which in turn makes the water warmer, which causes more ice to melt, and back around the loop we go.

This could mean that the IPCC's worst-case scenario will arrive a full century earlier than forecast! Consider the range of estimates in Figure 11.1.

But there are other, even more worrisome, potential feedback loops. For example, there is currently a vast amount of methane trapped at the bottom of the ocean, and in polar permafrost, in icy formations called *methane clathrates*. As these areas warm, massive amounts of methane could be released into the atmosphere. Now, as a greenhouse gas, methane is 21 times as destructive as carbon dioxide, so it could have a far more drastic warming effect than what we've seen so far, which would in turn cause the release of more methane.[15]

We know from geological records, such as the ice cores drilled from Antarctica, that the Earth can undergo extremely rapid changes, and flip from one climate state to another in just a few years. Such flips have occurred in the past, but none since the advent of complex human civilization.

This is probably the greatest worry climatologists have about climate change: that there won't be enough time for the masses of people at risk to migrate and adapt, making it impossible for them to survive such a flip today.

Unfortunately, climatology is still a very young science, and most of its practitioners will freely tell you that they're still at the stage of trying to identify all the important factors in climate modeling, let alone being at the point where their models would be considered accurately predictive. There are too many variables at work for us to really understand it, which is what allows global warming naysayers to refuse to take action because the data isn't all in yet.

## The Precautionary Principle

Rather than using that uncertainty to justify ignoring climate change, shouldn't it work the other way around? Shouldn't we be applying the *precautionary principle* instead?

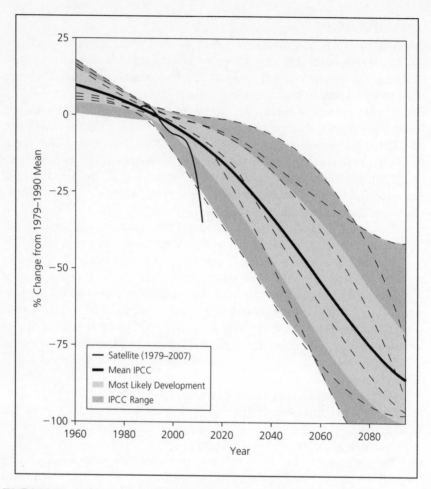

**FIGURE 11.1** *Arctic Sea Ice Loss Compared to IPCC Models*
*Source:* Dr. Asgeir Sorteberg, Center for Climate Research and University Center at Svalbarg, Norway, September 23, 2007, http://www.bjerknes.uib.no/pages. asp?kat=5&pid=101&lang=2 http://www.carbonequity.info/ images/seaice07.jpg.

The precautionary principle essentially boils down to such aphorisms as "Look before you leap" and "Do no harm," but there have been other interesting formulations.[16]

The Army's former chief of staff, General Gordon Sullivan, dismissed the Bush administration's position on that basis: "People are saying they want to be perfectly convinced about climate science projections," he said. "But speaking as a soldier, we never have 100 percent certainty. If you wait until you have 100 percent certainty, something bad is going to happen on the battlefield."

Put another way, the burden of proof that no damage will be done by some human activity should be upon its proponents, rather than allowing industry to do whatever it likes until somebody can prove beyond the legal shadow of a doubt that it's detrimental—which can be proved only after real damage is done!

It really comes down to something any child knows: If you can't fix it, don't break it. At the age of 12, Severn Suzuki, daughter of famed environmentalist and author Dr. David Suzuki, gave this scathing indictment of modern society at the UN 1992 Earth Summit:

> In my life, I have dreamt of seeing the great herds of wild animals, jungles and rainforests full of birds and butterflies, but now I wonder if they will even exist for my children to see.

> Did you have to worry about these little things when you were my age?

> All this is happening before our eyes and yet we act as if we have all the time we want and all the solutions. I'm only a child and I don't have all the solutions, but I want you to realize, neither do you!

> You don't know how to fix the holes in our ozone layer.

> You don't know how to bring salmon back up a dead stream.

> You don't know how to bring back an animal now extinct.

> And you can't bring back forests that once grew where there is now desert.

> If you don't know how to fix it, please stop breaking it!

If our leaders were children, instead of adults with vested interests in business, we'd wager that we wouldn't even be pretending to have a "debate" about global warming.

In fact, it's quite possible that it's already too late to stop climate change. It is estimated that if we were to cease all greenhouse gas emissions today, completely, worldwide, the emissions that are already in the atmosphere would continue to change the global weather patterns for some 100 years or more. We have already had an impact on the planet that we have no way to understand, let alone control.

## BUSINESS RISING TO THE CHALLENGE

With the worldwide scientific community making itself heard loud and clear, it only makes sense that the business community would brush politics aside and respond to the challenge. For example, eight American utility companies have "committed to investing $1 billion a year over three years to reduce carbon dioxide emissions by 5 million tons a year—the equivalent, they said, of taking about a million cars off the road."[17]

In fact, the developments from the business world have been coming fast and furious, faster than we can even keep up with. One such example came in 2007 from the Asia-Pacific Economic Cooperation (APEC), a WTO-like organization that promotes business and trade between the economies of Asia and North America.

The 21 member economies include the United States, Canada, Mexico, Russia, China, and Japan. They represent more than a third of the world's population and include the world's largest energy consumers, accounting for 60 percent of global energy demand.

Unlike the WTO, APEC makes purely voluntary agreements based on consensus, and makes nonbinding commitments. Thus, it is freer to operate outside the spheres of trade policy and treaty disputes.

Each year, APEC selects three key issues that it wants to address with presidents and prime ministers, and at its annual meeting, its members meet with the world leaders in small groups, to press for the changes they want to see.

So what burning issues do they want to bring to the attention of some of the most powerful people in the world this year? They want agreement on some common principles and goals on energy and global warming.

Again, the top businesspeople and leaders of more than half the world are going to seek agreement on a new path into the future. They see the twin challenges of peak oil and global warming straight ahead, just as we do here. And they're going to address them head-on, as if to prove once again that business is much more agile than politics.

For their part, the major banks have been hard on the heels of these forward-thinking businesses, ready to step up and provide solutions within their sphere of influence. A lobbying group called International Carbon Investors and Services is being established to urge industrialized nations to implement a carbon emission trading system based on the Kyoto Protocol, following the model set by the European Union's existing emission trading system.[18] The member banks include Morgan Stanley, Citigroup, Lehman Brothers Holdings, BNP Paribas, Barclays Capital, Deutsche Bank, Climate Change Capital, and Credit Suisse, along with a handful of major legal firms.

Of course, another major sector with plenty of skin in the climate change game is the insurance industry. An October 2007 report from the International Association of Insurance Supervisors found that many insurance companies are taking action to reduce their climate change risk and push for reduced emissions.

The report, "From Risk to Opportunity 2007: Insurer Responses to Climate Change,"[19] was commissioned by Ceres, a group of U.S. investors and clean energy supporters. Ceres directs the Investor Network on Climate Risk, which manages more than $4 trillion in assets. Mindy S. Lubber, president of Ceres, explained the report's findings:

*Insurers are beginning to respond to global warming—and not just by withdrawing from coastal markets with high financial exposure. We're seeing a rapid proliferation of products that will reduce climate-related financial losses, as well as the pollution causing global warming. Yet, insurer responses to date are not nearly sufficient given the scale of the challenge. We need more insurers, especially U.S. insurers, to step up.[20]*

The report found some 422 initiatives, incentives, and products offered by 190 insurers, reinsurers, brokers, and insurance organizations in 26 nations— more than double the number of products found in a similar report a year before.

Allianz, Europe's largest insurer, said that climate change–induced insured losses may increase by 37 percent within a decade. Other insurers, eyeing the billions in losses from unprecedented flooding, windstorms, and wildfires in 2007, believe climate change could put the future of the entire insurance industry in jeopardy.

## POLITICAL RESPONSE

Fortunately, the U.S. Congress and other political bodies have begun to take up the climate-change challenge, and the efforts are largely bipartisan. Despite the incredibly damaging divisive politics that have stymied dialogue in recent years, clearer heads on both sides of the aisle are recognizing that when the water levels rise to inundate our cities, they will drown the left and the right alike—or, to put it more positively, that free solar energy shines down the same on all of us.

One of the best examples is that of the Clinton Foundation. It has secured 187 commitments[21] from governments, banks, NGOs, foundations, educational institutions, and other groups, which has "avoided or reduced 20,070,524 tons of greenhouse gas emissions"[22] in just two years.

Several U.S. states have announced their own programs to build massive solar and wind electricity generation plants, such as a 300-megawatt solar plant that will be constructed in Florida, generating enough clean electricity to power nearly half a million homes.

Now, these measures are hardly a panacea, but they're a promising start, and we may reasonably expect as these major initial forays by the states into renewables prove their mettle that other states will quickly follow. Over half of the states in the union now have some sort of voter-approved renewable portfolio standard (RPS) to mandate production targets for electricity from renewables, and they're going to have to get it from somewhere.

For us, where they'll get it from is as clear as day: from all of the wonderful clean, green technologies we explore in this book.

## NATURAL CAPITAL

There is little doubt that the fundamentals of supply and demand are enough to dictate the future growth prospects and profitability of renewable energy. But the climate change angle provides even more value for renewable energy stocks, because finally, companies, individuals, and governments are attaching a price tag to environmental damage caused by carbon emissions.

Without decisive action, unchecked and unregulated man-made carbon emissions will lead to the deterioration of "natural capital." Natural capital includes all the resources we use on a regular basis, including water, minerals, fish, trees, oil, soil, air, and so on. It also encompasses living systems, such as grasslands, wetlands, estuaries, oceans, savannas, tundras, coral reefs, and rainforests.[23]

For years, little attention, if any, was given to natural capital. It was not valued. In fact, it was constantly being liquidated, further enabling the deterioration of ecosystem services that really represent the most important type of capital—things like the regulation of atmosphere and climate, the cycling of nutrients and water, pollination, control of pests and diseases, and the maintenance of biodiversity. These free, natural, and self-regulating services are worth trillions of dollars annually, but rarely has their value been reflected on balance sheets.[24] Now, however, all that is changing.

From extreme weather conditions to the destabilization of local climates, there is now little relevant debate over whether climate change contributes to the degradation of natural capital, and thus impinges on the overall profitability and long-term value of the corporate agenda.

This really is what gives the Kyoto Protocol the economic validation and support system it needs to move forward on the reduction of greenhouse gases responsible for climate change. And it is the basic framework of the Kyoto Protocol that has provided the economic validation and support system for carbon trading—just one more mechanism that adds even more value to renewable energy stocks. We'll discuss that in detail in the next chapter, as it has a direct effect on your renewable energy investments.

(For a more detailed analysis of natural capitalism, we strongly recommend reading *Natural Capitalism: Creating the Next Industrial Revolution.*[25] This is a book that no investor should be without.)

# CHAPTER

## 12

# PROFITING FROM POLLUTION

Renewable energy companies not only generate revenue by providing clean, green power for consumers, they can also generate additional revenue by simply offering an "offset" to companies that emit greenhouse gas emissions (GHG).

Through a system known as carbon trading, a market-based mechanism that helps mitigate the increase of carbon dioxide in the atmosphere, renewable energy companies (as well as other entities that provide offsets, such as forestry management companies, for instance) can sell carbon credits to companies that emit carbon dioxide into the atmosphere and want to balance out their emissions. The growing interest in carbon trading stems from emerging new legal requirements that investors expect to be established under the next administration in the United States.

According to analysts at New Carbon Finance, the U.S. carbon market could be valued at $1 trillion by 2020. Analysts at Point Carbon, a provider of analysis and news for carbon markets, have stated that the United States could be trading $600 billion in pollution credits annually by 2015. But what does that mean for Green Chip investors?

Well, for the companies in which we invest, it means a potentially huge valuation increase for those stocks. We'll get into the particulars of that in a moment. First, let's get into the meat and potatoes of how and why carbon markets exist.

## BUILDING MOMENTUM

The most recent data—though varying widely depending on the source—estimates that humans thrust anywhere from 26 to 36 billion metric tons of carbon dioxide into the atmosphere annually.[1] According to the U.S. Energy Information Administration (EIA), that number will rise to 40 billion by 2025 and to 43 billion by 2030, as seen in Figure 12.1.

Considering the potential global devastation that increased $CO_2$ emissions could cause, and more importantly, the acceptance of accurate, scientific data that supports this threat, it has been no surprise to see most of the global community come together over the past few years in support of levying a price on carbon emissions. This has been accomplished primarily through the framework set up by the Kyoto Protocol, which has made $CO_2$ either an asset or a liability—depending on which side of the trade one is on.

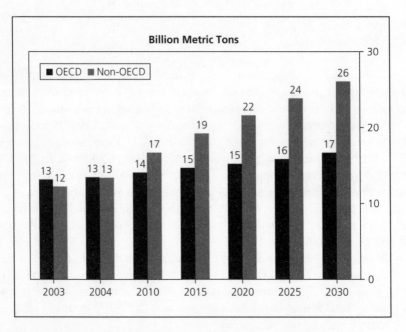

**FIGURE 12.1** *World Energy-Related Carbon Dioxide Emissions by Region, 2003–2030*
*Source:* Energy Information Administration, "International Energy Annual 2004" (May–July 2006), www.eia.doe.gov/iea.

Under the terms of the Kyoto Protocol, certain developed signatory nations must reduce their emissions by a determined percentage. If they do not, various trading mechanisms have been established to purchase Certified Emission Reductions (CERs) generated by carbon-offset projects certified by the UN.

Of course, it's impossible to continue without mentioning Australia's, Canada's, and the United States' abstention from Kyoto, primarily because the leaders of those countries have had their positions on Kyoto participation undermined by many of their constituents. In Australia, for example, Prime Minister John Howard—who opposed Kyoto—was ousted from his position in November 2007. He lost to Kevin Rudd, the Labor party leader who made climate change and the signing of Kyoto a large part of his campaign. Rudd ratified Kyoto immediately after taking the oath of office, and, almost instantly, there were calls for a booming Australian carbon trading operation. About a week after his election, representatives from the Australian Stock Exchange (ASX) indicated that a carbon futures market in Australia could be worth over $100 billion, based on a price of $25 per ton, and could be ready to launch as early as 2009.[2] It will take another three to five years for the system to be fully developed.

Canada, too, has shown signs of opposition to Kyoto. Although the Canadian government, under then liberal Prime Minister Jean Chrétien, ratified Kyoto in December 2002, the rise to power of conservative Prime Minister Stephen Harper in early 2006 has led to a straying from its policies. In April of that year, Canada reported it would have no chance of meeting its emission targets, and was thinking of pulling out. Then in May, it was announced that Kyoto-designated funding had been cut under the Harper administration while a new plan was developed to take its place. Since then, a number of bills have been introduced—some of them even passed by the House of Commons—but no real action has occurred, and the incumbent government has simply refused to cooperate, using many of the same hackneyed objections as its southerly neighbor.[3]

In the States, George W. Bush has been undermined by state governors who have formed regional partnerships to establish carbon trading networks. The first such partnership came in the form of the Regional Greenhouse Gas Initiative (RGGI—pronounced *Reggie*). RGGI was conceived in 2003, when then New York Governor George Pataki sent a letter to the governors of Northeastern and Mid-Atlantic states requesting their support in a new effort to help fight climate change. To date, 10 states participate in the initiative, including Connecticut, Delaware, Maine, Maryland, Massachusetts, New Hampshire, New Jersey, New York, Rhode Island, and Vermont. Pennsylvania, Washington, D.C., and eastern Canadian provinces participate as observers.

Action will commence in 2009 and is aimed at maintaining emissions at 2002-to-2004 levels by 2015. That period will be followed by a 10 percent reduction in those levels through 2020.

The second cooperative agreement to come out of the United States is the Western Regional Climate Action Initiative (WCI). Launched in February 2007, this initiative covers Arizona, California, New Mexico, Oregon, Utah, Washington, British Columbia, and Manitoba, with Colorado, Kansas, Nevada, Wyoming, Ontario, Quebec, Saskatchewan, and the Mexican state of Sonora participating in an observatory fashion. According to the group, "WCI is identifying, evaluating and implementing collective and cooperative ways to reduce greenhouse gases in the region."[4] An overall goal for reducing GHG emissions was set in August 2007 and, before the end of 2008, a market-based solution will be devised and implemented. In this context, "market-based" usually means a cap-and-trade mechanism.

On the heels of the WCI came the Midwestern Greenhouse Gas Reduction Accord (MGA). Signed in Milwaukee in November 2007, the MGA allows Illinois, Iowa, Kansas, Michigan, Minnesota, and Wisconsin to set GHG reduction goals and permits companies to buy and sell pollution credits to meet their targets. Illinois, Indiana, Kansas, Ohio, and South Dakota are participating more indirectly, calling for greater use of renewable fuels like wind and grain-based ethanol—of which the region has an abundance. Furthermore, as of December 2007, 740 cities in all 50 states have indicated support of Kyoto after Seattle Mayor Greg Nickels started a nationwide effort for them to do so.

Of course, there is also the consensus that once the Bush administration is replaced, the United States, based on new federal regulations and initiatives, will be ripe for a strong commodity bull market in carbon.

## COMMODITIZATION OF CARBON: HOW IT WORKS

Under the Kyoto Protocol, there are a few main Certified Emission Reduction (CER) mechanisms. The first, the Clean Development Mechanism (CDM), allows Kyoto signatories to offset their emissions—if they don't reduce them—by investing in clean technologies in developing countries or purchasing the resultant CERs from such projects. An industrialized country wishing to do this must first get consent from the developing country hosting the project. Then the project must be approved by the Executive Board of the CDM, which ensures the project would not have been developed if it weren't for the added incentives. Once the project is given the go-ahead, the saved emissions are calculated and approved by a third party, like the Norwegian company Det Norske Veritas, called a Designated Operational Entity (DOE). After all that, the difference in emissions is transferred into CERs at the rate of one per metric ton of prevented emissions, and sold.

The second, called Joint Implementation (JI), allows industrialized countries to do essentially the same thing as the CDM, only in other industrialized countries. There is also a government-backed trading program, which was created in conjunction with the Kyoto Protocol and adopted by the European Council in 2003, called the European Union Emission Trading Scheme (EUETS). Phase I of the EUETS commenced in January 2005 with all 27 member-states participating. In 2006, 1.1 billion CERs (each worth one metric ton of CO2) were channeled through the EUETS at a value of $24.3 billion. In the first half of 2007 alone, $17.3 billion had already made its way through the system.[5]

There is also a voluntary trading scheme implemented here in the United States, called the Chicago Climate Exchange (CCX). This market is still relatively small, but just about tripled its 2006 value by the end of 2007. Companies voluntarily join the CCX and agree to reduce their baseline emissions 6 percent by 2010. Once a company joins, it is then legally bound to meet its emission-reduction target.[6] To date, the CCX has more than 350 members, including market stalwarts like Ford, DuPont, and Motorola.

Companies can also join to supply the CCX with carbon credits. Emission reduction projects are certified by a third party and the resultant credits are sold on the exchange to companies that overshoot their emission limits. For example, the National Farmers Union has established a multistate program enabling crop growers to store carbon in their land through no-till cultivation practices and other land conservation efforts. The amount of carbon stored though these efforts is aggregated and then sold in the form of carbon credits on the exchange. The CCX has also initiated CER futures contracts through its exchange—the first such effort in the United States. Anyone with access to a clearing firm, like Barclays, Goldman Sachs, J.P. Morgan, or UBS, will be able to trade them.[7] The prices of the CERs are similar to the EUETS and can be affected by current supply and demand, as well as external factors like legislation and growing concern about climate change.

These futures contracts can be very lucrative. There are already over 750 carbon reduction projects registered with the United Nations. In one deal, a group of 10 investors bought 129 million credits from two projects in China. When sold in the Western market, the credits doubled in value and the investors stood to make over $1.35 billion.[8]

In 2006, companies in the United States, which didn't have mandatory emission caps, accounted for 68 percent of transactions in the voluntary carbon market, according to a report released by Ecosystem Marketplace and New Carbon Finance.[9] That same report stated that over 23.7 million metric tons of $CO_2$ equivalent were traded in voluntary carbon markets in 2006 at a value of $91 million, or $3.84 per metric ton.[10] But because the markets are voluntary, they're not always thoroughly regulated, and some of those emission cuts are not always verified. That has caused the voluntary carbon market to have its fair share of critics. Nonetheless, there is money to be made in carbon markets, both voluntary and mandatory, via carbon-offset projects, direct trading, and now even in carbon derivatives.

The carbon market, as a whole, is already worth $30 to $40 billion, depending on the source, and is forecast to grow to more than $1 trillion in less than 10 years.[11] According to a *New York Times* article, entitled "In London's Financial World, Carbon Trading Is the New Big Thing," "carbon will be the world's biggest commodity market, and it could become the world's biggest market overall."[12] A lofty assumption, no doubt, but consider this: Every year, humans generate 36 billion metric tons of $CO_2$—and counting—so the market is already potentially worth about $828 billion, using the current EU price in the mid-$20 range for a metric ton of carbon. As more and more governments start to regulate emissions, and as more companies—as we're already seeing—start to voluntarily limit their emissions, the demand for available carbon credits could skyrocket.

However, it should be noted that this is an industry dominated by the big boys of finance. The sudden surge of capital in the carbon market can be attributed to a flood of investment from large institutional firms. Those firms are investing billions and billions of dollars in what is known as project finance, or projects that are used to generate CERs. These projects can vary widely in type, from wind farms in the developing world to energy efficiency programs in downtown London, but in the end, either the UN or the verification arm of the EUETS must certify all projects. Then, once the CERs are reaped from a project, they are sold to companies or countries that need to meet their legally binding targets. Operations like this have become commonplace for big banks, hedge funds, and brokerage firms all over the world. In fact, many of those institutions now have dedicated carbon departments and have assigned positions such as Vice President of Carbon Markets or Senior Investment Officer for Carbon Finance.

Now, with rapid expansion in the carbon business, exchanges are looking for ways to get everyone in on the action, while turning a tidy profit for themselves in the process. The New York Stock Exchange has partnered with Caisse des Depot, a French bank, to launch a carbon trading market. This will permit $CO_2$ allowances and credits to be sold like any other commodity. Nymex Holdings, Inc., operator of the New York Mercantile Exchange and the U.S. home of crude oil futures trading has also thrown its hat into the carbon ring. In 2008, they began offering carbon futures contracts on their Green Exchange, much the same way crude is traded.[13]

Power players in the financial realm aren't just looking to finance carbon-reduction projects and trade CERs; they're also offering consulting and risk-mitigation strategies. Power generators are increasingly realizing that carbon has a price even before they generate emissions. That means corporations that generate emissions in any form now have to account for the price of carbon in their business models. Big banks are now calculating this new business risk before granting loans or underwriting IPOs. Morgan Stanley, for example, has created the Morgan Stanley Carbon Bank to aid companies in either reducing their emissions or going completely carbon neutral.[14] In February 2008, Citigroup, J.P. Morgan Chase, and Morgan Stanley announced that they were setting new "Carbon Principles" that would address carbon risks associated with financing electric power projects.[15]

## MORE BANG FOR YOUR CARBON BUCK

Although the generation and trading of carbon credits and the mitigation of carbon-associated risk is primarily dominated by large institutional firms, the profit potential for individual investors is still enormous. This is because the large funds that have been set up to finance emissions reduction projects are continually looking for new projects in which to invest—now more than ever. It's possible to invest directly in the companies that are pursuing and profiting from those projects.

Nearly any energy company operating renewable energy projects can sell carbon offsets to generate additional revenue, thereby adding even more value to the stock. For example, Italy's biggest utility, Enel (which trades in Milan under the symbol ENEL), has built up a portfolio of registered and implemented projects worth 56 million tonnes, with another 19 million tonnes of projects that are expected to be registered and implemented. The company has indicated that its CERs portfolio is worth more than $768.2 million.[16]

Consider the Chinese utility Huaneng (NYSE:HNP), which a couple of years ago struck a deal to sell credits to Spanish utility Endesa (which trades in Madrid under the symbol ELE). That deal alone set a negotiated price of $8.70 per ton, thereby generating about $375 million for Huaneng.[17]

## WHERE DO WE GO FROM HERE?

Under the Clean Development Mechanism (CDM), large investment firms first went after the low-hanging fruit. They went into China, India, and other developing countries and cleaned up the dirtiest operations they could find.

As of 2007, China was supplying the market with 61 percent of traded carbon credits.[18] When the CDM was in its infancy, these projects yielded huge returns. What's more, just 3 percent of the registered carbon-reduction projects accounted for 55 percent of total CDM carbon reductions.[19]

Currently, there are some 864 projects registered under the CDM. These projects are preventing 171 million metric tons of carbon from entering the atmosphere every year, but that number is growing every day.[20] The current demand for CERs is as high as 500 million metric tons. You can see why more projects are needed.

Although the United States hasn't ratified Kyoto, it is primarily the technology that's coming out of the United States that is driving these projects, especially as the carbon fruit gets harder and harder to pick. But with over 2,500 carbon-reduction projects in the pipeline, there are still plenty of opportunities to come, as evidenced by Figure 12.2.

The most promising opportunities for emissions-related profits will be in the realms of energy efficiency and demand-side management, which we discussed in detail in Chapter 7. But there are also opportunities for carbon

| CER Data by Host Country | | |
|---|---|---|
| CDM PIPELINE | Projects | Annual CERS |
| In Pipeline | > 2,600 | N/A |
| Registered | 844 | 174,268,851 |
| Requesting Registration | 53 | 12,986,794 |
| CDM PIPELINE—2012 CERS | | Expected |
| In Pipeline | | > 2,500,000,000 |
| From Registered Projects | | > 1,080,000,000 |
| Requesting Registration | | > 60,000,000 |

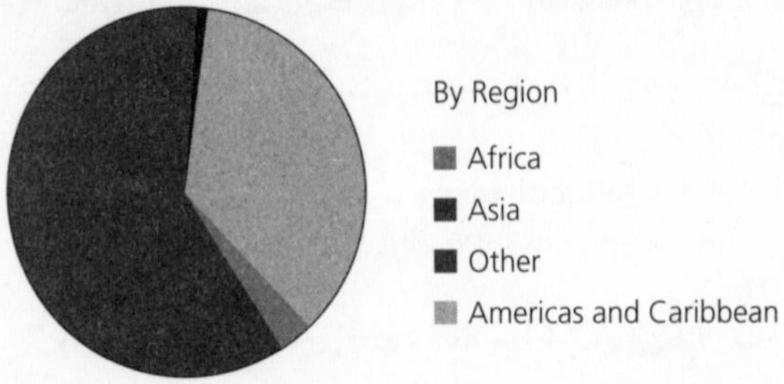

By Region
■ Africa
■ Asia
■ Other
■ Americas and Caribbean

FIGURE 12.2  *Certified Emission Reduction Data by Region*

aggregators, verifiers, and consultants. Companies like Climate Exchange Plc (which owns the Chicago Climate Exchange and trades in London under the symbol CLE), Trading Emissions (which trades in London under the symbol TRE), and the Ecosecurities Group (which trades in London under the symbol ECO) are all seeing, and will continue to see, a piece of the action. When the United States does enact some type of mandated trading scheme, we expect an increase in overall profitability for renewable energy companies as CERs become an additional source of revenue. A wealth of carbon-related IPOs will also likely flood the market pending such an announcement.

## BUYER BEWARE

For all the benefits and opportunities the carbon market presents, there are still a few possible drawbacks. It is, after all, a fairly new market, and there are still kinks to be worked out. Even those that have been involved since the beginning have less than 10 years' experience. Naturally, there have been claims of fraud, specifically about the verification—or lack thereof—of carbon credits, and about a scheme called "double counting" in which emission-reduction projects get more credits than they should. At one point, the pessimism about carbon markets was so high that the World Wildlife Fund called for more transparency in Kyoto controls, after claiming that up to 20 percent of UN carbon credits lacked "environmental credibility."[21] Also coming under scrutiny was an apparent loophole in the CDM allowing hydrofluorocarbon 23, a greenhouse gas, to be destroyed for the generation of carbon credits. This gas is a byproduct of refrigerant generation and is destroyed rather cheaply, rendering the sale of resultant CERs extremely lucrative. That loophole has since been closed.

Some of the questions surrounding carbon trading lie outside the realm of the market's maturity. A handful of environmental groups assert that the CDM is being used to deflect any meaningful domestic action to curb emissions because rich nations are simply outsourcing emission reductions to poorer countries, much as they do with manufacturing. Others have argued that capping emissions could slow the growth of the world's industrial markets, but the data on this is inconclusive, as there are widespread uncertainties in all the economic variables involved. To date, the most comprehensive reports have declared that emission reductions to Kyoto standards would cost countries about 1 percent of their gross domestic product (GDP). Other studies have claimed that doing nothing would cost those countries up to 20 percent of their GDP.[22]

Despite continuing debate, however, the Kyoto Protocol does not expire until 2012 and its successor is already being negotiated. The current participation of large global banks—in a long-term role—reflects the changing attitudes toward a cap-and-trade system. And with billions of investment dollars continually pouring in, it looks as though carbon trading will be around for years to come. The participation of the United States in any sort of international trading scheme would undoubtedly give the industry even more support and, more and more, it looks like that is eventually going to happen. In the mid- to long-term, we expect the easiest carbon cleanup opportunities in China and India to disappear, as those nations become increasingly developed. Future carbon-reduction projects may come from the continents of Africa and South America, where the development of renewable energy and the destruction of rainforests are both accelerating. Under the first phase of Kyoto, forestry projects were not allowed to generate CERs, but that seems likely to change in the next phase. If that does happen, Indonesia could also see a rise in CER generation and investment.

Indeed, the future of the carbon market looks strong and profitable, so long as it's played the right way. Profits from this sector will continue to flourish despite the opposition. Kinks will be worked out and loopholes closed, and soon the carbon market will be wholly adopted by financial communities and laypeople alike. We expect to see parts of the carbon market intrude into everyday life as retirement plans, hedge funds, and exchange-traded funds all begin to adopt some form of carbon practice. As this market continues to develop, we'll continue to show investors how they can profit from all of this at *Green Chip Stocks*.

# CONCLUSION

# THE GREATEST INVESTMENT OPPORTUNITY OF THE TWENTY-FIRST CENTURY

Imagine the year is 1908, and a skinny, middle-aged man by the name of Henry Ford asks you if you'd like to invest in his new company that's about to mass-produce a vehicle called the *horseless carriage*—a European invention that he believes will change the entire landscape of the United States. But not only that, he also asks you if you'd like to invest in a young, seven-year-old oil company called the Texas Company (also known as *Texaco*) and a tire manufacturer called Firestone that would soon be supplying the tires for these horseless carriages. Knowing everything you know now, would you take him up on his offer?

I know, it seems like a pretty dumb question. But back in those days, there were a lot of folks who couldn't wrap their minds around the idea that this new horseless carriage would actually be accepted, on a large scale, by the general public. In fact, many initially saw them as nothing more than expensive toys for the wealthy and eccentric. So, trying to convince the average investor that this industry would eventually become one of the most profitable in U.S. history was certainly a challenge. But investors who did believe, and had the foresight to look to the future instead of muddling around in the past, became some of the country's wealthiest individuals. And those who ignored it missed out, and most likely became one of the loyal Ford, Texaco, and Firestone customers for years to come—as well as their children, their children's children, and so on.

Today we are in a similar situation. Here we are, faced with an enormous opportunity to invest in something that's going to change the entire landscape of the world. Yet there are those who continue to question and doubt the validity of renewable energy, just like those before us who questioned and doubted many of the things we take for granted today. Take a look:

- "This 'telephone' has too many shortcomings to be seriously considered as a practical form of communication. The device is inherently of no value to us."—Western Union internal memo, 1878.

- "Radio has no future."—Lord Kelvin, British mathematician and physicist, 1897.

- "[Television] won't be able to hold on to any market it captures after the first six months. People will soon get tired of staring at a plywood box every night."—Darryl Zanuck, head of 20th Century–Fox, 1946.

- "Rail travel at high speed is not possible because passengers, unable to breathe, would die of asphyxia."—Dr. Dionysus Lardner, Professor of Natural Philosophy and Astronomy at University College, London, 1823.

- "Airplanes are interesting toys but of no military value."—Marshal Ferdinand Foch, French military strategist, 1911.

- "There is no reason for any individual to have a computer in their home."—Kenneth Olsen, president and founder of Digital Equipment Corporation, 1977.

And here's our favorite:

- In 1903, the president of the Michigan Savings Bank told Henry Ford's lawyer, Horace Rackham: "The horse is here to stay, but the automobile is only a novelty—a fad."

Fortunately, Rackham didn't listen, and invested $5,000 in Ford stock. He later sold it for $12.5 million.

As green chip investors, we have chosen not to accept the premise that renewable energy is merely a novelty or fad. Instead, we are embracing what we believe is an industry that will offer the greatest investment opportunity of the twenty-first century. And we're not alone. The fact is, some of the smartest, richest, and most innovative individuals and companies are investing in renewable energy right now:

- Billionaire Richard Branson is investing $3 billion in efforts to find renewable energy sources that will help get the world off oil and coal.

■ Oil tycoon T. Boone Pickens is investing in wind, building the country's largest wind-energy project in the Texas Panhandle.

■ Switching its light bulbs in its ceiling fan displays, Wal-Mart expects to save $7 million a year by investing in more efficient lighting. The company is also installing solar power systems in 22 of its Wal-Mart stores, Sam's Clubs, and distribution centers. It's estimated that these systems will save the company as much as 20 million kWh per year.

■ GE has committed $6 billion to investments in renewable energy by 2010.

■ John Doerr and his firm Kleiner Perkins Caufield and Byers have invested more than $200 million in alternative-energy companies.

■ Google invested in a 1.6 MW PV system at its headquarters, generating enough electricity to offset approximately 30 percent of the building's normal peak electricity consumption.

■ As of December 2007, Goldman Sachs has invested over $2 billion in renewable-energy projects.

There is no doubt that a movement is under way. It's being led by the world's largest corporations and investment banks as well as local businesses and, of course, individual investors like you. It is a movement that consistently battles against manipulated markets, politicians on the take, and a long history of misinformation; yet it continues to thrive because the basic fundamentals of supply and demand allow it to do so. As we've already discussed throughout this book:

■ The peak of global oil production (all liquids, including unconventional oil) will likely occur within two years.

■ Coal could peak in China (the world's largest coal producer) anywhere between 2012 and 2020. In the United States (the world's second largest coal producer), coal, in terms of energy content, may have already peaked nearly a decade ago.

■ The global peak of uranium production will likely be around 2025 to 2030.

■ The global peak of natural gas production will likely occur around 2025.

So what's left? What will fill the void in the next 10 to 20 years?

■ Enough electric power for the entire country could be generated by covering about 9 percent of Nevada with parabolic trough systems. This is a plot of land roughly 100 miles on each side.[1]

■ There are about 14 million quads of recoverable geothermal energy beneath U.S. soil.[2] That's about 140,000 times our current energy consumption.[3]

■ If all cars on the road were hybrids, and half were PHEVs by 2025, U.S. oil imports would be reduced by 8 million barrels per day.[4] That's roughly 80 percent of our total oil imports.

■ If we replaced every light bulb in the United States with an energy-efficient compact-fluorescent lamp, we would save enough energy to shut down, or avoid building, 90 power plants.[5]

■ The U.S. Department of Energy has estimated that there is enough potential offshore wind energy off the coast of the United States to cover nearly all the current installed U.S. electrical capacity.[6]

And that's just in the United States—a country with a long history of having perhaps the most hostile environment when it comes to integrating renewable energy. But all that is changing; because at the end of the day, no matter how you try to spin it, manipulate it, or downright lie about it, the end of our fossil fuel–based economy is near. And if you want to run computers, light and heat buildings, transport food, medicine, and clothing, and generally maintain the level of existence we enjoy today because of the robust availability of cheap energy, there is absolutely no other solution than renewable energy. This is not just an opinion shared by optimists, environmentalists, and forward-thinking capitalists, either. This is a fact, and continues to be proven as fact with every single watt we consume and every single mile we drive.

So the question is, *Do you want to get on board now, and have the opportunity to profit from all of this?* Or do you want to wait until renewable energy is integrated on a significant scale, use it on a regular basis, and talk about how you knew this was coming after reading this book, but didn't invest because it was too risky? The latter decision is one that could keep you from making a lot of money.

There is little doubt that the companies operating within this industry today will ultimately become the dominant players in the overall energy generation and transportation mix of tomorrow. Moreover, based on little more than our insatiable energy consumption and lack of conventional supplies to meet our growing demand, this is probably one of the safest long-term bets you can make.

Think about it. Do you really think that 10 years from now, nearly every single vehicle on the road won't be a hybrid? Better yet, how much longer do you think it'll be before PHEVs with a minimum 30-mile all-electric range are available at your local dealership? Based on what we're seeing now, you can expect to start seeing these in about two to three years.

And what about utility-scale generation? Solar fields, geothermal power plants, and miles and miles of new wind farms are being constructed right now. New transmission to move this power is being developed right now. New technology that will soon make renewables cheaper than conventional energy sources (though technically, many already are) is being tested in labs and deployed all over the world, right now. And right now, you have the opportunity to capitalize on all of this.

But keep in mind that this industry moves fast. What you've read in this book is merely the beginning—an introduction. That's why we encourage you to visit www.greenchipstocks.com, where every day we update our readers on market conditions that affect the integration and overall profitability of renewable energy. We keep close tabs on all the renewable energy and global warming legislation that's being introduced, debated, and passed all over the world, and consistently report on new companies and new technologies that will usher in the next round of renewable energy profits for green chip investors.

Of course, we wouldn't be completely honest if we didn't disclose the fact that we also favor renewable energy because it's going to enable a cleaner, safer environment for future generations. It's going to help strengthen the global economy, lessen our overall dependence on foreign oil, and support the emergence of an environmentally and economically sustainable energy economy.

My friend, this is an industry that will usher in a new way of life for everyone, and a new generation of wealth for investors. Welcome to the greatest investment opportunity of the twenty-first century!

# NOTES

## Preface

1. Clean Edge, January 8, 2008, http://www.cleanedge.com/story.php?nID=5094.

## Chapter 1: The Global Energy Meltdown

1. Matthew Simmons, "The World's Giant Oilfields," Simmons & Company International, www.nps.edu/cebrowski/Docs/energy/giantoilfields.pdf.

2. Steve Andrews's notes from "A Strategic Perspective on 21st Century Energy Challenges," a presentation by Tom Petrie on June 18, 2007, in Denver, to the Institute of International Education, as cited in *Peak Oil Review*, June 25, 2007.

3. ASPO Newsletter 77, May 2007, www.aspo-global.org/newsletter/ASPOGlobal_Newsletter77.pdf.

4. GAO Report on Crude Oil (GAO-07-283), March 29, 2007.

5. *Oil & Gas Journal*, last updated January 1, 2007, as reported by www.eia.doe.gov/emeu/international/reserves.xls with these data notes: PennWell Corporation, *Oil & Gas Journal* 104.47 (December 18, 2006); data for the United States is from the Energy Information Administration, U.S. Crude Oil, Natural Gas, and Natural Gas Liquids Reserves, 2005 Annual Report, DOE/EIA-0216(2005), November 2006.

6. Ibid., p. 122.

7. Energy Information Administration/*Natural Gas Monthly*, December 2007, 2006 data, http://www.eia.doe.gov/pub/oil_gas/natural_gas/data_publications/natural_gas_monthly/current/pdf/table_01.pdf and http://tonto.eia.doe.gov/oog/ftparea/wogirs/xls/ngm05vmall.xls.

8. "Natural Gas Has Eight Years Left," review of a David Hughes presentation, *The Republic of East Vancouver*, February 2 to February 14, 2006, No. 131.

9. J. David Hughes, "Natural Gas in North America: Should We Be Worried?" October 26, 2006, http://www.aspo-usa.com/fall2006/presentations/pdf/Hughes_D_NatGas_Boston_2006.pdf.

10. http://www.aga.org/Template.cfm?Section=News&template=/ContentManagement/ContentDisplay.cfm&ContentID=18979.

11. "Vast Energy Projects Feel Heat from Rising Costs," Reuters, February 21, 2007, http://www.reuters.com/article/idUSL2124373220070221.

12. J. David Hughes, "Natural Gas in North America: Should We Be Worried?" October 26, 2006, www.aspo-usa.com/fall2006/presentations/pdf/Hughes_D_NatGas_Boston_2006.pdf.

13. EIA, 2006 data, http://tonto.eia.doe.gov/dnav/ng/ng_cons_sum_dcu_nus_a.htm.

14. "High Risk of Underinvestment in Power Generation in Current Climate of Uncertainty," IEA press release, May 3, 2007, www.iea.org/Textbase/press/pressdetail.asp?PRESS_REL_ID=224.

15. Milton Copulos, "Averting Disaster of Our Own Design," *EvWorld*, March 30, 2006, www.evworld.com/article.cfm?archive=1&storyid=1003&first=12951&end=12950.

16. Matthew L. Wald, "Science Panel Finds Fault with Estimates of Coal Supply," *New York Times*, June 21, 2007, www.nytimes.com/2007/06/21/business/21coal.html?ref=business.

17. Richard Heinberg, "Museletter #179: Burning the Furniture," *Global Public Media,* March 22, 2007, http://globalpublicmedia.com/richard_heinbergs_museletter_179_burning_the_furniture.

18. Matthew L. Wald, "Science Panel Finds Fault with Estimates of Coal Supply," *New York Times,* June 21, 2007, www.nytimes.com/2007/06/21/business/21coal.html?ref=business.

19. "Coal: Resources and Future Production," March 2007, Energy Watch Group, http://www.energywatchgroup.org/fileadmin/global/pdf/EWG-Coalreport_10_07_2007.pdf.

20. Energy Information Administration, "International Energy Outlook 2007," 2007, www.eia.doe.gov/oiaf/ieo/pdf/electricity.pdf.

21. Princeton University, "Overview of Reactors," http://blogs.princeton.edu/chm333/f2006/nuclear/04_nuclear_reactors/01_overview_of_reactors/.

22. Georgia State University, "Fast Breeder Reactors," http://hyperphysics.phy-astr.gsu.edu/hbase/nucene/fasbre.html.

23. Thomas B. Cochran, Christopher E. Paine, Geoffrey Fettus, Robert S. Norris, and Matthew G. McKinzie, "Position Paper: Commercial Nuclear Power," *Natural Resources Defense Council,* www.nrdc.org/nuclear/power/power.pdf.

24. Australian Uranium Association, "Nuclear Power Reactors," May 2007, www.uic.com.au/nip64.htm.

25. Australian Uranium Association, "Nuclear Power in the World Today," www.uic.com.au/nip07.htm.

26. Information Administration, "U.S. Nuclear Generation of Electricity," www.eia.doe.gov/cneaf/nuclear/page/nuc_generation/gensum.html.

27. Council on Foreign Relations, "Prepared Statement before the Select Committee on Energy Independence and Global Warming, U.S. House of Representatives," April 18, 2007, www.cfr.org/publication/13128/.

28. John Vidal, "Nuclear Expansion Is a Pipe Dream, Says Report," *Guardian Unlimited,* July 4, 2007, http://business.guardian.co.uk/story/0,,2117711,00.html.

29. *Star Phoenix,* "Nuclear Demand Will Outstrip Supply: CEO," June 30, 2007, www.canada.com/saskatoonstarphoenix/news/business/story.html?id=a96783d2-7976-43f4-9879-c3ae3262677c.

30. Jan Willem Storm van Leeuwen and Philip Smith, "Can Nuclear Power Provide Energy for the Future: Would It Solve the CO2-Emission Problem?" *Great Change,* June 16, 2002, http://greatchange.org/bb-thermochemical-nuclear_sustainability_rev.html.

31. Jan Willem Storm van Leeuwen, "Energy Security and Uranium Reserves," *Oxford Research Group,* July 2006, www.oxfordresearchgroup.org.uk/publications/briefing_papers/energyfactsheet4.php.

32. Ibid.

33. John Vidal, "Nuclear Expansion Is a Pipe Dream, Says Report," *Guardian Unlimited,* July 4, 2007, http://business.guardian.co.uk/story/0,,2117711,00.html.

34. Energy Watch Group, "Uranium Resources and Nuclear Energy," December 2006, www.lbst.de/publications/studies__e/2006/EWG-paper_1-06_Uranium-Resources-Nuclear-Energy_03DEC2006.pdf.

35. Ibid.

36. Ibid.

37. Ibid.

38. We make an educated guess that 75 years from now, the production of renewable-energy machines will be constrained by the loss of fossil fuels with which to make them.

39. Robert Hirsch and Roger Bezdek, "Peaking of World Oil Production Impacts, Mitigation, & Risk Management," February 2005, www.netl.doe.gov/publications/others/pdf/Oil_Peaking_NETL.pdf.

40. Ibid.

41. Remarks at the ASPO-USA conference in Houston, October 18, 2007, http://www.getreallist.com/article.php?story=20060829200211917.

## Chapter 2: The Solar Solution

1. Cleveland, Cutler, "Energy Quality, Net Energy, and the Coming Energy Transition," Department of Geography and Center for Energy and Environmental Studies, Boston University, http://web.mit.edu/2.813/www/2007%20Class%20Slides/EnergyQualityNetEnergyComingTransition.pdf.

2. "Solar Energy Types," Solar Energy Industries Association, http://www.seia.org/solartypes.php#csp.

3. Ibid.

4. "U.S. Solar Cell Market Increased 33 Percent in 2006," U.S. Department of Energy, March 28, 2007, http://www1.eere.energy.gov/solar/news_detail.html?news_id=10675.

5. "Approximately 45% of the cost of a silicon cell solar module is driven by the cost of the silicon wafer . . . ," http://www.solarbuzz.com/FastFactsIndustry.htm.

6. D. Kammen, K. Kapadia, and M. Fripp, "Putting Renewables to Work: How Many Jobs Can the Clean Energy Industry Generate?" Energy and Resources Group/Goldman School of Public Policy at University of California, Berkeley (2004).

7. "Research News," Lawrence Berkeley National Laboratory, http://www.lbl.gov/Science-Articles/Archive/MSD-full-spectrum-solar-cell.html.

8. Nanosolar's thin-film cells are produced by a process that in many ways resembles printing. Light-sensitive semiconductor particles are mixed into a kind of ink, which is printed onto a thin substrate of metal foil that's continuously pulled off a series of rolls. This highly efficient *roll-to-roll* technology makes it possible to produce a large volume of solar cells in a relatively small manufacturing space, further reducing costs. See http://biz.yahoo.com/hbusn/061030/102606_solar_siliconvalley_biz2.html?.v=1.

9. "California Approves Legislation for Million Solar Roofs," August 23, 2006, EERE Network News, U.S. Department of Energy, http://www.eere.energy.gov/news/news_detail.cfm/news_id=10210.

10. "Solar Cell Production Jumps 50 Percent in 2007," December 27, 2007, Earth Policy Institute, http://www.earthpolicy.org/Indicators/Solar/2007.htm.

11. "PV Costs to Decrease 40% by 2010," Renewable Energy Access, May 23, 2007, http://www.renewableenergyaccess.com/rea/news/story?id=48624.

12. "Report: U.S. Solar Cell Market Increased 33 Percent in 2006," March 28, 2007, U.S. Department of Energy, http://www1.eere.energy.gov/solar/news_detail.html?news_id=10675.

13. "Solar Cell Production Jumps 50 Percent in 2007," December 27, 2007, Earth Policy Institute, http://www.earthpolicy.org/Indicators/Solar/2007.htm.

14. Makower, Pernick, and Wilder, "Clean Energy Trends 2007," March 2007, Clean Edge, Inc.

15. "Solar Power Set to Shine Brightly," Worldwatch Institute, May 22, 2007, http://www.worldwatch.org/node/5086.

16. "2007 Survey of Energy Resources," World Energy Council 2007, p. 425.

17. Ibid.

18. "Green Energy: Solar's Big Boom," September 26, 2007, *San Jose Mercury News*, http://www.mercurynews.com/business/ci_7001523?nclick_check=1.

19. "Sunny Outlook: Can Sunshine Provide All U.S. Electricity?" September 19, 2007, *Scientific American.* http://www.sciam.com/article.cfm?articleId=1FC8E87E-E7F2-99DF-3253ADDFDBEC8D41.

20. "Green Energy: Solar's Big Boom," September 26, 2007, *San Jose Mercury News*, http://www .mercurynews.com/business/ci_7001523?nclick_check=1.

21. "Google, Microsoft, and Yahoo faced spiking energy demands from running the hundreds of thousands of servers they need to power an economy increasingly conducted over the Internet." See http://biz.yahoo.com/hbusn/061030/102606_solar_siliconvalley_biz2.html?.v=1.

22. "Cleaning Up," *The Economist*, May 31, 2007, http://www.economist.com/opinion/displayStory. cfm?Story_ID=9256652.

23. "Solar Power Set to Shine Brightly," Worldwatch Institute, May 22, 2007, http://www.worldwatch .org/node/5086.

24. Daniel M. Kammen, "The Rise of Renewable Energy," *Scientific American,* Vol. 295, No. 3 (2006), p. 86.

25. Akeena press release, January 8, 2008, http://akeena.net/cm/Press%20Release/jan0208.html.

26. "It's also economically competitive in some parts of the United States now—including Hawaii, where electricity is very expensive; Massachusetts and New York, where energy costs are high and local governments often support solar power; and California and Arizona, which have large remote areas and much sunlight." See http://gtresearchnews.gatech.edu/reshor/rh-sf97/solar.htm.

27. Richard Heinberg, "Museletter #179," http://globalpublicmedia.com/richard_heinbergs_museletter_ 179_burning_the_furniture.

28. Suzanne Charlé, "When Addressing Climate Change Is Good Business," February 20, 2007, strategy+business magazine, http://www.strategy-business.com/li/leadingideas/li00014?pg=all.

29. "Final Report on the Implementation of the Task Force Recommendations," Natural Resources Canada and U.S. Department of Energy, September 2006, http://www.oe.energy.gov/Document sandMedia/BlackoutFinalImplementationReport(2).pdf.

30. Pau Preuss, "Research at Advanced Light Source Promises Improved Solar Cell Efficiency," October 3, 1997, http://www.lbl.gov/Science-Articles/Archive/pure-solar-cells.html.

31. "Sunpower Announces High Power, Higher Efficiency Solar Panel," *Sunpower*, October 16, 2006, http://investors.sunpowercorp.com/releasedetail.cfm?ReleaseID=214653.

32. Lisa Zyga, "40% Efficient Solar Cells to Be Used for Solar Electricity," Physorg.com, June 1, 2007, http://www.physorg.com/news99904887.html.

33. Phil LoPiccolo, "Applied Sees Sparkling Growth with Solar Plans," *Solid State Technology*, http:// sst.pennnet.com/Articles/Article_Display.cfm?ARTICLE_ID=272075&dcmp=WaferNEWS.

34. Charles Gay, "The Solar Industry Continues to Gain Momentum," Renewable Energy Access, January 22, 2007, http://www.renewableenergyaccess.com/rea/news/reinsider/story;jsessionid= CC52AA008F8B4511820D723933B1C970?id=47178.

35. "Department of Energy to Invest More than $21 Million for Next Generation Solar Energy Projects," U.S. Department of Energy press release, November 8, 2007, http://www.energy.gov/ news/5690.htm.

36. "CEC—New Solar Homes Partnership," Database of State Incentives for Renewables and Efficiency (DSIRE), last updated 10/18/2007, http://www.dsireusa.org/library/includes/map.cfm? State=CA&CurrentPageId=1.

37. Kammen, p. 86.

38. Pew Center on Global Climate Change, "States with Renewable Portfolio Standards," August 2007, http://www.pewclimate.org/what_s_being_done/in_the_states/rps.cfm.

39. "A Preliminary Examination of the Supply and Demand Balance for Renewable Electricity," NREL, October 2007, NREL/TP-670-42266, http://www.nrel.gov/docs/fy08osti/42266.pdf.

40. "2006 Net System Power Report," April 2007, California Energy Commission Publication #CEC-300-2007-007, http://www.energy.ca.gov/2007publications/CEC-300-2007-007/CEC-300-2007-007.PDF.

41. "Green Energy: Solar's Big Boom," September 26, 2007, *San Jose Mercury News*, http://www.mercurynews.com/business/ci_7001523?nclick_check=1.

42. "2007 Integrated Energy Policy Report." The report notes: "This number only includes generator-reported electricity, not electricity produced by many small-scale photovoltaic installations throughout the state. Based on the Energy Commission's Renewable Energy Program records, the state has financed approximately 135,517 kilowatts (kW) of solar photovoltaic capacity. Assuming that each installed kW of PV generated 1,500 kWh in 2005, then the combined output of these PV systems would add another 203.3 gigawatt-hours to the gross system power totals."

43. "2007 Integrated Energy Policy Report."

44. "Report: U.S. Solar Cell Market Increased 33 Percent in 2006," March 28, 2007, U.S. Department of Energy, http://www1.eere.energy.gov/solar/news_detail.html?news_id=10675.

45. "World Sales of Solar Cells Jump 32 Percent," 2004, Earth Policy Institute, http://www.earth-policy.org/Indicators/2004/indicator12.htm.

46. 50States.com, "California Facts and Trivia," http://www.50states.com/facts/calif.htm.

47. Gizmag, "Flexible Modules Could Transform Windows and Buildings into Solar Panel," October 11, 2007, http://www.gizmag.com/go/8156/.

48. See http://www.bosch-presse.de/TBWebDB/en-US/Presstext.cfm?CFID=85463&CFTOKEN=908664ea781f5efb-8B365A50-DB1C-C525-95CA3AF46A63175E&ID=3219.

49. Jesse Broehl, "A New Chapter Begins for Concentrated Solar Power," Renewable Energy Access, February 11, 2006, http://www.renewableenergyaccess.com/rea/news/story?id=43336.

50. Ibid.

51. "EPRI to Lead Multi-Party Concentrating Solar Initiative," Renewable Energy Access, July 2, 2007, http://www.renewableenergyaccess.com/rea/news/printstory?id=49195.

## Chapter 3: Global Winds

1. "Drought Could Force Nuke-Plant Shutdowns," January 23, 2008, Associated Press, http://news.yahoo.com/s/ap/20080123/ap_on_re_us/drought_nuclear_power.

2. One quad = about 172 million barrels of oil, or 45 million tons of coal. *Source:* AWEA wind FAQ, citing DoE, http://www.awea.org/faq/wwt_potential.html#How%20much%20energy%20can%20wind%20supply%20worldwide.

3. *2007 Survey of Energy Resources,* World Energy Council 2007, http://www.worldenergy.org/publications/survey_of_energy_resources_2007/wave_energy/760.asp.

4. The WEC report assumes a 15 to 40 percent "load factor," which basically describes an average of its uptime. Wind is often assumed to have a 30 percent load factor, meaning that over the course of a year, a wind-generation site will produce about 30 percent of the power it would have produced if it were running full time. *Source:* British Wind Association, http://www.bwea.com/energy/rely.html.

5. *2007 Survey of Energy Resources,* World Energy Council 2007, http://www.worldenergy.org/publications/survey_of_energy_resources_2007/wave_energy/760.asp.

6. 1 meter per second = 2.24 mph.

7. *2007 Survey of Energy Resources,* World Energy Council 2007, http://www.worldenergy.org/publications/survey_of_energy_resources_2007/wave_energy/760.asp.

8. Ibid.

9. Ibid.

10. IEA Wind Energy 2006 Annual Report, http://www.ieawind.org/annual_reports.html. True to the nature of energy reporting, the numbers here don't match up. According to IEA, the total world-wide installed wind capacity at the end of 2006 was 61,855 MW, as contrasted with the 72,000 MW cited by the WEC. To that we say, "close enough for government work."

11. Compared to data from the IEA Key World Energy Statistics 2007 report.

12. *2007 Survey of Energy Resources,* World Energy Council 2007, http://www.worldenergy.org/publications/survey_of_energy_resources_2007/wave_energy/760.asp.

13. "Continuing Boom in Wind Energy—20 GW of New Capacity in 2007," European Wind Energy Association, January 18, 2008, http://tinyurl.com/2u7hd6.

14. Makower, Pernick, and Wilder, *Clean Energy Trends 2007*, March 2007, Clean Edge, Inc.

15. "Wind Force 12," Global Wind Energy Council, 2005, http://www.ewea.org/documents/wf12-2005.pdf.

16. AWEA wind FAQ, http://www.awea.org/faq/wwt_potential.html#How%20much%20energy%20can%20wind%20supply%20worldwide.

17. "Alternative Energy Hurt by a Windmill Shortage," July 9, 2007, *Wall Street Journal.*

18. Ibid.

19. "U.S. Continues to Lead the World in Wind Power Growth," May 31, 2007, U.S. Department of Energy, http://www.energy.gov/pricestrends/5091.htm.

20. *AWEA Third Quarter Market Report*, November 2007, American Wind Energy Association, http://www.awea.org/Projects/PDF/3Q_Market_Report_Nov2007.pdf.

21. *AWEA 2007 Market Report*, January 2008, American Wind Energy Association, http://www.awea.org/projects/pdf/Market_Report_Jan08.pdf.

22. "U.S. Continues to Lead the World in Wind Power Growth," May 31, 2007, U.S. Department of Energy. http://www.energy.gov/pricestrends/5091.htm.

23. *AWEA 2007 Market Report*, January 2008, American Wind Energy Association, http://www.awea.org/projects/pdf/Market_Report_Jan08.pdf.

24. "U.S. Wind Energy Projects," American Wind Energy Association, as of January 16, 2008, http://www.awea.org/Projects/.

25. AWEA press release, "Installed U.S. Wind Power Capacity Surged 45% in 2007," January 17, 2008, http://www.awea.org/newsroom/releases/AWEA_Market_Release_Q4_011708.html.

26. "Texas Leads Nation in Wind Power Capacity," *Dallas Morning News*, January 17, 2008, with reference to the *AWEA 2007 Market Report.*

27. "Texas Wind Blows with Green Power," August 17, 2003, Reuters.

28. "Horse Hollow Wind Energy Center Now Largest Wind Farm in the World," September 7, 2006, press release from FPL energy, http://www.fplenergy.com/news/contents/090706.shtml.

29. "2007 Joint Outlook on Renewable Energy in America—Summary Report," http://www.nrel.gov/analysis/collab_analysis/pdfs/2007/workshop_pres/ws07_plenary_eckhart.pdf.

30. "The Outlook on Renewable Energy in America," ACORE, January 2007, http://www.acore.org/pdfs/Outlook_Preview.pdf.

31. "EU Countries Get Renewable-Energy Targets," *Wall Street Journal*, January 24, 2008, http://online.wsj.com/article/SB120111704860410651.html.

32. "EU Energy: Revolution for the UK?" BBC News, January 24, 2008, http://news.bbc.co.uk/2/hi/science/nature/7206008.stm.

33. "Britain Will Need 12,500 Wind Farms to Satisfy EU Targets," *Independent UK*, January 24, 2008, http://www.independent.co.uk/environment/climate-change/britain-will-need-12500-wind-farms-to-satisfy-eu-targets-773145.html.

34. "Massive Increase in Wind Turbines on Horizon for UK," *The Scotsman*, January 24, 2008, http://news.scotsman.com/latestnews/Massive-increase-in-wind-turbines.3705262.jp.

35. "Renewable Energy Could Power Half the Nation," CNNMoney.com, May 2, 2007, http://money.cnn.com/2007/05/02/news/economy/renewables/index.htm.

36. "U.S. Continues to Lead the World in Wind Power Growth," May 31, 2007, U.S. Department of Energy, http://www.energy.gov/pricestrends/5091.htm.

37. "Wind Power Beats Nuclear, Says AD," *Dutch News*, 12 July 2007, http://www.dutchnews.nl/news/archives/2007/07/wind_power_beats_nuclear_says.php.

38. *2007 Survey of Energy Resources,* World Energy Council 2007, http://www.worldenergy.org/publications/survey_of_energy_resources_2007/wave_energy/760.asp.

39. "U.S. Continues to Lead the World in Wind Power Growth," May 31, 2007, U.S. Department of Energy, http://www.energy.gov/pricestrends/5091.htm.

40. Ibid.

41. Ibid.

42. AWEA press release, "Installed U.S. Wind Power Capacity Surged 45% in 2007," January 17, 2008, http://www.awea.org/newsroom/releases/AWEA_Market_Release_Q4_011708.html.

43. "Slower Boats to China as Ship Owners Save Fuel," Reuters, January 19, 2008, http://www.reuters.com/article/ousiv/idUSL1831298320080120.

44. "Wind Energy Update," NREL, January 23, 2008, http://www.eere.energy.gov/windandhydro/windpoweringamerica/pdfs/wpa/wpa_update.pdf.

45. "Wind Force 12," Global Wind Energy Council, 2005, http://www.ewea.org/documents/wf12-2005.pdf.

46. Timothy Gardner, "Global Carbon Trade Rose 80 Pct Last Year—Group," Reuters, January 21, 2008, http://www.planetark.com/dailynewsstory.cfm/newsid/46518/story.htm.

47. "EPA Looking at a Full Plate This Year," MarketWatch, January 28, 2008, http://www.marketwatch.com/news/story/epa-has-full-plate-emissions/story.aspx?guid=%7BCAB30CEA-9519-49C9-AB69-888C50F17D02%7D.

48. "Wind Energy Update," NREL, January 23, 2008, http://www.eere.energy.gov/windandhydro/windpoweringamerica/pdfs/wpa/wpa_update.pdf.

49. Ibid.

50. "Cheap Alternatives," *The Economist,* print edition, July 5, 2007, http://www.economist.com/finance/displaystory.cfm?story_id=9447965.

51. "Installed U.S. Wind Power Capacity Surged 45% in 2007," American Wind Energy Association Newsroom, January 17, 2008, http://www.awea.org/newsroom/releases/AWEA_Market_Release_Q4_011708.html.

52. Vestas, About Section, http://www.vestas.com/en/about-vestas.

53. "Owens Corning Introduces New Fabric for Wind Industry," *Composites World*, http://www.compositesworld.com/news/cwweekly/2006/August/cw110614.

54. "Developing Affordable, Clean, and Smart Energy for 21st Century California," California Energy Commission, March 2007, http://www.energy.ca.gov/2007publications/CEC-500-2007-020/CEC-500-2007-020-SD.PDF.

55. "D-Var Solutions," *American Superconductor*, http://www.amsuper.com/products/transmissiongrid/dvar.html.

56. "Offshore Wind Worldwide," British Wind Energy Association, http://www.bwea.com/offshore/worldwide.html.

57. Andrea Thompson, "Study Sees Wind Power Potential on East Coast," MSNBC, February 15, 2007, http://www.msnbc.msn.com/id/17170505/.

58. Ibid.

59. "A Framework for Offshore Wind Energy Development in the United States," Resolve, Inc., September 2005, http://www.mtpc.org/offshore/final_09_20.pdf.

## Chapter 4: The Heat Below

1. "Geothermal FAQs," U.S. Department of Energy, http://www1.eere.energy.gov/geothermal/faqs.html.

2. Geothermal Education Office, http://geothermal.marin.org/GEOpresentation/sld051.htm.

3. 1921: John D. Grant drills a well at The Geysers with the intention of generating electricity. This effort is unsuccessful, but one year later Grant meets with success across the valley at another site, and the first geothermal power plant in the United States goes into operation. See http://www1.eere.energy.gov/geothermal/history.html.

4. U.S. Energy Consumption by Energy Source, 2004 (Quadrillion Btu)—Geothermal Energy: 0.340, Solar Energy: 0.063, Wind Energy: 0.143. *Source: EIA* http://www.eia.doe.gov/cneaf/solar.renewables/page/geothermal/geothermal.html.

5. 1960: The country's first large-scale geothermal electricity-generating plant begins operation. Pacific Gas and Electric operates the plant, located at The Geysers. See http://www1.eere.energy.gov/geothermal/history.html.

6. "Geothermal FAQs," U.S. Department of Energy, http://www1.eere.energy.gov/geothermal/faqs.html.

7. U.S. Dept of Energy, "Geothermal Power Plants," http://www1.eere.energy.gov/geothermal/powerplants.html#binarycycle.

8. Fifty-five degrees at five feet depth is an average; each location has its own depth and temperature at which the ground temperature stabilizes.

9. "About Geothermal Energy," Geothermal Technologies Program, http://www.nrel.gov/geothermal/geoelectricity.html.

10. "Solar Energy to Power Geothermal Plant," RenewableEnergyAccess.com, December 12, 2007, http://www.renewableenergyaccess.com/rea/news/story?id=50820.

11. Ruggero Bertani, "World Geothermal Production in 2007," Enel, http://geoheat.oit.edu/bulletin/bull28-3/art3.pdf.

12. "Peak Energy: Geothermia Revisited," http://peakenergy.blogspot.com/2007/11/geothermia-revisited.html.

13. Scaling Geothermal for Reliable Baseload Power," October 5, 2007, http://www.renewableenergyaccess.com/rea/news/story?id=50159.

14. "Geothermal Energy," http://geoenergy.org//publications/reports/May2007GEAUpdateonUSGeothermalPowerProductionandDevelopment.pdf.

15. "We Have Just Begun to Tap Geothermal Energy's Potential, Industry Leader Tells Congressional Hearing," press release from Geothermal Energy Association, May 17, 2007. Transcript of testimony: www.geo-energy.org.

16. DoE, Geothermal Technologies Program, "California State Profile," http://www1.eere.energy.gov/geothermal/gpw/profile_california.html.

17. "Scaling Geothermal for Reliable Baseload Power," October 5, 2007, http://www.renewableenergyaccess.com/rea/news/story?id=50159.

18. Karl Gawell and Griffin Greenberg, "Update on World Geothermal Development," May 2007, http://www.geo-energy.org/publications/reports/GEA%20World%20Update%202007.pdf.

19. Ibid.

20. Presentation to the Society of Petroleum Engineers by Adrian Williams, "A 'Hot' Opportunity," October 16, 2007, http://victas.spe.org/images/victas/articles/74/Geodynamics.pdf.

21. "Geothermia Revisited," *Peak Energy*, http://peakenergy.blogspot.com/2007/11/geothermia-revisited.html.

22. Ibid.

23. Ruggero Bertani, "World Geothermal Production in 2007," Enel, http://geoheat.oit.edu/bulletin/bull28-3/art3.pdf.

24. "Energy Efficiency and Renewable Energy," U.S. Department of Energy, http://www1.eere.energy.gov/geothermal/pdfs/egs_chapter_3.pdf—the power.

25. "Primary Energy Overview," Energy Information Administration, http://www.eia.doe.gov/emeu/mer/pdf/pages/sec1_3.pdf.

26. Karl Gawell, "Geothermal Potential in the Gulf of Mexico," July 3, 2007, Renewable Energy Access, http://www.renewableenergyaccess.com/rea/news/ate/story?id=49161; Bruce D. Green and R. Gerald Nix, "Geothermal—The Energy Under Our Feet," November 2006, NREL/TP-840-40665, NREL, http://www1.eere.energy.gov/geothermal/pdfs/40665.pdf.

27. Kevin Bullis, "Abundant Power from Universal Geothermal Energy," *Technology Review*, August 1, 2007, http://www.technologyreview.com/read_article.aspx?id=17236&ch=biztech&sc=&pg=1.

28. "Scaling Geothermal for Reliable Baseload Power," October 5, 2007, http://www.renewableenergyaccess.com/rea/news/story?id=50159.

29. Geothermal Energy Association, http://www.geo-energy.org/publications/reports/GEA World Update 2007.pdf.

30. "Geothermal Energy," http://geoenergy.org//publications/reports/May2007GEAUpdateonUS-GeothermalPowerProductionandDevelopment.pdf.

31. Daniel J. Fleischmann, "Geothermal Resource Development in Nevada—2006," Geothermal Energy Association (GEA), December 2006, http://www.geo-energy.org/publications/reports/Geothermal%20Resource%20Development%20in%20Nevada%202006.pdf.

32. "Advanced Geothermal Research and Development Bill Passed," *Technology News Daily*, January 3, 2008, http://www.technologynewsdaily.com/node/8871.

33. "Geothermal Energy in the Western United States and Hawaii: Resources and Projected Electricity Supplies," September 1991, Energy Information Administration, DOE/EIA–0544.

## Chapter 5: What May Wash Up in the Tide

1. "Marine Energy Can Be Forecast," *USA Today*, April 18, 2007, http://www.usatoday.com/tech/science/2007-04-18-wave-power_N.htm.

2. W. Wayt Gibbs, "Plan B for Energy," *Scientific American,* Vol. 295, No. 3 (2006), p. 112.

3. Ibid., p. 112.

4. Tom Edwards, "Wave and Tidal Power: Harnessing the Energy of the Sea?," briefing for the Scottish Parliament Information Centre (SPICe), February 12, 2004, http://www.scottish.parliament.uk/business/research/briefings-04/sb04-09.pdf.

5. "Wave Energy," DISCOVER, December 2, 2005. http://www.discover.com/issues/dec-05/features/ocean-energy/.

6. "Wave Power," *Technology Review*, MIT, January 2002, http://www.technologyreview.com/Infotech/12731/?a=f.

7. World Energy Council, *Survey of Energy Resources 2007*, http://www.worldenergy.org/publications/survey_of_energy_resources_2007/default.asp.

8. "Wave and Tidal Power: Harnessing the Energy of the Sea?," briefing for the Scottish Parliament Information Centre (SPICe), February 12, 2004, http://www.scottish.parliament.uk/business/research/briefings-04/sb04-09.pdf.

9. Electricity consumption data: EIA, 2006, http://www.eia.doe.gov/cneaf/electricity/epa/epates.html.

10. "Wave & Tidal Energy Technology," Renewable Northwest Project, April 4, 2007, http://www.rnp.org/RenewTech/tech_wave.html#_edn2.

11. "Overview: EPRI Ocean Energy Program," IEA Ocean Energy Systems, November 16, 2005, p. 8, http://oceanenergy.epri.com/attachments/ocean/briefing/IEABriefingRB111705.pdf, p. 13.

12. National Public Radio, "Potential Power Source: The Ocean?," July 23, 2007, http://www.npr.org/templates/story/story.php?storyId=12169705.

13. "EERE Network News," http://www.eere.energy.gov/news/enn.cfm#id_11125.

14. "Tides Hold Promise of Electricity," *The Daily Herald* (Everett, WA), February 11, 2007, http://www.heraldnet.com/stories/07/02/11/100loc_a1sunpower001.cf.

15. "San Francisco could tap enough wave power at Ocean Beach to keep the entire city lit. . . . " http://www.sfgate.com/cgi-bin/article.cgi?f=/c/a/2006/06/25/BAGATJK5D51.DTL.

16. Electric Power Research Institute, "Overview: EPRI Ocean Energy Program," slide deck, Duke Global Change Center, September 14, 2006, http://archive.epri.com/oceanenergy/attachments/ocean/briefing/Duke_Sep_14.pdf.

17. "EERE Network News," http://www.eere.energy.gov/news/news_detail.cfm/news_id=11125.

18. "Wave Energy Report," http://www.wavenergy.co.nz/wetnz-2006-06.pdf.

19. "Progress on Wave Power Development," *The Scottish Government*, August 30, 2006, http://www.scotland.gov.uk/News/Releases/2006/08/30103302.

20. "Wave Energy," DISCOVER, December 2, 2005, http://www.discover.com/issues/dec-05/features/ocean-energy/.

21. "Pelamis Wave Power," http://www.oceanpd.com/docs/Eon%20PR.pdf.

22. "Wave Farm Gets More Funding," BBC News, http://news.bbc.co.uk/player/nol/newsid_6590000/newsid_6596400/6596463.stm?bw=nb&mp=wm&news=1#; "Wave Hub Project Gets Final Go-Ahead," *UK Trade and Investment*, November 20, 2007, http://www.ukinvest.gov.uk/OurWorld/4016381/en-GB.html.

23. "Scotland Launches Consultation on Marine Energy Potential," *Renewable Energy Focus*, April 11, 2007, http://www.renewableenergyfocus.com/articles/wave/bus_news/070411_scotlandmarine.html.

24. "Scotland Vows Support for Wave Power," August 30, 2006, Edie (Environmental Data Interactive Exchange), http://www.edie.net/news/news_story.asp?id=11937&channel=0.

25. Le Havre, France, February 1, 2006 (*Refocus Weekly* magazine), "Marine energy could generate 20% of Britain's electricity and a global business opportunity worth £600 billion, estimates a UK consulting firm."

26. "Since 1999, the British government has committed more than £25 million, or $46.7 million, to research and development and £50 million to commercialize that research, plus money to bring the energy into the electrical grid, he said." See http://www.nytimes.com/2006/08/03/business/

worldbusiness/03tides.html?ex=1312257600&en=a0172afbc7c00d14&ei=5088&partner=
rssnyt&emc=rss.

27. Gibbs, "Plan B," p. 112.

28. "General Electric, Norsk Hydro of Norway and E.ON of Germany have recently pledged money for new projects or investments in tiny marine energy companies. Commercial investment from big energy companies is expected to top $100 million this year." See http://www.nytimes.com/2006/08/03/business/worldbusiness/03tides.html?ex=1312257600&en=a0172afbc7c00d14&ei=5088&partner=rssnyt&emc=rss.

29. "£600bn EU Marine Energy Market," Renew On Line (UK) 62, extracts from NATTA's journal *Renew*, Issue No. 162, July–August 2006, http://eeru.open.ac.uk/natta/renewonline/rol62/12.htm.

30. World Energy Council, Survey of Energy Resources 2007, http://www.worldenergy.org/publications/survey_of_energy_resources_2007/default.asp.

31. Energy Information Administration, Glossary, http://www.eia.doe.gov/glossary/glossary_l.htm.

32. "Wave & Tidal Energy Technology," Renewable Northwest Project, April 4, 2007, http://www.rnp.org/RenewTech/tech_wave.html#_edn2.

33. "Key Marine Energy Component Technologies for Cost Reduction R&D—Draft Report," Carbon Trust, October 2006, http://www.carbontrust.co.uk/NR/rdonlyres/E05EAF0B-6E9F-44D8-ADD9-1FFDB17C983B/0/KeyComponentTechnologies_CostReduction_PublicRev1.pdf.

34. "Wave Technology," Finavera Renewables, Inc., http://www.finavera.com/en/wavetech (accessed December 10, 2007).

35. "Kinetic Hydropower Systems," Verdant Power, http://www.verdantpower.com/2000/01/31/what-is-kinetic-hydropower-2/ (accessed December 10, 2007).

36. "Wave Test Site," EMEC Orkney, http://www.emec.org.uk/pdf/emecwave_test_site.pdf (accessed December 10, 2007).

37. Mario de Queiroz, "Riding the Wave of the Future," World Business Council for Sustainable Development, http://www.wbcsd.org/plugins/DocSearch/details.asp?type=DocDet&ObjectId=MjA2MTQ.

## Chapter 6: What's That Smell?

1. "Biogas," U.S. Department of Energy, http://www.eere.energy.gov/afdc/fuels/emerging_biogas.html.

2. "Landfill Gas," Energy Information Administration, July 2007, http://www.eia.doe.gov/cneaf/solar.renewables/page/landfillgas/landfillgas.html.

3. "Natural Gas," Combined Heat and Power Application Center, http://www.chpcentermw.org/pdfs/060216_Commercial-Instiutional-Light%20Industrial.pdf.

4. Brian Guzzone and Mark Schlagenhauf, "Garbage In, Energy Out," Cogeneration and On-site Power Production, http://www.cospp.com/display_article/307885/122/CRTIS/none/none/Garbage-in,-energy-out—landfill-gas-opportunities-for-CHP-projects/.

5. Cliff Haefke, "Using Landfill Gas as an Alternative Energy Option," Combined Heat and Power Application Center, August 9, 2006, http://www1.eere.energy.gov/femp/pdfs/energy06_cliffhaefke.pdf.

6. "Landfill Gas Energy Projects and Candidate Landfills," Landfill Methane Outreach Program, http://www.epa.gov/lmop/docs/map.pdf.

7. "About Waste Management," Waste Management, http://www.wastemanagement.com/wm/about/Overview.asp.

8. "Housing Units," U.S. Census Bureau, http://www.census.gov/popest/housing/HU-EST2006.html.

9. "A Guide to Clean Development Mechanism Projects Related to Municipal Solid Waste Management," United Nations, http://unescap.org/esd/environment/publications/cdm/Guide.pdf.

10. "Landfill Gas to Energy for Federal Facilities," Federal Energy Management Program, http://www.epa.gov/lmop/res/pdf/bio-alt.pdf.

11. Brian Guzzone and Chad Leatherwood, "Landfill Gas Use Trends in the United States," BioCycle, September 2007, http://www.jgpress.com/archives/_free/001417.html.

12. "Background Information," Methane to Markets, http://www.methanetomarkets.org/landfills/landfills-bkgrd.htm.

13. See http://www.epa.gov/methanetomarkets/faq.htm#4.

14. FAQ, U.S. Environmental Protection Agency, http://www.epa.gov/methanetomarkets/faq.htm#2.

15. "Landfill Methane Outreach Program," U.S. Environmental Protection Agency, http://www.epa.gov/lmop/overview.htm.

16. "Landfill Methane Outreach Program, Benefits," U.S. Environmental Protection Agency, http://www.epa.gov/lmop/benefits.htm.

17. "The AgSTAR Program," U.S. Environmental Protection Agency, http://www.epa.gov/agstar/overview.html.

18. *Global Warming News*, United Nations, http://www.un.org/apps/news/story.asp?NewsID=20772&Cr=global&Cr1=warming.

19. "An Analysis of the Benefits of Farm-Scale Anaerobic Digesters in the United States," Sierra Club, September 2006, http://www.sierraclub.org/factoryfarms/factsheets/manuredigesterpaper.pdf.

20. "GE's Jenbacher Product Line," General Electric, http://www.gepower.com/prod_serv/products/recip_engines/en/index.htm.

21. "Landfill Gas Solutions," General Electric, http://www.gepower.com/corporate/ecomagination_home/landfill_gas_sol.htm.

22. "About Waste Management," Waste Management, http://www.wastemanagement.com/wm/about/Overview.asp.

23. Jim Johnson, "WM Makes Big Investment in Landfill Gas," *Waste News*, July 2007, http://wastenews.texterity.com /wastenews/20070709/?pg=1.

24. "Microgy Technology," Environmental Power, http://www.environmentalpower.com/companies/microgy/technology.php4.

25. Ibid.

26. Tejoori Limited, http://www.tejoori.com/index.php?id=41&tx_ttnews[pointer]=1&tx_ttnews[ttnews]=6&tx_ttnews[backPid]=31&cHash=5bd400169d.

27. "Power & Industrial Projects," DTE Energy, http://www.dteenergy.com/businesses/powerIndustrial.html.

28. "Small Landfill = UNTAPPED Energy Potential," U.S. Environmental Protection Agency, http://www.epa.gov/lmop/res/pdf/landfills.pdf.

29. Capstone Turbine, http://www.capstoneturbine.com/prodsol/solutions/rrbiogas.asp.

30. "FirmGreen Technology," FirmGreen, http://firmgreen.com/tech_landfill.htm.

## Chapter 7: The Efficiency Advantage

1. "New Report Touts Vast Energy Efficiency Potential in Texas," Natural Resources Defense Council, January 17, 2007, http://www.nrdc.org/media/2007/070117.asp.

2. "Energy Efficiency, California's Highest Priority Resource," California Public Utilities Commission, ftp://ftp.cpuc.ca.gov/Egy_Efficiency/CalCleanEng-English-Aug2006.pdf.

3. "Green Action Team Meeting," Green Building Initiative, October 31, 2007, http://www.documents.dgs.ca.gov/green/meetings/statusMD071031.pdf.

4. "About USGBC," U.S. Green Building Council, http://www.worldworkplace.org/media/kits/us_green.pdf.

5. "A Green Foundation for Architecture," Allianz, http://knowledge.allianz.com/en/globalissues/energy_co2/energy_efficiency/green_buildings_climate.html.

6. "Green Building Basics," California Integrated Waste Management Board, http://www.ciwmb.ca.gov/GreenBuilding/Basics.htm.

7. Gregory Kats, "Greening America's Schools," A Capital E Report, October 2006, http://www.usgbc.org/ShowFile.aspx?DocumentID=2908.

8. Project Profile: Joe Serna Jr. California EPA Headquarters Building, U.S. Green Building Council, http://www.usgbc.org/ShowFile.aspx?DocumentID=3383.

9. "The Costs and Financial Benefits of Green Buildings," U.S. Green Building Council, October 2003, http://www.usgbc.org/Docs/Resources/CA_report_GBbenefits.pdf.

10. "Cost of Green Revisited," Langdon Davis, July 2007, http://www.davislangdon.com/upload/images/publications/USA/The%20Cost%20of%20Green%20Revisited.pdf.

11. Peter Morris, "What Does Green Really Cost?" Langdon Davis, http://www.davislangdon.com/USA/Research/ResearchFinder/What-Does-Green-Really-Cost/.

12. "Efficient Lighting," Lawrence Berkeley National Laboratory, http://eetd.lbl.gov/l2m2/lighting.html.

13. "Compact Fluorescent Light Bulbs," Energy Star, http://www.energystar.gov/index.cfm?c=cfls.pr_cfls.

14. Josef Hebert, "Bush Signs Law Requiring Greater Energy Efficiency, More Ethanol," *Ag Weekly*, http://www.agweekly.com/articles/2008/01/11/news/ag_news/news60.txt.

15. "TCP, Inc. Responds to Adoption of Federal Energy Bill," TCP, Inc., December 19, 2007, http://www.tcpi.com/corp/Federal_Energy_Bill.aspx.

16. "News," Energy Efficiency and Renewable Energy, http://www.eere.energy.gov/news/news_detail.cfm/news_id=10473.

17. "LED Lighting Market to Reach $1 Billion in 2011," *LEDs* magazine, February 2007, http://www.ledsmagazine.com/news/4/2/11.

18. "The Market for High-Brightness LEDs in Lighting," Strategies Unlimited, January 2007, http://su.pennnet.com/report_display.cfm?rep_id=181.

19. "Cree Achieves Highest Efficacy from a High-Power LED," Cree Press Room, September 13, 2007, http://www.cree.com/press/press_detail.asp?i=1189687350946.

20. "Online Guide to Energy Efficient Commercial Equipment," American Council for an Energy Efficient Economy, http://aceee.org/ogeece/ch4_index.htm.

21. Amory Lovins, "Profitably Getting Off Coal: Negawatts," Yahoo! Green, June 7, 2007, http://green.yahoo.com/blog/amorylovins/2/profitably-getting-off-coal-negawatts.html.

22. "Industrial Applications," Raser Technologies, http://www.rasertech.com/apps_industrial_motors.html.

23. "Performance Spotlight: Kodak," Motor Decisions Matter, http://www.motorsmatter.org/case_studies/kodak_doe.pdf.

24. "Motor Management Success: Woodgrain Millwork, Inc.," Motor Decisions Matter, http://www.motorsmatter.org/case_studies/Woodgrain.pdf.

25. "Case Study: Weyerhaeuser," Motor Decisions Matter, http://www.motorsmatter.org/case_studies/Weyer.pdf.

26. "Motors: AC Induction Motors," Platts New Mexico, http://www.pnm.com/customers/tech_guides/PA_MO_frame.html.

27. Alan Zibel, "U.S. Says Electricity Demand Lower This Summer than Last," Associated Press, http://www.telegram.com/apps/pbcs.dll/article?AID=/20070518/NEWS/705180373/1002/NEWSLETTERS10.

28. Joel Makower, et al., "Clean Energy Trends 2007," March 2007, http://www.cleanedge.com/reports/Trends2007.pdf.

29. Ibid.

30. "The Status of Utility Demand-Side Management in South Carolina, 2004," South Carolina Energy Office, http://www.energy.sc.gov/publications/2004%20DSM%20Report.pdf.

31. "Phantom Load," Open Computing Facility, University of California Berkeley, http://www.ocf.berkeley.edu/~recycle/ssec/download/Phantom%20Load.pdf.

32. "Home and Office Electronics," U.S. Department of Energy, http://www1.eere.energy.gov/consumer/tips/home_office.html.

## Chapter 8: Foreign Oil: The Path to Suicide

1. Colin Campbell interview in http://www.rte.ie/tv/futureshock/av_20070618.html.

2. "Newsletter No. 77," May 2007, http://www.aspo-global.org/newsletter/ASPOGlobal_Newsletter77.pdf.

3. Matthew Simmons, "The World's Giant Oil Fields," http://www.nps.edu/cebrowski/Docs/energy/giantoilfields.pdf.

4. The Association for the Study of Peak Oil and Gas (ASPO), Newsletter No. 82, October 2007, https://aspo-ireland.org/newsletter/en/pdf/newsletter82_200706.pdf.

5. "Newsletter No. 77," May 2007, http://www.aspo-global.org/newsletter/ASPOGlobal_Newsletter77.pdf.

6. "Oilwatch Monthly," ASPO Netherlands, June 11, 2007, http://www.peakoil.nl/wp-content/uploads/2007/06/oilwatch_monthly_june_2007.pdf.

7. Export data from EIA, "Top World Oil Net Exporters, 2006," http://www.eia.doe.gov/emeu/cabs/topworldtables1_2.html.

8. "Oilwatch Monthly," *The Oil Drum*, December 2007, http://www.theoildrum.com/tag/oilwatch.

9. *Source:* Jeffrey J. Brown and Samuel Foucher, "Commentary: Declining Net Oil Exports—A Temporary Decline or a Long Term Trend?" *Peak Oil Review,* September 24, 2007 (pdf), http://www.aspo-usa.com/index.php?option=com_docman&task=doc_download&gid=465&Itemid=66.

10. The *ultimately recoverable resources* (URR) of an oil field, also sometimes referred to as the *estimated ultimate recovery* (EUR), is the total amount of oil that will have been recovered at the end of the field's life. This is distinguished from the *original oil in place* (OOIP, also referred to as *oil initially in place*, OIIP), which is the total amount of oil in the field, irrespective of how much will ever be recovered. The URR of a field is the OOIP multiplied by the *recovery rate*, which can vary depending on many factors, such as the characteristics of the field and the recovery methods employed.

11. See http://www.aspo-global.org/newsletter/ASPOGlobal_Newsletter77.pdf. Groups that generally support this view include ExxonMobil, Chevron, OPEC, Cambridge Energy Research Associates, and ASPO-Ireland, plus government agencies (IEA and US-EIA); all shared this view in October 2005 in Washington, D.C.

12. ASPO USA, http://www.aspo-usa.com/index.php?option=com_content&task=view&id=160 &Itemid=76.

13. "Oil Demand Seen Rising, Piling Pressure on OPEC," *The Gulf Times*, June 13, 2007, http:// www.gulf-times.com/site/topics/article.asp?cu_no=2&item_no=154842&version=1&template_ id=48&parent_id=28.

14. ASPO USA, http://www.aspo-usa.com/index.php?option=com_content&task=view&id=160& Itemid=76.

15. "Oil Prices Rise," *Yahoo! News,* October 15, 2007, http://news.yahoo.com/s/ap/20071015/ ap_on_bi_ge/oil_prices_23.

16. *Peak Oil Review*, Vol. 2, No. 43, October 22, 2007, item 3.

17. "International Petroleum Monthly," Energy Information Administration, December 12, 2007, http://www.eia.doe.gov/emeu/ipsr/t12.xls.

18. Richard Heinberg, *The Oil Depletion Protocol*, New Society Publishers, July 2006, p.78.

19. "Peak Oil Review," ASPO USA, October 8, 2007, http://www.aspo-usa.com/index.php?option =com_content&task=view&id=225&Itemid=91.

20. CNN Money, http://money.cnn.com/news/newsfeeds/articles/prnewswire/TO12517092007-1.htm.

21. Bengt Söderbergh, Fredrik Robelius, and Kjell Aleklett, "A Crash Program Scenario for the Canadian Oil Sands Industry," http://www.peakoil.net/uhdsg/20060608EPOSArticlePdf.pdf.

22. "Canadian Oil Sands," http://www.peakoil.net/uhdsg/OilSandCanada.pdf; "An Inconvenient Swede," Canadian Business Online, 22 October 2006, http://www.canadianbusiness.com/ markets/commodities/article.jsp?content=20061009_81365_81365.

23. Canadian Association of Petroleum Producers, http://www.capp.ca/raw.asp?x=1&dt=NTV&e= PDF&dn=112820. Production was 383 kb/d of synthetic crude from mining, and 609 kb/d bitu-men. In 1998, the numbers were 308 kb/d synthetic, and 282 kb/d bitumen. Increase for synthetic is 3% per year. Increase for bitumen is 11% per year. Overall, the increase is 8% per year. See http://www.its.caltech.edu/~rutledge/Hubbert's%20Peak,%20The%20Question%20of%20Coal, %20and%20Climate%20Change.ppt#387,21,Canadian Oil Sands.

24. "Trillions in Spending Needed to Meet Global Oil and Gas Demand, Analysis Shows," *International Herald Tribune*/The Associated Press, October 15, 2007, http://www.iht.com/articles/ ap/2007/10/15/business/NA-FIN-US-Oil---Gas-Spending.php.

25. Vaclav Smil, *Enriching the Earth: Fritz Haber, Carl Bosch, and the Transformation of World Food Production* (2001), ISBN 0-262-19449-X.

26. David Pimentel, "Food, Land, Population, and the U.S. Economy," Cornell University, and Mario Giampietro, Instituto Nazionale dell' Nutrizione, Rome.

27. "Transforming the Way DoD Looks at Energy," study by LMI, quoting Milton R. Copulos. See http://www.boston.com/news/nation/washington/articles/2007/05/01/pentagon_study_says_oil_ reliance_strains_military/?page=2.

28. Bill Moore, "The Hidden Cost of Our Oil Dependence," *EV World*, April 23, 2006, http://www .evworld.com/syndicated/evworld_article_1018.cfm.

29. Milton Copulos, "Averting Disaster of Our Own Design," *EV World*, March 30, 2006, http:// www.evworld.com/article.cfm?archive=1&storyid=1003&first=4957&end=4956.

30. Alan Drake, "A 10% Reduction in America's Oil Use in Ten to Twelve Years," ASPO-USA, July 2007, http://www.aspo-usa.com/index.php?option=com_content&task=view&id=168&Itemid=91.

## Chapter 9: Biofuels: More than Just Corn

1. A more complete treatment of alternative liquid fossil fuels is given in the author's previous book, *Profit from the Peak,* Brian Hicks and Chris Nelder, John Wiley & Sons, 2008.

2. "Biofuels: Is the Cure Worse than the Disease?" September 2007, Organisation for Economic Co-operation and Development (OECD), http://media.ft.com/cms/fb8b5078-5fdb-11dc-b0fe-0000779fd2ac.pdf.

3. "Brazil Is World's Ethanol Superpower," March 13, 2006, AP, http://www.cbsnews.com/stories/2006/03/13/tech/main1394254_page2.shtml.

4. Pure ethanol can be used as fuel in specially designed engines that have higher compression ratios and other modifications that maximize miles per gallon. 5. E85, a blend of 85 percent ethanol and 15 percent gasoline, can be put into more than 5 million U.S. vehicles that also run on gasoline. These flex-fuel vehicles, however, get fewer miles per gallon on E85. The fuel economy of a Chevy Tahoe dropped 27 percent when running on E85 compared with gasoline, according to *Consumer Reports* magazine.

5. E10, a fuel that is 10 percent ethanol, is an octane booster that also helps fuel burn more cleanly. It can be used in all gasoline-powered vehicles, according to the federal Energy Department. See http://seattletimes.nwsource.com/html/businesstechnology/2003305110_biofuel15.html.

6. "A new car can be made flex-fuel-capable for about $35."

7. "E85 FYI Newsletter," National Ethanol Vehicle Coalition, January 23, 2008, http://www.e85fuel.com/news/012308fyi.htm.

8. Laura Meckler, "Fill Up with Ethanol? One Obstacle Is Big Oil," *Wall Street Journal,* April 2, 2007, reprinted at http://www.consumerwatchdog.org/energy/nw/?postId=7641.

9. See http://www.e85refueling.com.

10. Daniel J. Weiss and Nat Gryll, "Flex-Fuel Bait and Switch," June 18, 2007, http://www.americanprogress.org/issues/2007/06/flexfuel.html.

11. "Fill Up with Ethanol? One Obstacle Is Big Oil," *Wall Street Journal,* April 3, 2007, http://online.wsj.com/article/SB117547886199856472.html.

12. "E85 Stations," http://e85vehicles.com/e85-stations.htm.

13. Renewable Fuels Association Ethanol Industry Outlook 2007, February 2007, http://www.ethanolrfa.org/objects/pdf/outlook/RFA_Outlook_2007.pdf.

14. Renewable Fuels Association, Industry Statistics, http://www.ethanolrfa.org/industry/statistics/#B.

15. "False Hopes and Cellulose," ASPO-USA, January 23, 2008, http://www.aspo-usa.com/index.php?option=com_content&task=view&id=302&Itemid=91.

16. *Energy Assurance Daily,* December 18, 2007, U.S. Department of Energy, http://www.oe.netl.doe.gov/docs/eads/ead121807.pdf.

17. Tom Doggett, "Ethanol to Take 30 pct of U.S. Corn Crop in 2012: GAO," Reuters, June 11, 2007, http://www.reuters.com/article/scienceNews/idUSN1149215820070611.

18. "2007 Monthly U.S. Fuel Ethanol Production/Demand," Renewable Fuels Association, http://www.ethanolrfa.org/industry/statistics/#B.

19. "This Week in Petroleum," Energy Information Administration, http://tonto.eia.doe.gov/oog/info/twip/twip.asp.

20. Tom Whipple, *Peak Oil Review,* June 18, 2007.

21. "U.S. Energy Law Drives Alternative to Corn Ethanol," December 19, 2007, Reuters, http://www.reuters.com/article/environmentNews/idUSN1959731820071220.

22. Ibid.

23. M.R. Schmer, K.P. Vogel, R.B. Mitchell, and R.K. Perrin, "Net Energy of Cellulosic Ethanol from Switchgrass," U.S. Department of Agriculture—Agricultural Research Service, University of Nebraska, January 7, 2008, http://www.pnas.org/cgi/content/abstract/0704767105v1.

24. Stephen Long, "Miscanthus: A Solution to U.S. Dependence on Foreign Oil?," April 25, 2006, http://www.aces.uiuc.edu/news/stories/news3623.html.

25. Patrick Mazza, "Biofuel Breakthroughs and the Cellulosic Fuels Revolution," Renewable Energy Access, May 28, 2007, http://www.renewableenergyaccess.com/rea/news/printstory;jsessionid=4AEA3C078CEB37FC687D14ABAA58140B?id=48637.

26. DOE Office of Energy Efficiency and Renewable Energy, http://www.eere.energy.gov/afdc/altfuel/bio_made.html.

27. DOE Office of Energy Efficiency and Renewable Energy, http://www.eere.energy.gov/afdc/altfuel/bio_benefits.html.

28. ". . . biodiesel has immediate appeal in that it does not require modifications of a diesel engine." See http://www.nytimes.com/2006/09/12/business/smallbusiness/12bio.html?ex=1315713600&en=0f141e75db5758b0&ei=5088&partner=rssnyt&emc=rss.

29. John Van Gerpen, "Business Management for Biodiesel Producers," August 2002–January 2004, National Renewable Energy Laboratory," http://www.nrel.gov/docs/fy04osti/36242.pdf.

30. "Mali's Farmers Discover a Weed's Potential Power," *New York Times*, September 9, 2007, http://www.nytimes.com/2007/09/09/world/africa/09biofuel.html?_r=1&em&ex=1189483200&en=b8f0eb75c65f04f3&ei=5087%0A&oref=slogin.

31. "Poison Plant Could Help to Cure the Planet," Times Online, July 28, 2007, http://www.timesonline.co.uk/tol/news/world/article2155351.ece.

32. Green Star Products, Inc. press release, "GSPI Signs Contract to Build Algae-to-Biodiesel Facility," November 13, 2007.

33. "A Promising Oil Alternative: Algae Energy," *Washington Post*, January 6, 2008, http://www.washingtonpost.com/wp-dyn/content/article/2008/01/03/AR2008010303907.html.

34. "The Greenest Green Fuel," *Popular Science*, July 1, 2007, http://www.popsci.com/scitech/article/2007-07/greenest-green-fuel.

35. Ibid.

36. "A Promising Oil Alternative: Algae Energy," *Washington Post*, January 6, 2008, http://www.washingtonpost.com/wp-dyn/content/article/2008/01/03/AR2008010303907.html.

37. Ibid.

38. "The Greenest Green Fuel," *Popular Science*, July 1, 2007, http://www.popsci.com/scitech/article/2007-07/greenest-green-fuel.

39. Renewable Fuels Association statistics, Historic U.S. Fuel Ethanol Production, http://www.ethanolrfa.org/industry/statistics/#A.

40. "Biofuels: Is the Cure Worse than the Disease?" September 2007, Organisation for Economic Co-operation and Development (OECD), http://media.ft.com/cms/fb8b5078-5fdb-11dc-b0fe-0000779fd2ac.pdf.

41. George P. Shultz and R. James Woolsey, "Oil and Security," Committee on the Present Danger Policy Paper, August 5, 2005. Now appears to be available only at the Internet Archive: http://web.archive.org/web/20070403101414/ http://www.fightingterror.org/pdfs/O&S8-5-05.pdf.

42. "Biofuels: Is the Cure Worse than the Disease?" September 2007, Organisation for Economic Co-operation and Development (OECD), http://media.ft.com/cms/fb8b5078-5fdb-11dc-b0fe-0000779fd2ac.pdf.

43. "Commission Publishes Impact Assessment of the 10 Percent Biofuel Obligation," August 13, 2007, U.S. Department of Agriculture Foreign Agricultural Service, http://www.fas.usda.gov/gainfiles/200708/146291987.pdf.

44. M.R. Schmer, K.P. Vogel, R.B. Mitchell, and R.K. Perrin, "Net Energy of Cellulosic Ethanol from Switchgrass," U.S. Department of Agriculture—Agricultural Research Service, University of Nebraska, January 7, 2008, http://www.pnas.org/cgi/content/abstract/0704767105v1.

45. Overview of the controversy: "Study: Ethanol May Cause More Smog, Deaths," April 18, 2007, AP, http://abcnews.go.com/US/wireStory?id=3051493. Jacobson's paper: http://www.stanford.edu/group/efmh/jacobson/E85PaperEST0207.pdf.

46. Charles Hall et al., "Hydrocarbons and the Evolution of Human Culture," http://www.hubbertpeak.com/cleveland/OilAndCulture.pdf.

47. Charles Hall et al., presentation to the ASPO Third Annual Oil Conference, Houston, Texas, October 18, 2007. Notes by Chris Nelder, http://www.getreallist.com/resources/ASPO_Houston_10-07_cnelder.pdf.

48. M.R. Schmer, K.P. Vogel, R.B. Mitchell, and R.K. Perrin, "Net Energy of Cellulosic Ethanol from Switchgrass," U.S. Department of Agriculture—Agricultural Research Service, University of Nebraska, January 7, 2008, http://www.pnas.org/cgi/content/abstract/0704767105v1.

49. Private correspondence, with reference to as-yet-unpublished formal responses to the aforementioned study.

50. From a private meeting in 2007 with Nelder.

51. Ethanol only has about two-thirds the energy content of an equivalent volume of gasoline, so it takes about one-third more ethanol to move a vehicle the same distance. For this reason, ethanol is often measured in terms of energy content—such as barrels or tons of oil equivalent—rather than by volume.

52. "Biofuels: Is the Cure Worse than the Disease?" September 2007, Organisation for Economic Co-operation and Development (OECD), http://media.ft.com/cms/fb8b5078-5fdb-11dc-b0fe-0000779fd2ac.pdf.

53. Renewable Fuels Association, Industry Statistics, http://www.ethanolrfa.org/industry/statistics/#B.

54. Makower, Pernick, and Wilder, "Clean Energy Trends 2007," March 2007, Clean Edge, Inc.

55. Renewable Fuels Association, Industry Statistics, http://www.ethanolrfa.org/industry/statistics/#B.

56. Date from 2005 was the latest we could find on total vehicle fuel consumption, and comparing data across years is perilous when dealing with industries that are growing as quickly as these. However, U.S. total vehicle fuel consumption has likely risen only about 3 percent since 2005, so this percentage calculation is in the ballpark. Data source: Table C1, Estimated Consumption of Vehicle Fuels in the United States, by Fuel Type, 2003–2005, EIA. See http://www.eia.doe.gov/cneaf/alternate/page/atftables/afvtrans_c1.xls.

57. "Biofuels Coming Online," July 2006, FASWorldwide, U.S. Department of Agriculture, http://www.fas.usda.gov/info/fasworldwide/2006/07-2006/BiofuelsOverview.htm.

58. Lester Brown, "Exploding U.S. Grain Demand for Automotive Fuel Threatens World Food Security and Political Stability," Earth Policy Institute, November 3, 2006, http://www.earth-policy.org/Updates/2006/Update60.htm.

59. "Renewable Fuels Association," New York Times, May 27, 2007, http://www.nytimes.com/2007/05/27/business/yourmoney/27view.html.

60. Patrick Mazza, "Biofuel Breakthroughs and the Cellulosic Fuels Revolution," Renewable Energy Access, May 28, 2007, http://www.renewableenergyaccess.com/rea/news/reinsider/story?id=48637.

61. "2007 Joint Outlook on Renewable Energy in America—Summary Report," http://www.nrel.gov/analysis/collab_analysis/pdfs/2007/workshop_pres/ws07_plenary_eckhart.pdf.

62. Patrick Mazza, "Biofuel Breakthroughs and the Cellulosic Fuels Revolution," Renewable Energy Access, May 28, 2007, http://www.renewableenergyaccess.com/rea/news/reinsider/story?id=48637.

63. Department of Energy press release, "DOE Selects Six Cellulosic Ethanol Plants for Up to $385 Million in Federal Funding," February 28, 2007, http://www.energy.gov/news/4827.htm.

64. Range Fuels press release, "Range Fuels Breaks Ground on the Nation's First Commercial Cellulosic Ethanol Plant," November 6, 2007, http://www.rangefuels.com/Range-Fuels-Breaks-Ground-on-the-Nations-First-Commercial-Cellulosic-Ethanol-Plant.

65. BlueFire press release, "BlueFire's Southern California Project to Receive Initial Funds from $40 Million DOE Grant," October 9, 2007, http://bluefireethanol.com/pr/40/; and "BlueFire Files for Construction Permits for California's First Cellulosic Waste to Ethanol Plant: Demo Facility for Bio-Butanol," August 1, 2007, Green Car Congress, http://www.greencarcongress.com/2007/08/bluefire-files-.html#more.

66. Pacific Ethanol press release, "Pacific Ethanol Among Four Companies Selected by U.S. Department of Energy to Research Commercial Cellulose Technology," January 29, 2008, http://biz.yahoo.com/prnews/080129/nytu149.html?.v=101.

67. "Establishment," Mascoma web site, http://www.mascoma.com/welcome/market_leadership.html.

68. Mascoma press release, "Mascoma Corporation to Build Nation's First Switchgrass Cellulosic Ethanol Plant," September 27, 2007, http://www.mascoma.com/welcome/pdf/09.27.07%20-%20 Mascoma%20News%20Release%20-TENN%20-%20FiNAL.pdf.

69. Verenium press release, "Verenium Commends Congressional Passage of Energy Legislation and Urges Farm Bill Action in Early 2008," December 18, 2007, http://ir.verenium.com/phoenix.zhtml?c=81345&p=irol-newsArticle&ID=1088569.

70. "Termite-Derived Enzymes," Verenium web site, http://www.verenium.com/Pages/Specialty%20 Enzymes/Biofuels/AltFuelsTermites.html.

71. "Novozymes and NREL Reduce Cost of Enzymes for Biomass-to-Ethanol Production 30-Fold," Green Car Congress, April 14, 2005, http://www.greencarcongress.com/2005/04/novozymes_and_n.html.

72. FPL Energy press release, "FPL Energy Enters into Agreement with Citrus Energy for First of its Kind Ethanol Plant," July 19, 2007, http://www.fplenergy.com/news/contents/2007/071907.shtml.

73. "U.S. Energy Law Drives Alternative to Corn Ethanol," December 19, 2007, Reuters, http://www.reuters.com/article/environmentNews/idUSN1959731820071220.

74. POET History/Legacy, from their web site, http://www.poetenergy.com/about/history.asp.

75. "Biofuels Coming Online," July 2006, FASWorldwide, U.S. Department of Agriculture, http://www.fas.usda.gov/info/fasworldwide/2006/07-2006/BiofuelsOverview.htm.

76. Susan Moran, "Biofuels Come of Age as the Demand Rises," New York Times, September 12, 2008, http://www.nytimes.com/2006/09/12/business/smallbusiness/12bio.html?ex=1315713600&en=0f141e75db5758b0&ei=5088&partner=rssnyt&emc=rss.

77. Green Star Products, Inc. press release, "GSPI Signs Contract to Build Algae-to-Biodiesel Facility," November 13, 2007.

78. "How Liposuction Can Lead to Cleaner Air," December 12, 2006, Pittsburgh Post-Gazette, http://www.post-gazette.com/pg/06346/745390-294.stm.

79. Directory of Lipo.com, http://www.lipo.com/mtree/.

80. "Poison Plant Could Help to Cure the Planet," Times Online, July 28, 2007, http://www.timesonline.co.uk/tol/news/world/article2155351.ece.

81. Data source: EIA International Energy Annual 2005, table 6.4, http://www.eia.doe.gov/pub/international/iea2005/table64.xls.

82. "Poison Plant Could Help to Cure the Planet," Times Online, July 28, 2007, http://www.timeson-line.co.uk/tol/news/world/article2155351.ece.

83. "With Help, Could Ethanol Be the Next Internet?," New York Times, May 27, 2007, http://www.nytimes.com/2007/05/27/business/yourmoney/27view.html.

84. "U.S. Energy Law Drives Alternative to Corn Ethanol," December 19, 2007, Reuters, http://www.reuters.com/article/environmentNews/idUSN1959731820071220.

85. "False Hopes and Cellulose," ASPO-USA, January 23, 2008, http://www.aspo-usa.com/index.php?option=com_content&task=view&id=302&Itemid=91.

86. "Q&A: European Commission Climate Change Laws," The Times Online, January 24, 2008, http://www.timesonline.co.uk/tol/news/environment/article3241359.ece.

87. "Biofuels Coming Online: International Biofuel Use Expands," U.S. Department of Agriculture, FAS Worldwide, July 2006, http://www.fas.usda.gov/info/fasworldwide/2006/07-2006/Biofuels Overview.htm.

88. "Vertigro and SGCEnergia Form European Biodiesel Feedstock Company," July 26, 2007, Marketwire, http://www.marketwire.com/mw/release.do?id=755069.

89. "Japan Plans to Support Replacing Petrol with Wood," Reuters, January 25, 2008, http://www.reuters.com/article/environmentNews/idUST8125820080125.

90. "Interview: Japan's First Rice Ethanol Plant Sees 2009 Start," Reuters, January 18, 2008, http://www.reuters.com/article/latestCrisis/idUST33749.

91. U.S. Department of Agriculture Foreign Agricultural Service, Attaché Reports. See http://www.fas.usda.gov/scriptsw/AttacheRep/default.asp.

## Chapter 10: Plugged-In Profits

1. Kelly Olsen, "OPEC Chief Wants Political Tension Eased," CBS News, June 5, 2006, http://www.cbsnews.com/stories/2006/06/05/ap/business/mainD8I24RA82.shtml.

2. "President Signs Historic Renewable Fuels Standard Calling for 36 Billion Gallons of Ethanol Use," American Coalition for Ethanol, December 19, 2007, http://www.ethanol.org/news/index.php?newsid=29.

3. "GM EV1," Seattle Electric Vehicle Association, http://www.seattleeva.org/wiki/GM_EV1.

4. Green Car Congress, November 5, 2007, http://www.greencarcongress.com/2007/11/toyota-has-sold.html.

5. "National Household Travel Survey," U.S. Department of Transportation, http://www.bts.gov/programs/national_household_travel_survey/daily_travel.html.

6. Ibid.

7. "Blueprint, Set America Free," http://www.setamericafree.org/blueprint.pdf.

8. Lucy Sanna, "Driving the Solution: The Plug-In Hybrid Vehicle," http://mydocs.epri.com/docs/CorporateDocuments/EPRI_Journal/2005-Fall/1012885_PHEV.pdf.

9. Ibid.

10. Ibid.

11. "Battery Innovation, Electrovaya," http://www.electrovaya.com/innovation/battery_tech.html.

12. "Our Companies," Ener1, http://www.ener1.com/enerdel.html.

13. FAQ, Phoenix Motorcars, http://www.phoenixmotorcars.com/faq/index.html#8.

14. William Tahil, "The Trouble with Lithium," Meridian International Research, December 2006, http://www.evworld.com/library/lithium_shortage.pdf (top of page 5).

15. Ibid., top of page 6.

16. Ibid., top of page 6, converted from metric.
17. Ibid., page 6, converted from metric/bottom of page 9 for zinc.
18. Ibid., bottom of page 9.
19. Ibid., page 11.
20. Ibid.

## Chapter 11: Global Warming: The Not-So-Great Debate

1. Many of these headlines were taken from the excellent blog, "Survival Acres," from its October 3, 2007 entry: http://survivalacres.com/wordpress/?p=953.
2. "California to Sue EPA Over Air Standards," CBS News, April 25, 2007-10-29, http://www.cbsnews.com/stories/2007/04/25/tech/main2728241.shtml.
3. "UN Chief Urges Immediate Climate Action," StopGlobalWarming.org, September 24, 2007, http://www.stopglobalwarming.org/sgw_read.asp?id=1148229242007.
4. "States Set to Sue the U.S. Over Greenhouse Gases," *New York Times*, October 24, 2007, http://www.nytimes.com/2007/10/24/nyregion/24emissions.html?ref=nyregion.
5. Intergovernmental Panel on Climate Change, http://www.ipcc.ch/.
6. "Scientists Offered Cash to Dispute Climate Study," *The Guardian,* Friday, February 2, 2007, http://www.guardian.co.uk/environment/2007/feb/02/frontpagenews.climatechange.
7. "Scientists' Report Documents ExxonMobil's Tobacco-like Disinformation Campaign on Global Warming Science," Union of Concerned Scientists, January 3, 2007, http://www.ucsusa.org/news/press_release/ExxonMobil-GlobalWarming-tobacco.html.
8. GMO Quarterly Letter, January 2007, https://www.gmo.com/America/CMSAttachmentDownload.htm?target=JUBRxi51IIDqLlslDnruR1dLYeIb4f1Zj24xTe1xQqat6DiJszZo1izByKuEauvH gGv7s%2fG%2f6c7lgXNMfwZNVjdo0fsQ6Jl8MsQjFAaDW%2f0%3d.
9. United Nations Environment Programme, "Global Environment Outlook 4," http://www.unep.org/geo/.
10. Peter Schwartz and Doug Randall, "Imagining the Unthinkable: An Abrupt Climate Change Scenario and Its Implications for United States National Security," October 2003, http://www.grist.org/pdf/AbruptClimateChange2003.pdf. Peter Schwartz is a CIA consultant and former head of planning at Royal Dutch/Shell Group, and Doug Randall is from the California-based Global Business Network. Report was leaked to *The Observer*, 2003.
11. "National Security and the Threat of Climate Change," Center for Naval Analyses, 2007, http://securityandclimate.cna.org/report/National%20Security%20and%20the%20Threat%20of%20Climate%20Change.pdf.
12. Jeff Goodell, "The Prophet of Climate Change: James Lovelock," *Rolling Stone*, October 17, 2007, http://www.rollingstone.com/politics/story/16956300/the_prophet_of_climate_change_james_lovelock.
13. Julian Borger, *The Guardian*, "Climate Change Disaster Is Upon Us, Warns UN," Friday, October 5, 2007, http://www.guardian.co.uk/environment/2007/oct/05/climatechange?gusrc=rss&feed=12.
14. "The Earth Today Stands in Imminent Peril," *The Independent*, October 29, 2007, http://environment.independent.co.uk/climate_change/article2675747.ece.
15. Tim Flannery, "The Weather Makers: How Man Is Changing the Climate and What It Means for Life on Earth," *Atlantic Monthly Press,* January 27, 2006, ISBN-10: 0871139359, ISBN-13: 978-0871139351.
16. Environmental Research Foundation, "The Precautionary Principle in the Real World," January 21, 2008, http://www.precaution.org/lib/pp_def.htm.

17. "Bill Clinton's Bid to Save the World," *Los Angeles Times*, September 28, 2007, http://www
    .latimes.com/news/nationworld/politics/la-na-bill28sep28,1,4874110.story?coll=la-news-
    politics-national&ctrack=1&cset=true.

18. "Banks Urging U.S. to Adopt the Trading of Emissions," *New York Times*, September 26, 2007,
    http://www.nytimes.com/2007/09/26/business/26bank.html?_r=1&oref=slogin&page
    wanted=print.

19. "From Risk to Opportunity 2007: Insurer Responses to Climate Change," CERES, October 2007,
    http://insurance.lbl.gov/opportunities/Risk-to-Opportunity-2007.pdf.

20. See http://www.insurancejournal.com/news/national/2007/10/18/84392.htm.

21. As of October 29, 2007. Clinton Global Initiative, Energy and Climate Change Commitments,
    http://commitments.clintonglobalinitiative.org/projects.htm?category=51.

22. *Source:* The Clinton Foundation. As reported by Reuters, "FACTBOX: Clinton Global Initiative
    Achievements," Tuesday, September 25, 2007, http://www.reuters.com/article/smartThinking/id
    USN2533574220070925.

23. Paul Hawken, Amory Lovins, and L. Hunter Lovins, eds., *Natural Capitalism: Creating the Next
    Industrial Revolution*, New York, Little, Brown, 1999.

24. See http://www.abanet.org/genpractice/magazine/2005/mar/naturalcapitalism.html.

25. Paul Hawken, Amory Lovins, and L. Hunter Lovins, eds., *Natural Capitalism: Creating the Next
    Industrial Revolution*, New York, Little, Brown, 1999.

## Chapter 12: Profiting from Pollution

1. "International Energy Outlook 2007," Energy Information Administration, May 2007, http://www
   .eia.doe.gov/oiaf/ieo/emissions.html.

2. Glenda Korporaal, "$100 bn in Carbon Futures Coming Soon," *The Australian*, December 5,
   2007, http://www.theaustralian.news.com.au/story/0,25197,22871100-643,00.html.

3. "Kyoto Bill Sparks Constitutional Questions," CBC Canada, February 15, 2007, http://www.cbc.
   ca/canada/story/2007/02/15/kyoto-bill.html.

4. The Western Climate Initiative, http://www.westernclimateinitiative.org/.

5. Andrei Marcu, President and CEO, International Emissions Trading Association.

6. "Overview," Chicago Climate Exchange, http://www.chicagoclimatex.com/content.jsf?id=821.

7. Timothy Gardner, "Chicago Climate Exchange to Offer Kyoto Contracts," Reuters, August 24,
   2007, http://www.planetark.com/dailynewsstory.cfm/newsid/43925/story.htm.

8. Ibid.

9. "State of the Voluntary Carbon Markets 2007," Ecosystem Marketplace, http://ecosystemmarket-
   place.com/documents/acrobat/StateoftheVoluntaryCarbonMarket17July.pdf.

10. Ibid.

11. James Kanter, "In London's Financial World, Carbon Trading Is the New Thing," *New York Times*,
    July 6, 2007, http://www.nytimes.com/2007/07/06/business/worldbusiness/06carbon.html?_r=1
    &oref=slogin.

12. Ibid.

13. Anupreeta Das, "U.S. Exchanges Explore Carbon Trading," Reuters News Service, November 7,
    2007, http://www.planetark.org/dailynewsstory.cfm?newsid=45190.

14. "Morgan Stanley Announces Creation of Carbon Bank," Renewable Energy Access, August 15,
    2007, http://www.renewableenergyaccess.com/rea/news/story;jsessionid=A0DFB1BAB2CB5AC
    68191FC077EC4410?id=49655.

15. "Leading Wall Street Banks Establish the Carbon Principles," Morgan Stanley, February 4, 2008, http://www.morganstanley.com/about/press/articles/6017.html.

16. "Update 2-Enel Sees 75 mlnt of CO2 Offsets in 2008–2012," Reuters, March 13, 2008, http://www.reuters.com/article/rbssIndustryMaterialsUtilitiesNews/idUSL1382411120080313.

17. "Chinese Power Giant to Sell Carbon Dioxide to Spain under CDM Contract," Worldwatch Institute, January 23, 2006, http://www.worldwatch.org/node/3876.

18. Karen Degouve, Investment Manager, European Carbon Fund.

19. Ibid.

20. "CDM Statistics," United Nations, http://cdm.unfccc.int/Statistics/index.html.

21. "Poor Countries Need Billions to Cut Emissions," EurActiv, December 6, 2007, http://www.euractiv.com/en/climate-change/poor-countries-need-billions-cut-emissions/article-168903.

22. Jill Duggan, Head Phase II EUETS.

## Chapter 13: The Greatest Investment Opportunity of the Twenty-First Century

1. "Concentrating Solar Power," Solar Energy Systems, http://www.cogeneration.net/concentrating_solar_power.htm.

2. "Geothermal Energy Resources," Department of Energy, http://www1.eere.energy.gov/geothermal/pdfs/egs_chapter_3.pdf

3. "Primary Energy Overview," Department of Energy, November 2007, http://www.eia.doe.gov/emeu/mer/pdf/pages/sec1_3.pdf.

4. "A Blueprint for U.S. Energy Security," Set America Free, http://www.setamericafree.org/blueprint.pdf.

5. "How to Spread the Word about Global Warming," Maui Media, http://an-inconvenient-truth.com/CFL.pdf.

6. "A Framework for Offshore Wind Energy Development in the United States," Resolve, Inc., http://www.mtpc.org/offshore/final_09_20.pdf.

# ABOUT THE AUTHORS

**Jeff Siegel** is the co-founder and managing editor of *Green Chip Stocks*, an investment advisory service that focuses exclusively on renewable energy and organic food markets. He is often cited in the media, and has been a featured guest on Fox, CNBC, and Bloomberg Asia. Siegel also works as a consultant, and is a frequent speaker at investment and renewable energy conferences and seminars.

**Chris Nelder** is a self-taught energy expert who has intensively studied peak oil for five years, and written hundreds of articles on peak oil and energy in general. Chris also founded and published an online magazine called *Better World* in the mid 1990s, as part of his lifelong interest in fostering environmental and social responsibility. Chris is the co-author of *Profit from the Peak*, a frequent contributor to *Green Chip Stocks*, among other publications, and is an active investor in energy.

**Nick Hodge** is the managing editor of *Alternative Energy Speculator*, an investment advisory service that focuses primarily on clean energy and emission-reduction technologies. Nick has also written extensively on water and infrastructure investing, and has been featured on Canada's Business News Network (BNN).

# INDEX

**247**